AIR MOBILE: THEY STRUCK SUDDENLY AND ALL AT ONCE

During the last few minutes of the tube artillery preparation, transport helicopters took off from "Mustang" PZ with the first two platoons of C Company. The artillery fire was lifted, at which time the Aerial Rocket Artillery shot ahead to continue the fire for about a minute.

The birds were on the final approach to the landing zone, the door gunners picking up fire with their M-60 machine guns. Then the birds were on the ground, landing eight at a time. The infantry from C Company made their first assault, sprinting from the birds to the distant tree line.

YEAR OF THE HORSE— VIETNAM

1st Air Cavalry in the Highlands

COLONEL KENNETH D. MERTEL
Infantry, United States Army

BANTAM BOOKS
NEW YORK · TORONTO · LONDON · SYDNEY · AUCKLAND

The views of the author do not purport to reflect the position of the Department of the Army or the Department of Defense.

YEAR OF THE HORSE—VIETNAM

A Bantam Book / published by arrangement with the author

PRINTING HISTORY
Exposition Press edition published 1968
Bantam edition / January 1990

Drawings by Greg Beecham.

Maps by Alan Mcknight.

Bantam Books are published by Bantam Books, a division of Bantam Doubleday Dell Publishing Group, Inc. Its trademark, consisting of the words "Bantam Books" and the portrayal of a rooster, is Registered in U.S. Patent and Trademark Office and in other countries. Marca Registrada. Bantam Books, 666 Fifth Avenue, New York, New York 10103.

PRINTED IN THE UNITED STATES OF AMERICA

O   0 9 8 7 6 5 4 3 2 1

DEDICATION

This book is dedicated to the "Sky Troopers," living and dead, of the 1st Air Cavalry Division, and especially to those courageous troopers of the "Jumping Mustangs," the 1st Battalion, Airborne, 8th Cavalry. "Drive On, All the Way."

For freedom's battle, once begun,
Bequeath'd by bleeding sire to son,
Though baffled oft, is ever won.

from "The Giaour"
LORD BYRON

CONTENTS

FOREWORD

In this book Colonel Kenneth Mertel recounts his experiences and the doings of his splendid "Jumping Mustang" battalion during the organizing, training, deploying to and fighting in Vietnam as a unit of the 1st Air Cavalry Division.

Colonel Mertel, affectionately dubbed "the Grey Beret" by his men, had served a previous tour of duty in Vietnam which sharpened his understanding of the cunningness of the enemy and the physical demands of combat in the tropics. His own Army aviation background helped him understand and exploit the all-important helicopters. The esprit-de-corps and teamwork that he instilled in his men in training served them well in combat. The "Jumping Mustangs" had a can-do attitude which new replacements quickly absorbed.

Under the flexible organization of the Air Cavalry Division, the "Mustangs" fought under each of the three brigades in varied environments ranging from the heavily populated coastal lowlands to the almost uninhabited, extremely rugged central highlands near the Cambodian border. The speed with which the helicopter could put men into battle placed heavy demands upon combat leaders and troops alike. A state of readiness to do battle under rapidly changing circumstances became a way of life with the Air-Cavalrymen.

This book is about pioneers—men who fought a new kind of airmobile warfare before the textbooks on such warfare were written. In documenting his experiences, Colonel Mertel has added an important chapter to the history of airmobile warfare.

—HARRY W. O. KINNARD
Lieutenant General, US Army

ACKNOWLEDGMENTS

I wish to express my sincere thanks and appreciation to the many officers and men of the "Jumping Mustangs" for their help and assistance in refreshing my memory and providing notes concerning our experiences in Vietnam.

My appreciation is also given to Lieutenant General Harry W. O. Kinnard, for the Foreword; Brigadier General S. L. A. Marshall, for his review and comments; War Correspondent Charles Black, of the Columbus *Enquirer*, for his notes on the night air assault of 3-4 November, 1965; my secretaries, Mrs. Velva B. Lebo and Mrs. Doris Wagner, for their excellent clerical work; and my wife, Molli, for the grammatical review.

K. D. M.

INTRODUCTION

The "Year of the Horse," according to the Chinese calendar, was the year 1966.

The year 1966 was also the "Year of the Horse" for troopers of the 1st Air Cavalry Division. The "Sky Troopers" arrived in the Republic of South Vietnam in September, 1965, and immediately began offensive operations against the Viet Cong and the rapidly infiltrating North Vietnamese Army, who were attempting to seize and occupy the II Corps Tactical Zone in the Pleiku area.

It was this offensive action, begun in 1965 and culminated in 1966, that stopped the enemy cold in their tracks and proved that the United States soldier could beat them at their own game.

This book tells a small portion of the story of one Airborne Infantry battalion of the 1st Air Cavalry Division, the "Jumping Mustangs," the 1st Battalion, Airborne, 8th Cavalry.

YEAR OF THE HORSE— VIETNAM

THE NEW
1ST AIR CAVALRY DIVISION

1 July 1965, Fort Benning, Georgia

There was excitement in the air, in the barracks, at the Officers' Club, and throughout the city of Columbus, Georgia. We had known for several days that the 11th Air Assault Division was no more and soon would be the new 1st Air Cavalry Division. This could mean only one thing—Vietnam, and an opportunity to utilize this new airmobile-weapons concept that so many had worked hard and long to test and try out—a chance now for the ultimate test, combat against an armed enemy.

The initial announcement came from Defense Secretary McNamara, indicating that he had authorized the Army to organize a new division, the Airmobile Division. To be organized at Fort Benning, Georgia, the new sixteen-thousand-man outfit would be ready for action by mid-August. It placed the Army on the threshold of an entirely new approach to the conduct of land battle. Airmobile combat troops, artillery, and ground vehicles were to be flown into combat with the division's more than four hundred UH-1, OH-13, and CH-47 helicopters. The division would also have six twin-engine OV-1 Mohawks with infrared scanning devices, radar, and cameras for reconnaissance duty. One of the division's three brigades would be made up entirely of trained paratroopers, and therefore would be capable of conducting Airborne operations.

OV-1 Mohawk

Based in the United States, the Airmobile Division would be ready to move at a moment's notice to any trouble spot in the world and get there within a matter of hours, employing the Air Force's C-130's to carry all men and equipment except the largest helicopters, which would be flown in giant C-133 turboprop cargo planes. The United States already had airfields in South Vietnam and Thailand capable of handling such planes and was rapidly building more. The Airmobile Division had little armor, but could make up for that with mobility and fast striking force. It would be capable of conducting operations in all types of terrain; it could react quickly and maneuver rapidly over large areas. It could reconnoiter, screen, delay hostile forces, and conduct raids deep behind enemy lines. The Division would be especially effective in locating and maintaining contact with the enemy. In other words, the 1st Air Cavalry Division seemed tailor-made for Vietnam.

Two days previous had been one of the proudest days of my Army career as I assumed command of the 1st battalion, 188th Infantry, of the 11th Air Assault Division. In the short ceremony on the parade ground, before a token assembly of the battalion, Brigadier General Richard T. Knowles, Assistant Division Commander, and the Brigade Commander, Colonel Elvey B. Roberts, pinned on me the battalion crest and green tabs indicating a combat leader. How do you explain the feeling of pride that sweeps through you? Command of an

Infantry battalion—the career goal of every Infantry leader. How fortunate I was!

Today it was no longer the 188th, but as of 1 July the 1st Battalion, Airborne, 8th Cavalry, of the 1st Air Cavalry Division.

The following day I had a chance to look over my new command. The battalion was being converted from straight leg to Airborne Infantry. Prior to sailing, at an unannounced date, we would convert to Airborne and accomplish maximum small-unit combat training in preparation for Vietnam. The major task was to accomplish the first mission of becoming Airborne. Arrangements had been made for all volunteers within the battalion, both enlisted men and officers, to attend the Basic Airborne Course at Fort Benning, Georgia, the home of the Airborne School.

Almost all of the officers in the battalion volunteered for Airborne training. A few noncommissioned officers and about one-third of the troops also signed up. In addition to myself there were but a handful of Airborne-qualified officers currently in the battalion. Additional fillers of all ranks would come from the Airborne School when they were graduated. A large number of noncommissioned officers would be levied from one of the other Airborne units in the Army in order to round out the battalion.

Similar organizational and training problems were faced by the 2nd Battalion, Airborne, 8th Cavalry, our sister battalion, and other members of the Airborne Brigade throughout the Division. There was little other training that could be accomplished at this moment because all of the men who were not going Airborne were to be transferred from the battalion. Everything was in turmoil. The main activities were Airborne training and preparations for movement to Vietnam.

How do you start to build a new battalion? As Colonel Elvey B. Roberts, our Brigade Commander, said, "This is one of the rare opportunities, the first since World War II, in which a Battalion or a Brigade Commander has the opportunity of building his battalion or brigade, training it and then taking his troops into combat."

Nearly a week later our jump training began! I conducted a campaign to encourage and convince key personnel within the battalion to go Airborne. There was more to becoming a paratrooper than just desire. Many of the outstanding noncommissioned officers of the former 1st Battalion, 188th Infantry, who were not Airborne-qualified (Airborne troopers call them "straight legs," or "legs") did not have the requisite physical capability or the adaptability.

Airborne is its own way of life. A man might be well motivated to try for his jump wings, but unless he was physically fit, mentally alert, young in attitude in spite of his physical age, and determined, he would never make it.

A good example was the Acting Battalion Sergeant Major, a straight leg, fifty-two years of age, who wanted to go with the battalion. He tried to become Airborne and started training. However, in view of his age and his physical condition, there was little hope of his being able to successfully complete it. Failure was certainly not due to any lack of motivation on his part or to his own physical efforts to become Airborne. The flesh simply would not permit.

I spent my days getting thoroughly familiar with the battalion and meeting the many newly assigned Airborne lieutenants. I also interviewed a number of Airborne Infantry captains who had recently completed the Career Course at the Infantry School. They were desperately seeking assignment to the 1st Air Cavalry and specifically to the Airborne Brigade.

One of this group was my new Adjutant, Captain William Mozey, whom I had met earlier in the day. He and Captain Roy Martin arrived at the same time. Both were tentatively assigned to the battalion subject to my acceptance; both were eager to obtain permanent assignment. Captain Mozey seemed most fitted to be S-1, although his first request was command of a rifle company. Since I had already firmed up the slate of rifle company commanders, actually keeping those who were already in command, all I could do at that time was to promise Captain Mozey that he would have his chance at a later date. Captain Roy Martin also wanted a rifle company, but the same thing applied to him. He was extra at the moment and became an Assistant S-3 to be held for later use.

A few days later, Major John R. Herman arrived. He came from the Special Forces at Fort Bragg, North Carolina, and from the beginning appeared to be an outstanding officer.

I was impressed with him at once and decided to make him S-3. The Assistant S-3, captain Norman C. Propes, attending Airborne School, was experiencing difficulties because of his large size. His six-foot-four-inch frame prevented him from performing some of the physical exercises required in completing Airborne training. Should he not make it, he would accompany the battalion anyway as the Assistant S-3. He would be one of the few "legs" within the battalion.

The new Battalion Surgeon soon arrived, Dr. Richard B. Odom. A fine athlete and a soldier by first impression, although completely new to the Army, he impressed me with his ability both as a soldier and as a doctor.

I thought I had lost the Chaplain, Captain Ralph Spears, who was scheduled to be transferred from the battalion to brigade. He wanted to remain with the battalion. I went to bat for him with the Brigade Commander, who decided that Captain Spears would remain with us.

I was much impressed with the new lieutenants who arrived. All were inexperienced but eager. Some received their commissions from Officer Candidate School, others came from the Reserve Officer Training Corps and West Point. All had completed Airborne School and were eager and ready for work. A few were weak. As I reviewed the platoon leaders in the battalion, I determined those with whom I was going to spend more time in order to correct their weak points.

There remained only fifty days to form the battalion, train it, and depart for Vietnam and the combat missions that were certain to come. A sobering and challenging thought.

The following day the Jumping Mustang Battalion made its first battalion jump at Friar Field, Fort Benning, Georgia. This was a part of the 1st Airborne Brigade jump, the first brigade-size jump for the division in the history of the organization since its activation as the 1st Air Cavalry. This first jump of the Jumping Mustang Battalion included the fifty-five men and officers previously Airborne-qualified. Take-off was from Lawson Army Airfield in a C-130, parachuting into a wet field on the Alabama side of the Chattahoochee River at 1845 hours. The jump was made without injuries. The fifty-five members of the battalion who made the jump

C-130

became charter members of the battalion. A plaque was prepared to be hung in each Company Orderly Room listing the names of all fifty-five officers and men.

It is not easy to put into words the meaning of a soldier's pride in his unit. It could be the one ingredient which might be the difference between winning and losing. The soldiers in the 1st Air Cavalry Division realized the significance of the big black and gold patch because it was the insignia of the "First Team." These men were out in the field for months on end and proved that they had a way of fighting which earned them the honor of being the first Airmobile Division in the history of the Army. This parachute jump was the first chapter in a new history of the 1st Air Cavalry Division.

Jump training was progressing well. The battalion had been permitted to go through Jump School as a unit, under its own officers and noncommissioned officers. This fact helped encourage many of the men through some of the more rigorous training because of unit spirit—the fact they were members of the battalion who perhaps under other conditions might not succeed. The Basic Airborne Course was exactly the same given any paratrooper, with the exception of physical training.

The physical condition of the troops was excellent prior to the beginning of jump training. In view of the tight training schedule in this phase, physical training was eliminated from Jump School. We were on an accelerated program with the physical training accomplished within the units.

I made a daily visit to battalion elements participating in jump training, usually in the morning and afternoon to see how the men were doing. I was most impressed with the young officers, former members of the 188th, going through jump training in order to stay with their unit; and also by the NCO's, especially the young, aggressive squad leaders who stayed with the battalion, as well as the many fine young soldiers who also remained. I did not know yet where the troops who would fill the battalion would come from, but had taken a close look at the regular classes of jumpers currently going through training. Many of these men would join the battalion.

I visited Colonel Lamar Welch, Director of the Airborne Department, almost daily in the hopes of obtaining some of the senior NCO's from the Airborne Department to join the battalion. Senior NCO's were extremely short. None of the first sergeants would remain. It appeared that the Sergeant Major would be transferred to brigade as the Brigade Sergeant Major. The battalion was also short of platoon sergeants. It was necessary to recruit from any and all places, although higher headquarters had guaranteed that senior NCO replacements would arrive prior to departure to Vietnam.

The officers' ladies sponsored a coffee at the home of Mrs. Pat Eberhardt, hostess and wife of Major Guy Eberhardt, the Executive Officer. I put in my appearance at this first coffee in the Jumping Mustang Battalion, partook of a cup of coffee and a piece of cake with the ladies, and spent about fifteen minutes talking about the battalion, what their husbands were doing, and what it would be like when we eventually reached Vietnam.

My purpose was to inspire the ladies, inform them concerning what was going on, so that they would understand better what their husbands were going through, and encourage them. The coffee turned out to be an outstanding success and was well received by the husbands of the battalion as well.

On 1 July, Lieutenant Colonel Bob Shoemaker, who commanded the 1st of the 12th, and I joined Colonel Roberts in the first jump in the history of the 1st Air Cavalry Division, which was the first jump in the history of the 1st Airborne Brigade and my first jump in thirteen years.

Huey

My last Airborne experience had been with the 82nd
Airborne Infantry Regiment, during 1948 to 1951. I left the
82nd with thirty-six jumps; the thirty-seventh was made from
a HU-1D helicopter from the 1st Brigade Aviation Section
that morning in company with the other officers. The chute
was similar, now a T-10 instead of the old T-7. The only major
difference was the aircraft, or bird—this time a helicopter.
The bird picked us up from the Brigade Helipad, where we
had already rigged chutes, and flew to the drop zone a few
minutes away. We jumped. The chute opening was as I
remembered from before. The landing was no different. The
helicopter dropped down and snatched us up. A few minutes
later we were back in the brigade area, where we posed for
pictures in front of the 1st Airborne Brigade sign with Colonel Roberts.

This day marked the first qualifying jump by the neo-
phyte paratroopers of the battalion. I joined, to make my
third jump in the battalion, this time in a C-130. It was the
first training jump for members of the battalion who were
taking jump training. The company commanders were with
me on the jump. We scattered throughout the various aircraft

to provide inspiration for our own troops, since the first jump in Jump School was always a "great big step," and anything we could do to assist our troops we would. This action was most important to the morale and spirit we aimed to develop as we built a battalion.

Parachute training was completed. I made the last jump with the battalion, as did the company commanders. After the jump the graduating members of the battalion, as well as others of the Airborne Brigade and the Airborne Task Force, received their wings in a ceremony on the drop zone. It was a good day. I was most pleased. All of the officers, except one or two who had been injured in the process of jumping, completed their training. The majority of the NCO's and men of the battalion who had started out had also received the prized Jump Wings.

Authority was granted to complete jump training of those few men who were injured during their training and had completed one or more jumps, at such time as they were physically fit. We would complete their jumps and then notify the Airborne Department of the Infantry School, who were to award the Jump Wings.

A battalion officers' party was scheduled at the Officers' Club. This was my first party as the Battalion Commander and host. All officers and their wives were present at the Corregidor Room of the Officers' Club, where we had a chance to meet each other and renew acquaintances.

This was important for the officers' ladies of the battalion, for this was the first time that they would, particularly those of the old 188th, have the opportunity to meet the many new wives. Mrs. Pat Eberhardt acted as hostess. I made a short speech to the assembled group to congratulate the officers on the tremendous achievements of the battalion thus far, to indicate my pleasure for our successes, and to wish them the best of luck for the future. I also congratulated the wives on the part that they were playing.

A highlight of the party was the awarding of the Jumping Mustang Crest to Charlie Black, the military news reporter for the Columbus *Enquirer*. Charlie Black had been writing news for the 11th Air Assault Division and especially for the old 188th Infantry for a number of months. Lieutenant Colonel Bob Kellar, the former commander of the 188th, had presented a 188th Infantry Crest of the battalion to Charlie Black a few months past for the outstanding job that he had accomplished. On the changeover to the 1st Air Cavalry Division and to the 1st of the 8th, Charlie was with us many times to see what was going on and to write about the troopers.

I think he probably came closer than any other news reporter in the Vietnam War to writing in the style and manner of the Ernie Pyle of World War II fame. He was well liked by the troops and was a friend to all. He wrote of the soldier, of what he was doing and feeling. He had a great knack for this, because his trips took him out to the field and to the troops, whom he joined on their hikes and their marches. You would see him in fatigues and boots, usually sporting a twelve-day beard and topped with a beat-up red beret.

Charlie was a true friend to us, and I recognized this by awarding him the Jumping Mustang Crest on behalf of the battalion. He unofficially became our Battalion Information Officer. We were destined to see much of him in the future in Vietnam.

The 8th Cavalry Regiment from which our history came had a crest consisting of a demi-horse or a horse's head on the crest, below which were eight five-pointed stars. The motto on the crest was "Honor and Courage." The name of the battalion was the "Mustang Battalion." This name was applicable to both the 1st and 2nd Battalions of the 8th Cavalry.

In agreement with Lieutenant Colonel Jim Nix, who commanded the 2nd of the 8th, I had taken the name "Mustang." He selected another name. Since we were Airborne, I added the word "Jumping" to our name to make us the "Jumping Mustangs." It was essential that we build additional unit history and unit accomplishments as soon as possible. To help in this a special Infantry Blue Battalion guidon was adopted which had a large white stallion standing on its hind legs and above the horse the word "Jumping" and below it "Mustang," thereby indicating the "Jumping Mustang Battalion."

We soon would receive our new company guidons. In the meantime, although actually a cavalry unit, I considered this an Infantry battalion. I had fabricated individual company guidons of Infantry Blue. The companies carried these new guidons.

Spirit was rapidly building. I concentrated at the battalion level and tried to form a team, using the Jumping Mustang flag as my standard. Each of the companies adopted a special flag. Alpha Company, commanded by Captain Ted Danielsen, was known as the "Alphagaters." Bravo Company, commanded by Captain Oliver Dillon, was the "Bravo Bulls." Charlie Company, commanded by Captain William Smith, was the "Road Runners," and Delta Company, commanded by Captain Vandoster L. Tabb, was known as the "Delta Dogs." We were also getting good spirit within the Headquarters Company, commanded by Captain Russell W. Ramsey.

One means of building the battalion was the physical training program. Initially the individual companies conducted calisthenics and running each morning at 0700 hours. My two radio operators and I, with the battalion guidon, joined the companies from time to time and exercised and ran with each of them in turn. The members of the battalion staff joined individual companies. Our Air Force Liaison Officer (ALO), Captain Edward Holland, our Blue Suiter, was a real athlete. He joined each company of the battalion at different times to help encourage and provide inspiration. Our Artillery Liaison Officer (Arty LNO), Captain Dave Wilkie, ran with us occasionally. We were busily trying to weld all members of the battalion team as one. Our doctor and chaplain easily kept up with any and all of the companies. The whole battalion operated as a team.

I forecast we would complete a five-mile run without rest breaks the last week prior to shipment. This would be done by the entire battalion in formation. The reaction to this announcement from the troops was disbelief and a hope that it would not occur. They had a surprise coming.

On 28 July 1965 we were notified the 1st Air Cavalry Division would go to Vietnam. This information was on a need-to-know basis. The sailing date for the 1st Airborne Brigade was to be about 20 August. We could expect a thirty-day ocean voyage and should be in Vietnam sometime around 20 September. The battalion leaders were notified, providing considerable pep to all preparations from that point on.

I concentrated on squad and platoon-level training within the companies. Our fillers and NCO's had arrived. The best sight I ever witnessed had occurred two days before, at 0800 hours, when I greeted my new Sergeant Major, Herbert McCullah; the new first sergeants; most of the new platoon sergeants; a total of 140 noncommissioned officers from the 101st and the 82nd Airborne Divisions who were assigned to the Jumping Mustang Battalion. I cannot adequately describe my feeling in seeing this large group of stripes with their sharp, professional appearance. The number of stripes and ribbons displayed indicated the experience we desperately needed. I knew that these men would make the battalion complete. Overnight we became an Airborne battalion.

This group of Airborne NCO's provided in one group—one assignment—an Airborne capability. From the few jump masters formerly in the battalion—principally myself and a couple others—we now had over one hundred. These were men who could lead the sticks, who knew what to do both in the airplane and on the ground. I no longer had any worries about our abilities or capability as an Airborne battalion.

First Sergeant Ray E. Poynter, B Company, expressed the feelings of this whole group of NCO's when he stated:

> I must go back to 30 June 1965 at 101st Airborne Division Ready Force Formation and explain the exact feelings I had when a runner came out to tell me there was a big levy out for Vietnam and that all 1st Sergeants were to meet immediately.
>
> At this time, the news to date gave me the impression that Vietnam was a small place where snipers were shooting at the civilian population and we had advisors trying to tell the people how to stop it. All of a sudden, in a second thought, perhaps Vietnam was a World War III in the making. My own eighteen years of service came to my mind as I wondered just how I would tell my wife and six children I was to leave again for war. I had never shirked my duty and I thought of the oath I had taken to defend my country and to give my life if that's what it would take to keep this country free. So it seemed this was the big moment.
>
> I was briefed and found out that we had four-

teen days to clear Post, settle families, visit friends, and to do whatever we had to do to be ready to reform the 1st Cavalry Division for deployment to Vietnam. After looking over the list of names from my battalion, it seemed more like a battalion move to Fort Benning than a group of men used as replacements. This eased the feeling somewhat as I knew we had a group of the finest noncommissioned officers ever assembled in one area. This was proved while in Vietnam.

I kissed my family good-bye and left to form the new unit. I knew I would not be able to take the time out to come back home until my tour in Vietnam was over.

Now with NCO's and almost all fillers present, those remaining from the battalion who would not stay with us were employed to prepare the battalion for movement—the logistical end of the operation. This was true also in the case of officers. The rest of the battalion—those going to Vietnam—continued an intensified training program, concentrating at platoon level.

In a series of Rifle Platoon firing tests, I followed each platoon through the course, observing the abilities of the platoon leader and the NCO's as they led their platoon through a live firing exercise. This series of training exercises was most important to the battalion and especially to me. I was able to judge the ability, fire control, and proficiency of each platoon leader as he led his platoon through simple exercises, conducted on one of the ranges at Fort Benning. At the same time we concentrated on firing all other weapons. It was our goal to master, in a short period of time, squad and platoon tactics, as much at company level as possible, at the same time continuing to concentrate on weapons and physical conditioning.

Having been in Vietnam once before in 1963, I knew that the jungle environment and heat could be faced only by a man in topnotch physical condition. This was the major reason for the concentration on this important aspect. I knew that weapons, including operation, maintenance, and the shooting ability, were most important. Ours was a rifle battalion. Rifles would be the key to success, with the support of

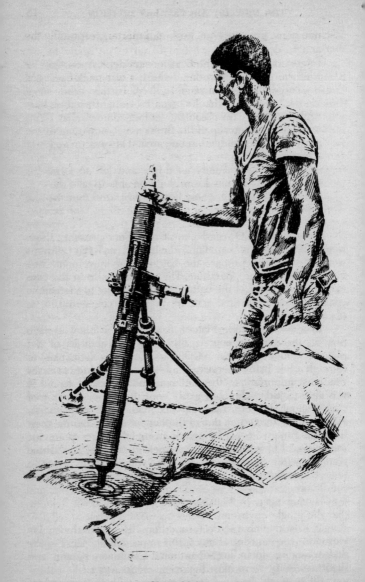

81mm Mortar

machine guns, grenade launchers, and mortars, especially the mortars.

I was most disappointed in observing the conduct of 81mm mortar fire the first day. In fact, I was so discouraged that I personally concentrated my efforts on those most important elements of the battalion in order to whip them into shape so that they could be ready for combat. This included the three-gun section of each rifle company and the four-gun platoon of Delta Company. Placing Captain Vandoster Tabb, the Delta Company commander, in charge of this important activity, I supervised and harassed him and his mortarmen until they could meet my standards.

One highlight of training was Escape and Evasion, in which we pitted one company against the other. One company on the Escape and Evasion Range had the job of operating the prison camp, setting up patrols to try to capture as many as they could of the opposing company as it moved through a predetermined piece of terrain going from Point A to Point B, some fifteen kilometers distance at night. The objective was to get through the course without being detected by the enemy and, if captured, to resist the interrogation and try to escape. I observed this outstanding training on several nights. The training was most valuable to all personnel and in helping me determine the quality and type of NCO's, as I observed them by name, performing both as captors and as the captured. These fine young soldiers did anything to resist divulging information. They endured considerable torment in the mock prison camp and as a "reward" for being captured the tortures ran from being covered with sorghum molasses, rolled in the dirt, and then standing for insects to do their best, to sitting with legs wrapped around a greased pole, one foot locked behind the opposite knee and the other behind the pole under the buttocks. Woe to the man who exhibited a fear of snakes, because he was usually spread-eagled over a pit of several snakes, face down, supported by his hands and feet on the top corners of the pit.

The final departure time was rapidly approaching. We received containers to begin loading equipment. Most of the equipment would be loaded in metal Connex containers and sent to ports prior to our departure on 20 August.

It was quite an operation to pack up what we needed for

combat and for use in Vietnam. Having been there, I knew some of the things that we would require for convenience. We had been trying to locate as many of these items as possible. Included were any and all types of construction materials. It was most important to assure that our equipment was in topnotch condition, since we would have little resupply, at least in very large quantities, for a number of months after our arrival.

The S-4, Captain Jerry Plummer, did a fine job of overseeing the preparations. We conducted a series of inspections at platoon and company level. I participated from time to time on a spot-check basis, to assure that every soldier's equipment was ready.

Word was received that all underclothing, handkerchiefs, socks, and fatigues were to be dyed a deep forest green. There would be some work accomplished by the Quartermaster; however, shortage of time required our accomplishing the task ourselves. Word was passed to the companies, and the dyeing operations began in earnest, both within the units and at home with the wives, as well as with many of the laundries throughout Columbus.

When it was all over, just prior to sailing, every soldier had green underwear, socks, handkerchiefs, and the majority of his fatigues dyed a darker forest green to help us blend in with the jungle terrain. In addition, all insignia were colored a dark green or black to decrease the possibility of being spotted by the enemy. Thus we would make less of a target for snipers.

I doubt if wives and girl friends of 1st Air Cavalry Sky Troopers ever forgot the color of green dye.

The brigade commander directed that the entire brigade, most of whom would sail on one ship, be prepared to wear, as a uniform on the voyage, athletic shoes and socks, shorts, and T-shirts. This uniform was required for a number of reasons. It was comfortable and cool on the ship; second, it was easier to keep clean, for there would be few laundry facilities aboard ship. Fatigues were difficult to keep clean. Wearing the khaki athletic shorts, which we had been able to obtain for every man, simplified the entire problem.

An item in the Columbus *Enquirer* noted the first and

last jump of the Jumping Mustangs in the United States as a battalion, as follows:

"The Jumping Mustangs of the 1st Battalion Airborne, 8th Cavalry, made their first and last drop this week. Lieutenant Colonel Kenneth D. Mertel, Battalion Commander, led the drop exiting over Friar Field Drop Zone. Following the drop the companies were deployed up to the northern corner of the reservation for three days of patrolling, squad and platoon tactics, and raids. For many of the Jumping Mustangs, this was their first time in the field together. Squad and platoon leaders stressed individual combat actions and getting to know the chain of command. The significance of this jump was that this was the first time that the entire battalion, after having received parachute training, was functioning together as companies and as a battalion. This drop was made without incident and no injuries."

We were now a real paratroop outfit, "all the way."

The advance party was scheduled to leave on 18 August from Travis AFB in California by air for Vietnam. The battalion would send sixteen men. I sent the Battalion Executive Officer, Major Guy Eberhardt; the Assistant S-3, Captain Norman Propes; the S-4, Captain Jerry Plummer; and the Executive Officers and three men from each of the four line companies. Their primary task was to prepare our base and to receive the battalion on its arrival in Vietnam. Little did we know at that time what was really awaiting them. Had we known, we would not have sent so many leaders but more "doers," for the advance party's mission turned out to be primarily a "doing" mission in which everyone, regardless of rank, participated.

I was proud of the manner in which the battalion was performing. Many of the men who had been off at the various service schools, particularly the technical schools, were now with us. The platoons were shaping up rapidly. I carefully observed the company commanders to learn all about them and their abilities as well as those of their units.

I was most pleased with the progress of the platoon leaders. They were really coming of age and developing rapidly. I had been working hard on the staff. Major Herman, the S-3, was whipping the Operations Section into shape.

The S-1 section rapidly shaped up. The S-2 section was doing well and I was most pleased with the S-4. It appeared that the S-4 was a great scrounger, almost, I suppose you could say a thief, but all for a good cause. He obtained the things we needed and made certain that the battalion was properly equipped.

In the field we concentrated on day and night land navigation and cross-country movement, using the compass. Strong emphasis was also placed on crossing streams and rivers using various field expedients. We conducted a series of practical exercises in the Chattahoochee River. Each soldier was required, in conjunction with another soldier, to construct a two-man raft from their clothes and equipment. Then they swam across the river, pushing the raft in front of them and using it as a float when necessary. Next, we practiced crossing streams using a rope bridging that would be valuable both for stream crossing and for crossing narrow defiles. The men seemed to like this water activity. First of all, it was hot this time of the year, and training meant a chance to get in the water either through the actual crossing or when a luckless trooper fell from the dangling rope bridge into the stream. Captain Ramsey, the Headquarters Company Commander, took charge of water training for the entire battalion, performing in an outstanding manner.

Another important thing concerning myself. I finally selected my radio operators. The two men were part of my personal team and would be with me from then on. They were most important to the success of the battalion and improved my own effectiveness as a leader. First I selected a young soldier who impressed me one day in training, Private Edward Desner. He learned to be a driver and then concentrated on operating the PRC-25 radio.

In the battalion I had a policy of selecting for three days at a time a Colonel's Orderly. When selected as the Outstanding Young Soldier within the battalion, it was his job to stay with the Battalion Commander for those three days, going with me wherever I went, assisting as needed. I was most impressed by one particular young corporal, Corporal Byrl Ballew, whom I decided to select as my Senior Radio Operator and Chief of the Team. I took him from his job as a Fire Team Leader in Charlie Company.

Corporal Ballew was one of the original members of the battalion and had successfully completed jump training. He was a well-trained soldier who could shoot well, was physically fit, and could keep up with me any time, any place.

These two young soldiers had a difficult job. It was their mission to carry and operate two PRC-25 radios for me, one in the Battalion Command Net and the other in the Brigade Net. Second, they had to look after me more or less as my bodyguard in combat. Both these young soldiers were conscientious and strongly motivated. It was particularly challenging for them to keep up with the things that every soldier did within the battalion and also to accomplish all of the various special training and responsibilities in connection with being a radio operator for the Battalion Command Team.

Now that Airborne training was completed, a Prop Blast for the officers was in order to ready everybody of age as a paratrooper. This meant Prop Blasting almost all of the officers within the battalion. The only ones who had been Prop Blasted previously were Major Herman, myself, and one or two others.

A Prop Blast was organized and conducted at the Pistol and Rifle Club, Fort Benning, Georgia, one evening at about 1800 hours. General Richard Knowles, the Assistant Division Commander, was our guest of honor. He, Major Herman, two other members of the board, and I ran all of the officers through the Prop Blast ceremony, a tradition which had its beginning with the first history of the Airborne.

This was an excellent ceremony, one in which everyone had a lot of fun, and it did accomplish a great deal to unify and build the spirit within the battalion. It was most interesting to have our ALO, Captain Edward Holland, who was a jumper and had never been Prop Blasted, join us, along with our Artillery Liaison Officer and all of the new lieutenants. All in all, it was a successful Prop Blast with our own special Jumping Mustang cards, which Captain Mozey, the Adjutant, came up with, plus our own special Prop Blast Mug, made from a 75mm shell casing with two brass handles attached, one on each side.

The officers talked of the many humorous incidents that occurred during the "blast," especially to Captains Holland and Mozey, and then we were "on the way."

* * *

Time was getting close. We tried to give every man a short leave in order that he might settle his personal affairs and look after his family. This was difficult because we had so much to accomplish.

I was unable to take any leave. However, I managed to take one weekend pass in which I flew by commercial jet to see my daughter, Maria, in Philadelphia; my older brother, Bill, in Seattle; and my younger brother, Bob, in Los Angeles, all within the space of thirty-six hours. It was a fast trip and only a few hours with each of them, but sufficient to say good-bye.

In the meantime we were all getting our households packed up, stored, and moved, or what have you, so that the last two or three days would be spent only in worrying about the battalion.

On August fifteenth we completed the five-mile run—the run which had been forecast as the battalion goal and which most believed would never occur.

At 1530 hours, I joined the formation. We were all stripped to shorts and jump boots. The Guidon and my radio operators were with me. The staff was present and ready to go.

We started in company formations, a battalion of five companies in line, four men abreast in column. We commenced the run a little faster than a double time—a good, fast paratroop shuffle.

The headquarters commandant had laid out the course so that we wound back and forth through the battalion and brigade area in the Harmony Church. Two miles, three miles, everybody wondering if we would be able to do it. The Battalion Guidon, the "Jumping Mustang," was flying at the front of the column. Ballew and Desner shifted it back and forth. Although the guidon was an added burden for them to carry they were proud to be doing so.

At four miles we were all beginning to hurt, but we drove on. I was not really certain that I personally could make the run. I was not sure that we were going to make a five-mile one, because certainly if I could not, we would not complete the run. At four miles I was feeling good, and seeing the Jumping Mustang guidon up there, I could not quit. The battalion, seeing that flag and seeing me up there, were not about to quit either.

At four and a half miles we were all blowing hard but continuing. A few minutes later we completed the five miles, the flag still at the head of the column.

We came through in excellent shape and everyone, with the exception of a half a dozen who received minor sprains in the run, had completed it, including the Air Force Liaison Officer, the Artillery Liaison Officer, the chaplain, and doctor.

The unit was "one," and this was, I think, the major factor that helped us form such an excellent spirit.

Most of the officers and men long remembered the eighteen-hour days from 1 July to 20 August prior to loading up. It was rather unfortunate for those who were married, because they saw little of their families during that period. The working day began in the companies at 0400 hours and in most cases did not end, at the earliest, until about 2100 hours in the evening, and that was barring an exercise which took the units out overnight.

First Sergeant Ray E. Poynter, of B Company, best described this period: "I worked for twenty hours out of every twenty-four trying my best to learn the men, meet my subordinates and commanders, and get all the important rosters and reports accurate for the move. I'll never forget the hustle and all at Fort Benning. One can never forget the five-mile run."

There were so many things to do that one wondered in retrospect how they were ever accomplished: the training of the men, their own individual training, welding into squads and platoons, and getting together all of the various equipment necessary for both the troops and the unit. Not only having the equipment, but having it in topnotch, serviceable condition, meant repeated inspections in order to achieve the necessary standards. Not all supplies were available because of the tremendous demand on the supply agencies. Therefore, this whole process was spread out over a longer period of time. Necessary clothing and equipment could be obtained only in certain quantities and in certain sizes. It was only at the last minute prior to sailing that we finally reached one hundred per cent on equipment.

Everybody was thinking about Vietnam and about combat. We all read and studied everything we could find from the units that were over there ahead of us, especially the 173rd Airborne Brigade. Captain Danielsen, of A Company, and one sergeant in the S-2 Section and myself were the only Vietnam veterans in the outfit. We'd been there way back in sixty-two and three. We tried to pass on to battalion everything that had transpired before that might be of value. In addition, two other officers in the old 188th Battalion, who had been in Vietnam but were not going with us, lent a helping hand.

My usual day began with breakfast in one of the companies at 0500 hours followed by a chance to catch up on paperwork in my office until 0700. At that time, in PT uniform, I joined in physical training that lasted from thirty minutes to an hour. After a quick change of clothes and perhaps a shower, I would then observe field training.

The platoons and companies trained hard, concentrating on weapons, physical training, and information about Vietnam, including some of the language. We especially concentrated on ambush and counter-ambush and Viet Cong tactics and techniques. We were to receive the M-16 rifle during the last ten days prior to sailing. M-16 rifle training was accelerated as first priority when the rifles were received in order to make sure that we were proficient in mechanical training, minor repair, and, of course, in marksmanship.

Many, including myself, had misgivings about this weapon to begin with, having been unimpressed with it in Vietnam the first time when it was initially being tested. However, the M-16 turned out to be an excellent weapon if kept clean and only nineteen rounds were loaded in the magazine. It later proved efficient and effective in combat. The rifle was easy to shoot, and delivery of accurate fire was much simpler than with the M-14 rifle.

I mentioned that we concentrated on land navigation and map reading. Every platoon went through a compass course over the worst possible terrain we could find at Fort Benning, Georgia. This included a series of swamps as part of a prelude to an exercise in the Vietnam Village that the Infantry School used for training. We obtained permission to use this course to run each platoon through, both on the land-navigation

M-16

phase and through an attack on the village. Instructors from the Infantry School assisted on the phase in the Village to teach and demonstrate proper techniques.

I recall one platoon in which both the company commander and myself were present. We followed this platoon through the land-navigation phase. A total trip through the swamps and heavy vegetation should have taken about two and a half hours. We were still tramping the jungle and swamps some four hours later, and it looked at though we would not arrive in time for the Vietnam Village portion of the exercise.

The platoon leader was badly disoriented and learned a real lesson. His artilleryman, a forward observer from the company, kept insisting that they were going in the wrong direction. The platoon leader would not believe him and kept plugging on. The result was complete disorientation until the platoon leader finally got together with the artillery observer.

They coordinated their position and found out where they were and decided on an azimuth that would take them out.

The company commander and I both simply went along for the ride, letting the lieutenant make his mistakes and find his own way out of the swamp. This lieutenant was harassed considerably later on by his buddies, who I had made certain were aware of his misfortunes in the swamp, thus assuring a lesson that would be learned and not repeated again, by either him or the others.

The officers and the ladies of the battalion assembled this night at one of the small clubs at Fort Benning, Georgia, for a farewell party. This was a somewhat sad occasion, for we knew that we would be leaving in a few days and that it would be some time before wives and husbands, fathers and daughters and sons, would be together again. There was some gaiety, though, because the party marked the climax of our intensive training. I was happy to pass again on to the officers and ladies my appreciation for the outstanding job the battalion had accomplished.

In keeping track of the training and preparation for Vietnam and the many, many things going on in the battalion, I put in my appearance everywhere, or at least made the troops think I did. I had heard comments wondering how this was accomplished. It was not really hard. By knowing what was going on in the battalion, making use of the jeep and my drivers, making use of my feet and occasionally the helicopter, I was able to be in many places in a short period of time.

It was not necessary to spend a long time with the troops to observe a particular exercise or a platoon; it was enough to be there a few minutes and show the troops that you were concerned and interested. Most important, it showed them that you might pop up anytime, any place, in the future. This technique proved to be of great value and one which I carried on in Vietnam, not so much to check the troops, but to show my interest and so as to know what was happening and what was going on. The soldiers always knew I would be there if ever things went wrong.

One company commander indicated to me later that he never would understand how I could be in so many places at so many different times. He never knew exactly when I would show up or where, and sometimes not only under embarrassing conditions to him but also in interesting tactical situations.

A few words are necessary to give a proper understanding of the organization of the 1st Air Cavalry Division and the portions that might make up a battalion combat team.

First of all, the basic fighting elements in the Division were eight Infantry battalions; the ninth one joined us later in Vietnam. These eight battalions were organized into three brigades of: three battalions, including the ones I have already mentioned, in the 1st Airborne Brigade; three in the 2nd Brigade; and two in the 3rd Brigade. In addition, there was an Air Cavalry Squadron, which consisted of three Air Cavalry troops mounted in helicopters, plus one ground troop, mounted and mobile by the use of light, wheeled vehicles. The Air Cavalry Squadron was used to assist in seeking out the enemy.

There were the usual artillery battalions, one per brigade in direct support, and, most important, an Aerial Rocket Artillery Battalion (ARA) consisting of thirty-six rocket ships. These were UH-1B or D helicopters mounting thirty-six 2.7 rockets on either side. Some of these birds were also armed with 7.62-caliber machine guns. They provided rocket artillery fire when tube artillery was not available and in addition were used to supplement tube artillery.

The helicopter lift of the battalion was found in the Aviation Group, the primary elements being two assault helicopter battalions, one assault transport helicopter battalion, and supporting aircraft to include the reconnaissance Mohawk and command and control helicopters.

Each one of the assault helicopter battalions—the 227th and 229th—had sixty UH-1D helicopters. These were organized into three companies of twenty birds each. In addition, there was a gun company consisting of twelve UH-1B helicopters, armed with machine guns and rockets. The combination of four M-60 machine guns and sixteen rockets were mounted eight rockets and two guns on either side. A second assault helicopter battalion was organized the same way. The Chinook Battalion, the 228th Assault Support Helicopter Battalion, was equipped with forty-eight Chinook helicopters, sixteen birds in each of three companies. These helicopters were capable of carrying one rifle platoon.

CH-54 Flying Crane

The Division Support Command contained all of the logistical elements. Of major interest were four flying Cranes, the CH-54, capable of lifting by slingload a total weight of nine tons. These cranes were used to carry artillery pieces and ammunition. There were twelve UH-1D helicopters in the Medical Battalion, employed to evacuate casualties from the battlefield.

Last in the Division were the Signal Battalion, the Engineer Battalion, and the necessary command and control elements for the Commanding General and his staff in the Division Headquarters Company.

A battalion combat team consisted usually of the Infantry battalion, supported by at least one battery or more of 105mm tube artillery, perhaps reinforced by additional tubes. An Engineer Platoon or more was attached. Elements of Pathfinders from the Aviation Group were available to assist in selecting landing zones and controlling air traffic. The medical evacuation helicopters were available through the Forward Support Element (FSE), a portion of the support command that provided the logistical support. A number of helicopters were made available for a lift from the assault helicopter battalion. Usually, coordination and control effort were through one helicopter company reinforced with additional birds to whatever extent was required. The Chinook helicopters might work separately or through the assault helicopter company commander.

Often a portion of one of the Air Cavalry troops, or even the ground troop, would work with an Infantry battalion. Most important in the Air Cavalry Troop were the three teams: first, the White Team, made up of two OH-13 scout helicopters; second, the Red Team, which was made up of a platoon of gun ships mounting rockets and machine guns; and last, a Blue Team, essentially a rifle platoon mounted in UH-1D helicopters and used to search out the enemy when the indications were that some might be present.

These combined elements made up the basic support that was either attached to a battalion or under its operational control or in support of it to form a Battalion Task Force or Battalion Team.

Major General Harry W. O. Kinnard was the Commanding General of the 1st Air Cavalry Division. He was the chief architect and engineer who gave birth to the idea of the 11th Air Assault Division in 1963 and nursed it carefully forward through the major tests of Air Assault I and Air Assault II to the changeover to the 1st Air Cavalry Division, and then led it to fight in Vietnam.

Brigadier General Richard T. Knowles was the Assistant Division Commander who was concerned primarily with operations. I saw quite a bit of him when he visited my battalion.

Brigadier General Jack Wright was the other Assistant Commander, concerned primarily with logistics and the logistical elements. He would also be responsible for the Barrier or Green Trace in Vietnam, having planned, organized, and supervised its construction. He would also be the principal figure who kept logistics in operation in Vietnam, including supply and helicopter maintenance, in the same manner and with the same splendid record that he did in the latter stages of Air Assault II.

Colonel George S. Beatty was the Chief of Staff of the Division, having commanded the original Airborne Brigade of the 11th Air Assault. On changeover to the 1st Air Cavalry Division, he became the Chief of Staff. He had served for three months prior to that as the Commander of the 11th Aviation Group in the Division.

2

SHIPBOARD

On 20 August 1965 the Jumping Mustang Battalion began post clearance operations at 0300 hours. Large air-conditioned buses arrived a few minutes later, beginning the orderly departure from the battalion area and Fort Benning, Georgia.

Movement in a total of twenty-one buses to Savannah, Georgia, was completed by 1000 hours. The arrival at Savannah, arrangements there, and loading aboard the USN *Geiger* was completed without difficulty. The troop transport lifted anchor at 1745 hours and departed for Vietnam serenaded by music from a United States Army WAC band.

The movement down the Savannah River to the Atlantic Coast took approximately two hours. During this period people bid us farewell by cheering from the shore line, as well as from the ships that we met en route to the ocean.

Seven hundred fifty-three officers and men were aboard ship. This group, along with forty men and officers from the Reconnaissance Platoon of D Company, who sailed aboard the USN *Patch* the day before, and the sixteen men and officer of the advance detachment that had departed by air on the 17th, made up the Jumping Mustang Battalion en route to Vietnam.

The battalion had accomplished everything I asked, and had, to a man, declared themselves ready to go. I was impressed by the spirit, morale, and individual attitude of all the soldiers, including the young ones. For many of my noncommissioned officers and officers, this was an old war that they were returning to. The lieutenants were a gung-ho group with most of them Ranger-trained as well as Airborne. With the large, recently assigned group of noncommissioned officers from the 101st and 82nd Airborne Divisions, the entire battalion had acquired an Airborne capability in rapid order.

I was particularly pleased with our unit in comparison with others. Many of the fine points I harped upon really began to highlight the battalion's appearance and performance. This was especially true in those areas pertaining to quick and effective compliance with orders, which would be of major importance when we reached Vietnam.

The troops rapidly became accustomed to the ship, even though about 95 percent had not previously made an ocean voyage. The first night we were all weary and tired from completion of an intensive fifty-day training program. As soon as personnel were permitted to hit the sack, they really conked out. I finally went to bed at about 2200 hours and did not stir until 0600 the following morning.

We spent most of the next day simply relaxing, along with the reorganization and reassembly of troops within the holds. The entire battalion was in two holds or compartments, Bravo 6 and Charlie 6. The troops were billeted by squads under squad leaders, by platoon and company. It was a relief to get all the troops aboard the ship and to know that I had them definitely under my control for the next twenty-five days unless they should jump overboard. This was unlikely!

The food was excellent. I was afraid we would all be waddling ashore in Vietnam were it not for our PT program scheduled to commence on the twenty-third.

The sea was calm and quiet; this was excellent because it enabled the troops to get accustomed to the ocean and to the slight pitch and roll of a ship. Few of us had ever sailed before.

One thing was in our favor: the brigade was traveling on the ship as a single, complete unit. All of the rules and regulations were our own, with the exception of a few mandatory naval regulations. Thus the control was exercised only through our single chain of command, reducing the individual harassment of the troops.

All of the young troopers were on deck leaning over the

rails, sprawled on the deck, sleeping, or sunbathing. They were quick to take advantage of this day of unaccustomed leisure and rest.

Sunday was another day of relaxation and a chance to attend church services and generally take life easy. Relaxation included more sunbathing and the main occupation on board a ship: hanging one's head over the rail and simply staring at the horizon or the water. The troops were relaxed and talkative. I talked with many each day. They were all eager to "get on" with the job we had been selected to accomplish. Morale was high. As I compared the Mustangs with the other battalions, I could not help but be proud and feel privileged to be their commander. I was sure that the "Jumping Mustangs" would give a good account of themselves.

At 0500 hours we passed off the coast of San Salvador, one of the many islands of the Bahamas. At 1915 hours, we were a few miles off the coast of Communist Cuba, a short distance from Guantanamo Base. It was dark and we could see little of Cuba itself.

Tuesday morning, the following day, we were scheduled to pass through the Panama Canal. This was to be quite an experience and something new for most of us. I understood that it takes about a day and a half to go through the Panama Canal, that is, to cross the entire Isthmus of Panama. I would try to get a few pictures of the Panama Canal and of the activities of American troops sailing into combat.

It was about time to go out and take a look around the deck. On a ship one alternates between eating, sleeping, walking around the deck, and peering over the rail.

Tomorrow would begin a training program which would continue as long as we were on ship. This would include a large amount of physical training. At the rate that I had been eating the last couple of days, I would have to accomplish a great amount of physical training to keep my military figure.

Training began in earnest, and six days had passed since our passage through the Canal. Life aboard ship evolved around three activities: eating, sleeping, and training. The food was excellent and the Navy was taking good care of us! The sea was calm, except for the previous afternoon and

night, when we experienced some severe pitching and rolling. Even the normally agile waiters lost their balance (and a
few dishes), to the applause of our officers and NCO's, who
continually maintained a good sense of humor.

We had been receiving excellent physical training on the
sundeck, including forty-five minutes of calisthenics and the
stationary run, which had expanded to eight minutes. Corporal Ballew and PFC Desner and I generally went through two
and a half sessions of physical training. Each company took its
own separate PT. Thus one could take PT five times each day
if desired; however, two and a half periods were enough for
me! I was getting into pretty good physical condition and
feeling fine.

The troops had shown little seasickness; however, both
Ballew and Desner had been a bit under the weather for a
short time the previous night. The troops were taking the
voyage in stride and having a grand time.

Training was progressing well on the ship. We concentrated on jungle warfare subjects; mines and booby traps;
weapons; ambushes—both how to set up an ambush and how
to counter one; and a little about the country of Vietnam and
a study of basic Vietnamese phrases.

We had now completed about one-third of our trip and
were one week from Honolulu. We were due to arrive in
about six days, on Saturday, 4 September. It was unlikely that
many of the troops would be permitted ashore. The ship was
to be in port for twenty-four hours to take on additional fuel
and supplies. Supplying nearly three thousand active (and
hungry) paratroopers was a demanding task.

It would be nice to be in port, especially to replenish our
supply of potable water. We had adequate water, but strict
rationing was required to insure that none was wasted. Water
was cut off from 2000 hours to 0700 hours in the morning,
and again from 1300 to 1600 hours in the afternoon. We could
not wash clothes. This created somewhat of an inconve-
nience! Fortunately, as far as the troops were concerned,
wearing the shorts and T-shirts resulted in a sparse wardrobe
and there was sufficient water to enable everyone to wash
shorts and socks whenever necessary.

The western end of the Panama Canal was 4,400 miles
from Honolulu. From Honolulu, it was another 5,000 miles to
Vietnam. Our route passed just north of the Philippine

Islands, between the Philippines and Formosa, and then on into Vietnam.

On the ship relations with the crew and officer personnel of the ship were cordial. We had quite a joke as to where the ship's captain was. No one had seen him. We began to doubt whether there actually was a captain aboard. Maybe the ship was operated by a computer? He had not yet made himself known even to the senior officer on the ship, Colonel Roberts. They were equals as the ship captain's rank was equivalent to a full colonelcy. Thus far there was a contest going as to "who was going to see the Skipper first." We had been at sea nine days and no one had observed him yet. There was a rumor floating around today that one of our officers supposedly saw him, but this report proved erroneous. Will the ship's captain sign in, please?

I was pleased with the progress of the battalion. Being grouped in close quarters on the ship tended to draw us together. Everyone was getting to know one another. The fact that you are with one another twenty-four hours a day has numerous benefits. It's amazing what a unit can accomplish when their only concern is their specific mission to fix and destroy the stubborn enemy that is awaiting them.

I had been having a series of skull sessions with my staff each day. We got together and discussed the various problems we might encounter in Vietnam. What was the best way to accomplish a particular facet of the mission? In other words, what were our best operating procedures? These studies created interest and provided food for thought. Beginning the following day, we would include the company commanders in our meetings. I was certain that these sessions would prove to be valuable. We were also revising our tactical standard operating procedure to change from a training atmosphere to one of combat.

Morale and attitude of the entire battalion continued to be high. This was most pleasing. Daily inspections were held in the troop compartments. The commander of Compartment C-6, Captain William Smith, worked hard to win the top compartment designation on the ship. There were nine or ten troop compartments; competition for top honors was keen. Two days before Captain Smith had succeeded and captured the "best compartment" award. Unfortunately, that same day the brigade commander decided to no longer make a "best compartment" award, but simply to rate the compartments as satisfactory or unsatisfactory. Thus Captain Smith was never presented the award he had labored so hard to win.

My Executive Officer, Major Herman, or I personally inspected the compartments once a day at 1000 hours to see that everything was shipshape. It was amazing that 375 men could live in a space about a third the size of a football field, but it could be done. The men were bunked three and four in a stack on top of one another, in some cases in iron-bunk type beds or World War II canvas bunks, with very little head room. Latrines and showers were also crowded. These close conditions required that everyone cooperate and work closely together to the fullest extent. Our well-disciplined troops were doing a magnificent job.

The troops continued to be fed excellent food. I received few complaints. We had only limited PX facilities aboard, and each of the four battalions aboard took its turn, a day at a time, in numerical order. Such goodies as candy, cookies, and other comfort items of this sort were available but were rationed to insure that everyone would receive his fair share.

It was amazing to see how these young soldiers ate. At chow they filled their mess trays completely full, yet an hour later you would see them in the PX line with either a milkshake or a big box of cookies.

We had gained two hours' time thus far, and we turned our clocks back. Tonight we were on Pacific Daylight Time and would turn the clock back one more hour at midnight. This meant that for the past few days the ship had not been far off the United States Pacific coast. Commencing tomorrow our course would be more westward, to complete the 2100-2200 miles from San Francisco to Honolulu.

1st Sergeant Ray E. Poynter, B Company:

"I'll never be able to explain the many thousands of thoughts that ran through my mind aboard ship as we headed for the Panama Canal—thoughts I had not experienced since World War II. I was only a private first class then, and I tried to think how I felt then. Could these young men, ten of them only seventeen years old, do the job they had volunteered or been assigned to do? Would they fight, could they stand up in the awful storm of conflict, war, killing, and living from day to day? Not knowing yet what it was like, they seemed to me as a group of children going on a picnic. After a few days out and the saying 'Kill VC's' got around and 'Drive on—All the Way' talk developed among them. I realized I had nothing to worry about. We had a good outfit and were going to be hard to beat.

"The spirit of the unit rose to an all-time high with the constant training program, physical training, talks, decisions, and hearing all the leaders talk about their different tasks that lay ahead."

We arrived in Honolulu September 4th, pulling into Pearl Harbor at about 1000 hours. Approaching Pearl Harbor from the ocean was a beautiful and thoughtful experience. I had been in Pearl Harbor once before on a sight-seeing tour when I returned from Vietnam in 1963. As we came into the Harbor, we passed by the battleship *Arizona*, still a commissioned US Navy ship; but now a memorial to some 1200 sailors who still lie entombed within its sunken hull.

We docked at one of the piers in Pearl Harbor, and shortly a team headed by a Lieutenant General from the US Army, Pacific, came aboard to greet us and brief us on the forthcoming twenty-four hours. The entire ship was to be given liberty for approximately twelve hours. Welcome news to all! Troops were to go ashore at 1200 hours as fire-teams under supervision of their noncommissioned officers, who would accompany them, to return by 2200 hours. Officers and senior noncommissioned officers were to return by 2400 hours. We were scheduled to sail the next day at 1300 hours.

I accompanied Colonel Roberts to US Army Pacific Headquarters, where we received an excellent briefing on Vietnam, including the latest tactical situation with emphasis on our area of operation. We spent a few minutes in the Post Exchange at Fort Shaftner and then drove over to Fort De Russy, a military recreation center located in the middle of Honolulu on Waikiki Beach. Here most of the troops had been brought by bus to enjoy their liberty.

We strolled around Waikiki Beach, pleased with the excellent behavior of the uniformed paratroopers who seemed to have taken over the whole area. We adjourned to the Officers' Club at Fort De Russy, and spent the evening there having dinner and a few drinks, took in a fine Polynesian floor show, and then returned to the ship at about midnight.

At the ship I received the report that the Mustang Battalion had behaved themselves in an excellent manner. We experienced only a few minor incidents.

The short period of shore leave was worth while. We all had a chance to "recharge batteries" and enjoy a "last visit" on American soil. After two weeks at sea it was a welcome relief to be walking around on old Mother Earth again.

The following day was Sunday. The morning was spent in relaxation. The troops were tired and recovering after a night out on the town.

We lifted anchor at 1300 hours and sailed out of Pearl Harbor while Hawaiian music bade us a fond farewell. The sky was pretty and Honolulu beautiful in the midafternoon sunshine as we moved out past the battleship *Arizona*; I recorded our departure on film.

Soon we were on the open sea again, headed west toward Vietnam and whatever destiny held in store for each of our nearly three thousand troopers.

As we crossed the International Date Line, the date actually jumped from the seventh to the ninth, with no 8 September.

One of my associates, Colonel Joe Bush, who commanded the 2nd of the 19th, had a birthday on the eighth. He missed the birthday as a result of crossing the date line. However, we still had a party for him, complete with cake and coffee.

The sea had been calm the last two or three days, and the weather was beautiful.

We were busy training. The highlight of our training was still the physical-conditioning training. Each company had forty-five minutes on the sundeck, which, by careful maneuvering, would accommodate 175 troops in the necessary formation to go through vigorous calisthenics, the Army dozen. This week we executed fifteen repetitions of each exercise, which provided a good workout. This took about twenty minutes, followed by a twenty-minute stationary run conducted in cadence, sounded by the sergeants and officers. Many of the noncommissioned officers developed singing chants similar to the Jody Chant, to go with the running, which made everyone feel spirited. Chaplain Spear also wrote a popular Jody Chant, which we used:

Wake up Sunday, get out of bed,
Go to the washroom, wash my head.
Going to go to Church and Bible School,
Learn about Jesus and the Golden Rule.

Now we're headed for Vietnam,
You better run, you Viet Cong.
Going to fight for peace and liberty,
To make a new home for Democracy.

The Chaplain, Doctor and the CO too,
May lead a stick from the sky so blue.
When we have descended, you better run,
Can't go home till the combat's done.

Freedom, Freedom is our game,
For the People, by the People is the claim.
The right to worship, vote and love our liberty,
That's why we're going to have a victory.
Victory, victory, that's our claim
1st of the 8th, 1st Cavalry, that's our name.

Stand up, hook up, shuffle to the door.
Jump right out and count to four.
If my main don't open, gonna pull my reserve,
If that don't open, gonna lose my nerve.

All five of the companies demonstrated excellent esprit; the attitude and the morale of the soldiers, the noncommissioned officers, and officers were outstanding. That they were in such a mental condition, in spite of the long sea voyage was reassuring; we had completed about two-thirds of the trip.

The troops were informed on this day of our exact destination in Vietnam. We would be landing at Quin Nhon on the nineteenth of September. There was no harbor there, so we would debark into landing craft and land on the beach, executing, we hoped, a "peaceful invasion" of this beautiful country. Peace and security were about to become scarce commodities. The beach was sandy, similar to Miami Beach, as I recalled from prior visits to Quin Nhon. From Quin Nhon we would fly directly to our Division Base at An Khe along famed Highway 19, on which the Viet Minh had soundly defeated the French forces over twelve years before. An Khe was located along this highway about forty-five miles west of Quin Nhon, in the middle of the lush An Khe Valley.

I conducted a series of noncommissioned officers' and officers' schools every other evening. The daily skull sessions continued with emphasis on combat techniques. For example, with the company commanders and staff, we discussed the best way to employ our weapons, artillery, and tactical air support.

The Adjutant was busily engaged in preparing a decoration policy, something we had not been concerned with at Fort Benning. Our casualty reporting system had been updated. Since promotions would probably be a little bit more liberal in Vietnam, a new and revised promotion policy had been published. However, the realities of war had not been forgotten, and the latest casualty reporting system was being taught to all our officers and NCO's, who would be the ones to initiate casualty reports.

Commanding a unit is a stimulating experience, and I was fortunate in having an outstanding staff and an excellent group of company commanders.

However, I did have a problem with one lieutenant who was below par in one of the companies and who was also overweight. He was not performing well and everyone wanted to fire him. I decided to place him under my wing and put my thumb on him, so to speak. Between his company commander and me, we placed him on a rough schedule. He inspected the troop mess at 0400 to 0500 hours every morning and made a report to me at 0730. He completed physical training with his own company for forty-five minutes, then accompanied me on at least one of two other sessions with other companies for forty-five minutes each. He was on a diet and weighed himself every night and stuck to his diet, which was prescribed by our Battalion Medical Officer, Dr. Odom. He had to list for me every night exactly what he consumed during the day and the total number of calories. In the following seventeen days this had been an effective program. He had shaped up, had lost five pounds, and was fast becoming a good lieutenant. He could now do physical training more effectively on the second or third daily session.

This was just an example of how, working with some officers and men, you could watch and help them develop.

I concentrated on my own physical condition to assure that there would be no problem in my keeping up and leading the battalion in combat. On this day I increased my pullups on a horizontal bar from five or six when I began to thirteen. In a little contest with some of my staff, I managed to knock out forty-five push-ups, one right after the other, much to the astonishment of the staff. I had made them stay with me, and about had it by the time we finished. Anyway, I was getting into excellent condition and, although I had not lost any weight, it had reshifted, particularly from the stomach area. I was getting slim and trim again.

My lieutenant who was engaged on the diet came in to give me his report this night. He absorbed a total of 983 calories that day: 413 for breakfast, 202 in a light lunch, and 368 for dinner. He lost an additional pound, making a total of six since we started this program. The program had been effective and also had a desirable effect on some of the other officers in the battalion. I would not be surprised if this lieutenant would become one of my best before his return to CONUS.

We went ashore on Guam. We were scheduled to be there for only a few hours, but we had been given the opportunity of going ashore for at least a little exercise and some relaxation.

We docked on the Navy side of Guam alongside several destroyers and cruisers. The Adjutant, Captain Mozey, had gone ashore to make arrangements for a PX truck or beer wagon to join us on the beach area, where we assembled the entire battalion.

It was our turn to disembark. Dressed in PT uniform, companies were formed with guidons flying, including the Jumping Mustang flag. Under battalion control, a two-mile run was made to the beach area.

The battalion was in high spirits because of a chance to be ashore, get a little exercise, and drink some beer. On a fast paratroop run, our route took us alongside the piers where the Navy ships were tied up. The battalion was looking sharp; everyone was in step, each individual company counting cadence. As we passed the Navy ships the sailors were drawn up in white uniforms, observing us in silence, respectful or stunned—I was not sure which! This was quite a sight to them, I am sure, seeing a formation of approximately 800 troops, the uniform we were wearing, and the smoothness and precision as well as the spirit demonstrated in both the running and the counting of cadence. I had the impression that had one sailor given a catcall or had anybody tried to laugh, the entire battalion of Mustangs would have assaulted the offending ship and its crew. The spirit was evident to all.

I was extremely proud as the battalion ran by, because this was marked evidence of a well-trained and high-spirited organization. We were only a few days out of Vietnam, and it was obvious that we were ready for whatever might come.

We completed the run to the beach, where Captain Mozey met us with the first PX truck loaded with beer which he had managed to slip through the other battalions. The units were kept under company control on various locations or areas of the beach which had been assigned to them. There they swam and relaxed and did whatever they wished for the next two or three hours.

I provided a few cases of beer for each of my companies. We planted the battalion flag on a sand dune on the beach, where my staff, drivers, and I enjoyed a cool beer and relaxed on the beautiful seashore. There was quite a bit of sharp coral around the shore line, and the first thing one young trooper decided to do was jump in, head first; he smacked against a chunk of coral, and blood was streaming from his cuts. Fortunately, he was not seriously injured.

The sun was hot, there was plenty of beer, and the troops were taking full advantage of it. We all received a good addition to our suntan. The relaxation was well worth while.

After three hours it was time to reassemble the battalion and return to the ship. Again we moved by formation, and on the run, back to the ship, past the same waiting and watching sailors aboard the cruisers and destroyers. Quite a few of the troops had had considerable beer to drink; this fact, along with the hot sun, had made a few sick troopers, though nothing serious. These few hours had been a most welcome change here on Guam, one which helped not only our physical condition, but our morale. We were back aboard ship by 1400 hours. A short time later the ship hoisted anchor and sailed from Guam on the last leg to Vietnam.

PRC-25 Radio

*　　*　　*

In training we concentrated on the best method of carrying equipment and verifying equipment SOP's within the battalion. Within my own command group, we had been working on the best method to carry and camouflage the PRC-25 radios and the necessary equipment that we had to have in our small command group. Each of the radio operators was equipped with an M-16 rifle. One carried a machete and one an entrenching shovel. I carried my 45-caliber pistol. We all carried two fragmentation hand grenades. I carried two smoke grenades of various colors and each of my radio operators one.

As for our sleeping gear within the battalion, we each carried a combat pack. We used a two-man buddy system, one man carrying a poncho liner (a lightweight silk blanket) and the other an air mattress. Normal procedure was for one man to sleep while the other was on guard. This was called a 50 per cent alert. A system such as this cuts down on the extra equipment that must be carried.

Every man carried a poncho and his pistol belt, harness, and approximately three to five hundred rounds of M-16 ammunition, in addition to two fragmentation hand grenades.

A minimum amount of toilet articles was required because I insisted that the battalion maintain its personal sanitary condition and that every man shave habitually and keep clean to avoid disease.

In our training periods in the battalion we had been concentrating on airmobile techniques which the original 11th Air Assault Division perfected in Air Assault I and II. The officers were familiar with these techniques, but many of the NCO's were new to the air assault, having come from the Airborne 82nd and 101st. It was difficult for them to really understand the differences and the actual techniques. Those techniques were much like Airborne, so that it did not take long, with a series of classes and evening NCO and officers' schools, to ingrain what an air assault was and how the battalion and companies would perform them.

The techniques of the air assault include the maximum use of aircraft in movement of troops, employment of fire power, command and control and communication, intelligence and reconnaissance, and logistics.

The next day we would arrive in Vietnam.

3

ARRIVAL IN VIETNAM—GREEN TRACE

There was great excitement throughout the ship. Vietnam had been sighted and "Land ahoy" was sounded throughout the ship. All troops were on the deck at the best vantage point to observe the approaching landfall.

This was my first time to approach Quin Nhon harbor from the seaward side. I was most familiar with this area from 1962 to 1963, then a quiet little Vietnamese seaport and village, a smaller airfield able to land twin-engine Army aircraft at best, and the small harbor. I wondered what it would look like now with the extensive United States buildup for combat operations in Vietnam.

Land loomed larger on the horizon. Soon we approached the harbor itself and the anchorage with twenty or thirty ships at anchor.

After anchoring there was a period of suspense as Lieutenant Colonel Harlow Clark, advance party representative from the brigade, came aboard to brief us. We had thought it would probably be necessary to make some kind of assault combat landing, an amphibious landing, or perhaps even an air assault immediately after hitting the beach. This was not to be the case. The entire harbor and vicinity were secure, courtesy of the 101st Airborne Division.

We were disappointed that this would not take place, as we were all primed and ready to make some kind of combat landing. It was to our advantage, however, not to have to fight immediately, because it gave us time to go ashore, move to our base, and have a few days for preparation before operations began.

There were no piers for debarking, as had been the case at Savannah. Landing was to be from lighters, "ship-to-shore," then we would go by helicopter to An Khe, our new base camp.

At our base at An Khe, the advance party had been working feverishly to improve the camp. Security was provided by a battalion of the 1st Brigade of the 101st Airborne Division. We were expected to accomplish only our own local security and would have the few days necessary to shake down, get used to the terrain, the temperature—which was ninety-five to one hundred degrees—and the initial stages of combat.

No one went ashore on this day. After receiving the briefing from Colonel Clark, updating us on the tactical situation, final preparations for landing continued. What load to carry ashore? What should be the composition of the rear detail, which would stay aboard ship and oversee the unloading of the cargo and its movement, including the vehicles, to An Khe?

The entire battalion's equipment was now in the harbor. All ships were being unloaded by lighter, ship-to-shore. The aircraft carriers, loaded with helicopters, were in the harbor. Aircraft were rapidly assembled on the deck, engines run up, and the aircraft flown to An Khe.

We remained on board ship this final night. The company commanders were busy with plans for the following day—principally, the movement ashore and to An Khe. We would meet our advance detachment at An Khe and receive details on the specific situation facing the battalion.

Most of us spent the remainder of the day leaning over the rail, staring at the city of Quin Nhon and the surrounding terrain, fascinated with the strange sights. Binoculars were handy and at a premium, since they provided a detailed close-up of the other ships and of outposts on the surrounding hills which form a U-shape around the harbor and anchorage itself. One could see the squad tents, tactical wire, and men on the hilltops who were securing the harbor. There was little active evidence of war or combat except for the many busy ships in the harbor. No firing could be heard or seen during the afternoon or that night.

I was glad that we were finally here. It had been a pleasant voyage. The battalion was in fighting condition. I had not realized how valuable thirty days on a ship could be, with the entire battalion there, organized in squads, platoons, and companies, and no other mission except thinking, planning, and working toward preparedness for combat. Physically the battalion was in top condition and ready for whatever might lie ahead in the jungles, swamps or mountains. We were well polished in procedures and SOP's at squad, platoon, company, and battalion level. We had practiced hours of dry runs and skull sessions, what to do and when to do it, for every conceivable situation. We now would see how well those techniques were going to work. I had the utmost confidence and faith in the battalion, all the way.

As I evaluated the companies, I was pleased with the efficiency of C Company, commanded by Captain William H. Smith. B Company was commanded by Captain Oliver Dillon.

A Company, commanded by Captain Ted Danielsen, was coming along well. Captain Danielsen was the only commander with previous Vietnam combat experience, having been an Advisor in Vietnam in 1963. His company would perform well.

Delta Company, commanded by Captain Vandoster Tabb, was effective as far as the Reconnaissance Platoon and the Anti-tank Platoon went. I was not happy with the Mortar Platoon. This platoon required live firing, which it soon received on arrival—then it would be able to carry its load.

I was pleased with the battalion staff. Major John R. Herman, the S-3, was an outstanding officer and on the voyage had been acting as both the Executive Officer and the S-3. The S-2, Captain Charles B. Stone, was equally outstanding. The S-1, Captain William B. Mozey, was performing well. The S-4, Captain Jerry Plummer, was with the advance party in Vietnam. I had no doubts about his performance. Headquarters Company, commanded by Captain Russell W. Ramsey, was probably the finest headquarters company that I had ever been privileged to work with. The Service Platoon was weak, but certain changes made on the ship were correcting that. I was sure this platoon would be able to accomplish its combat mission as required.

The Jumping Mustangs were to be the second battalion to go ashore. Debarkation began at 1100 hours—down a single gangway to a large landing craft with capacity for three hundred soldiers. Headquarters Company and C Company were the lead elements, followed by A, D, and B Companies. There was a short run from the ship, a half-mile to the beach; the ramp was lowered, and we were ashore, much different from the anticipated assault landing.

Loaded up on two-and-a-half-ton and stake-and-platform trucks, we were transported a half-mile to the airfield to the staging area. There we assembled in groups, packet size CH-47 loads, twenty-five men per packet. The first packet, of which I was a member, numbered seventy troopers, to be transported in a Flying Crane, carrying us in the pod suspended beneath the crane itself. This would be my first time to fly in the Crane.

A three hours' wait for the aircraft to come. Meantime we had a C-ration dinner and stood in small groups watching the activities around us—those common at any airfield; many civilians were gathered around the outer perimeter of the airfield observing us with equal fascination. The soldiers were giving portions of their leftover C-rations, jam, coffee packet, sugar, and so forth, to the many children eagerly awaiting these handouts. I do not think the children were hungry, but these were nice tidbits and certain portions would end up on the black market.

1st Sergeant Poynter: "As we pulled into Quin Nhon Bay, we saw the black-pajama characters all around, many who were supposed to be Viet Congs. It did not take long to realize that everyone over there wore black pajamas. I realized right away that if we shot them all, we would be way behind on ammunition resupply before the battle started."

Finally my Flying Crane landed and we boarded the pod. I rode in the jump seat just behind the pilot and copilot. Takeoff was easy and, with seventy troops of the Jumping Mustangs suspended in the pod beneath us, we headed up Highway 19 toward An Khe deep in Viet Cong territory. Airborne, we climbed to 1500 feet. I had an opportunity to renew my acquaintance with the Quin Nhon area once again. It looked most familiar, including Highway 19.

There was a quick briefing by the pilot and copilot, who has been making this trip for several days as the division was being unloaded and moved to An Khe. Flight altitude of 1500 feet above the ground avoided enemy sniper fire, of which several rounds have been received in the past flights. Memory flashed back to my former flights over Highway 19 between Quin Nhon and Pleiku and the history of this famous highway, especially the era of the French back in 1953 and 1954 and the many battles that were fought along here. These battles included the complete destruction of Group Mobile 100, a French paratroop commando force, wiped out by the Viet Minh between An Khe and Pleiku.

I was struck again by the beauty of Vietnam. Vietnam was probably one of the most beautiful countries I had ever seen. It had everything—azure seashores along the areas of Quin Nhon and further south to Nha Trang. Flatlands or ricelands grow every conceivable agricultural product, including continuous rice crops—two and three each year. The mountains were covered with many types of trees, including valuable hardwoods such as mahogany and teak. There was every type of natural resource imaginable in the country. Were it not for the enemy situation, the country would be the type of place where you would gladly spend a two- or three-month vacation. Some day when this war is over, it will be a wonderful land. These thoughts slipped through my mind as we completed the short twenty- to twenty-five-minute flight to An Khe.

Our flight passed over the An Khe Pass, a small, narrow, winding pass through the range of mountains just east of An Khe, marking the beginning of the beautiful Song Ba River valley or plain, of which An Khe was the hub or center. The Song Ba valley was surrounded by mountains. To the west was the famous Mang Yang Pass. The first look at An Khe revealed a broad, flat, fertile valley with high ground in the distance and low hills several hundred feet high immediately adjacent to the camp, particularly to the south and southeast. Hong Kong Mountain, 700 feet high, also called Mustang Mountain, dominated the camp itself and eventually would become part of the perimeter. Memory flashed back to the famous French battle of Dien Bien Phu, that decisive defeat suffered by the French in 1953.

When word came of the plan for defense of the An Khe base and the fact that the entire Division would be located in one area, and when we saw the maps and terrain, I wondered if this might be the beginning of another Dien Bien Phu. The situation and circumstances were different here. The biggest difference, which I'll have more to say about later, was the present existence of an Airmobile Division. The mobility of the helicopter provided the capability to move troops any time, anywhere. An Khe was simply a base, selected primarily because it was the center of the Vietnamese Second Corps Tactical Zone and was astride the important Highway 19. One of the Air Cavalry's first missions was to keep this highway open from Quin Nhon to An Khe, now held partly by Division elements and others, and also to open the road between An Khe and Pleiku initially and from time to time and finally on a permanent basis.

1st Sergeant Poynter: "The ride up to An Khe seemed like a Sunday cruise—we didn't even get shot at. I thought, could the VC really be down there? Would we really get into a fight? Well, it didn't take long for us to find that out!"

The Flying Crane made a circle of the An Khe Camp, at the moment simply a big clearing carved deep in the subjungle. The jungle growth was not heavy, consisting of small twenty-, thirty-, and forty-foot trees. There were some large trees, including one in the middle of the camp, known as "The Banyan Tree," a huge banyan tree standing in solitary splendor on the Golf Course, a designation for which the An Khe Base and the 1st Air Cavalry Division would become famous. Sufficient to say now, the Golf Course was (or soon would be) the world's largest heliport and had nothing to do with the game of the same name.

Landing, we were met by guides from the battalion. Here was Major Guy Eberhardt, the Executive Officer, whom I was happy to see. He did not have time to tell me too much, but he started us walking on the rough, muddy trails. It had been raining, as it does so much of the time in Vietnam and as it was doing this day. It took fifteen or twenty minutes to make the short march with our gear, less the duffle bags, which had been stacked in piles to be moved later by trucks, to that portion of the An Khe jungle clearing belonging to the Jumping Mustangs.

We finally arrived there. I was pleased with the progress made in carving out this portion of the jungle camp. The advance detachment of sixteen men had had little time to work on this area for the battalion itself. The entire advance detachment of the Division had been held under central control by General Wright, one of the Assistant Division Commanders and the general officer in charge of the advance

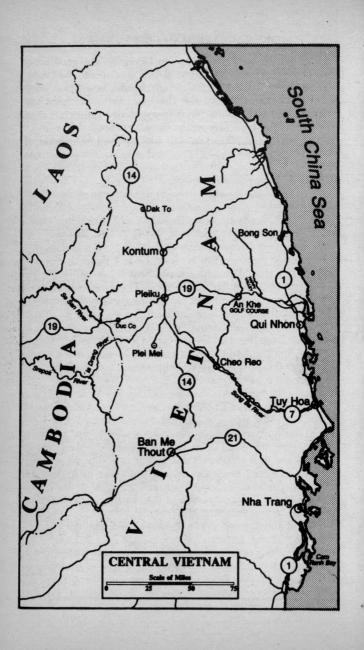

LAOS

South China Sea

14

Dak To

Bong Son

Kontum

Se San River

Pleiku

19

1

19

Duc Co

An Khe
GOLF COURSE

Ia Drang River

Plei Mei

Qui Nhon

VIETNAM

Cheo Reo

Srepok River

14

Song Ba River

Tuy Hoa

7

CAMBODIA

Ban Me
Thout

21

Nha Trang

1

Cam
Ranh Bay

CENTRAL VIETNAM

Scale of Miles

0   25   50   75

party, to develop certain key division installations, particularly the Golf Course, or the Helipad, in order to land the birds, or helicopters, on arrival. The helicopters were the most important single asset to the division. Without them we simply ceased to function. The first priority and mission of the advance party was to create the Golf Course.

The companies were quickly guided to their portion of the Jumping Mustang area. Pup tents were pitched and the

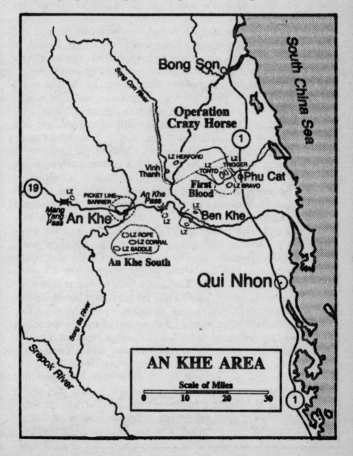

battalion established for the night. A portion of our tentage had arrived. At least, we had a squad tent for Operations with radio and wire communications to the brigade and our sister battalions. There were two small tents up for the Executive Officer and me. A temporary shelter had been erected for the kitchen so that hot food could be served as soon as kitchen equipment arrived from the ships; this would not be for several days. Meantime, we were eating C-rations, our fare for a few days until we could get the kitchens ashore and prepare B-rations (canned rations) for the men.

All were weary and tired and thankful that we did not have to fight, that we were here and ready to go. I made a quick circuit of all company areas, visited the company commanders, and ascertained that we were set for the night.

This first night, none of our troops were on the line or on that portion of the perimeter for which our battalion would ultimately be responsible. This was fine, because, despite all our training and the excellent leadership of our officers and NCO's, I had anticipated that we might be a bit trigger-happy that first night in Vietnam. Fighting positions were prepared and areas carefully assigned: a certain portion of the battalion bivouac to each company, including coordination points. Security or listening posts were established in each company area. Weapons were not to be loaded. There would be no shooting unless positive that the target was a Viet Cong, or unless an officer or NCO directed the fire. We were within a perimeter, and personnel from the advance party and the 101st Airborne Division were securing the perimeter or, as we would soon be calling it, the "Green Trace."

Major Eberhardt, the Executive Officer, spent considerable time bringing me up to date on what had transpired in the advance party, the latest situation in the area, latest intelligence, and what would be expected of us. We were not to have a specific mission for a few days, at least for a week, other than improvement of the bivouac and commencing work on the barrier that marked the Green Trace.

The troops turned out to be calm this first evening, although there was some shooting during the early part of the evening and the night from troops on the Barrier, an occasional rifle shot or flare, and a few outgoing mortar rounds. It was a much quieter evening than was expected—probably a disappointment to some, a relief to others. Finally, at 2300 hours I decided to call it quits and hit the bunk myself for a few hours' much-needed sleep, knowing that we would have a busy day on the morrow.

One sergeant: "The advance party right away started telling combat stories about how they were the bush hogs, how they had been waging war on the bushes and trees where Bravo Company would be set up. They didn't tell me enough about the big ants in the area, and it took only a couple hours to find out about them. I made the mistake of placing a used C-ration can under my bunk. I believe every ant in the area came to roost under my bunk. I found out about this about 3:00 A.M. when I got up for a moment. I had ants all over me—in my sleeping bag, in my boots, and inside my underwear. I latched onto a bottle of mosquito lotion that night and kept it with me until I left Vietnam in August, 1966."

It was a new day and the beginning of a busy period, spent improving the bivouac, establishing and ditching tents, and checking equipment. Some equipment arrived from the ship. In about three days the vehicles began to arrive. We were well off for wheeled transport because a few of our vehicles had come in on earlier ships and were already on hand. These were the gun jeeps, mounting the battalion's eight 106 recoilless rifles.

Drinking water was a major problem and had to be procured from one of the water points established by the Division Engineer. We were fortunate to have three 500-gallon water trailers and could handle this requirement with ease.

We were still eating C-rations but tried to heat them under central control in each company and to at least prepare hot coffee.

On this morning the Brigade Commander called the battalion commanders together. We had been given initial assignments for defense and for construction of a portion of the barrier. Fortunately, the 1100-yard portion allotted to the Jumping Mustangs was adjacent to our bivouac area. I divided the area into three company sectors, A, B, and C. The company commanders were shown these areas and commenced immediate work on hasty positions, that is, foxholes, with gun positions for the machine guns and other crew-served weapons. We laid wire and each night placed booby traps on enemy avenues of approach.

The intelligence situation indicated that there was little likelihood of a major attack but that we could expect guerrilla attempts to penetrate our perimeter and create local disturbances. Tonight was the first night we occupied the Barrier or Green Trace, assuming responsibility from the advance party. The 101st Brigade Battalion now moved out to what was called the "Picket Line," a series of hilltops five to seven kilometers distant, designed to keep the Viet Cong out of mortar range of the camp. They would be responsible for occupying those hills and conducting patrols.

Our mission for the next few days was protection of the perimeter of our base. The "Green Trace" or the "Barrier," described as both, was actually the outer perimeter of the Division camp, formed as a circle or a wheel. In the center of the wheel were the Division agencies, including the headquarters and supply units. Around the rim or outer perimeter were positioned the eight Infantry battalions.

These Infantry battalions were responsible for defending the perimeter itself, patrolling out to a distance of five hundred meters in each one of the sectors. It was visualized that this fortified barrier would eventually consist of bunkers, trenches, electric lights, barbed wire, and mines and be practically impenetrable, so that minimum numbers of troops could defend it yet be able to resist any type of attack, including a major attack.

Contributing to the defense by the eight Infantry battalions were the tube artillery battalions in position with howitzers covering every portion of the sector. The 2nd of the 19th Artillery provided support for the 1st Airborne Brigade. We had carefully prepared fire plans for both the artillery and our own mortars in the rifle companies and D Company, and had commenced to register where terrain would permit. Unfortunately, a portion of the Jumping Mustang area was in an area heavily populated by Vietnamese civilians. There was little registration that we could actually accomplish in a portion of this civilian area. We had to be particularly alert if under attack, for when we did shoot, we were probably going to kill some civilians; so we took utmost care and maintained absolute fire discipline, unless the VC were really there.

This first night on the Barrier was most interesting indeed. Through our emphasis on leadership and fire discipline, our battalion proved its discipline and self-control in not firing a single round that first night, in spite of continuous firing on the left from a sister battalion and on the right where the other battalion was. This latter unit shot up a storm almost every night. Everyone was a bit nervous. I was in contact by telephone and radio with the company commanders, and they with their platoon leaders. Every time we heard a series of weapons firing cut loose on our flanks from our sister battalions, we were all concerned. Questions start flowing back and forth in the chain of command by both telephone and radio. I tried to find out what was going on from brigade and the adjacent battalions and passed this information to the companies. They talked with their platoon leaders and the platoon leaders with their squad leaders, thus attempting to keep a calm and controlled situation within the Jumping Mustang Battalion this first crucial night.

We carried out more of the same type of preparations as on our first day on this our second day at the battlefield, improving the bivouac and continuing the work on the barrier. You could hear the signature of the 1st Air Cavalry overhead, the beat of blades of the ever-present helicopters, slapping the air as they lifted in and out of An Khe.

The weather was very humid, rainy, and hot.

A *sergeant:* "We saw nothing but rain for the first nineteen days. I thought it rained in Texas, but I found somebody upstairs just plain opened a spigot and let it run wide open in Vietnam."

Right now there was a lot of both mud and rain. Trying to keep the men dry and taking care of weapons and equipment became a major task for all leaders. I spent most of my time touring the various company areas, conducting spot checks and detailed inspections of weapons, ammunition, and equipment. Our weapons suffered from the continued wetness. They had to be kept thoroughly clean and lightly oiled or we were going to have problems. Ammunition became unusable rapidly in this type of weather. We established SOP's on how ammunition was to be maintained on Barrier positions and how it would be carried by each trooper.

Weapons safety was paramount. There were two degrees

of loading weapons in the battalion, always on order of a
leader. The first degree was insertion of a magazine or a clip
into the weapon without chambering a round; this was accomplished only on the order of a leader. The second degree
of loading was to put a round in the chamber, with the
weapon ready to fire with but a touch of the trigger, after
removing the safety. During the day weapons were unloaded
with magazines in magazine carriers or pouches. At night on
positions on the line, magazines were inserted in the weapons and machine guns were half loaded, but that was as far as
it went. There were to be no rounds in chamber and no full
load in the machine guns. In this manner we had avoided
wild shooting and accidental shooting thus far.

Instructions to squad leaders and men, if they saw or
heard something, were to watch and listen and call for an
illuminating flare from one of the mortars to see what was
there. My standing order was simply, if you fire a round,
there better be a dead VC body. This system worked well
within the battalion. I made maximum use of the poor
examples of other units and their wild shooting to impress on
our units and leaders that fire-control discipline was mandatory.

Everybody was anxious to shoot the first Viet Cong, but
thus far we had not had a real chance. There had been two or
three reports that Claymore mines, placed out in front of our
unit positions at night, had been reversed 180 degrees. This
meant that apparently a Viet Cong had sneaked in close and
turned the Claymore mine around. Then, believe it or not,
someone from that same vicinity threw rocks at the troops in
the hopes that they would detonate the Claymore, thereby
injuring or killing our own men. We were wise to this enemy
technique, having been made aware of it from after-action
reports we had read. We now booby-trapped the Claymores,
so that if one was moved, it would blow up and destroy
whoever was fooling around. We made it SOP to not put the
Claymores out in firing positions until the last light just prior
to dark and to retrieve them early the next morning. People
out in the bushes watching us during the day did not have too
good an idea where our Claymores were. We also pulled the
machine guns back from positions during the day and covered
them with canvas so that someone outside, where there were

Claymore Mine

many civilians, could not spot our troops or machine guns and so aid a possible attack in the evening.

On this evening, while preparations continued for the defense, we suffered our first casualty. One of our sergeants in setting out a trip flare accidentally set one off in his jacket. He had been carrying a trip flare inside his jacket along with two or three fragmentation hand grenades. The flare accidentally went off. As it started to burn inside his jacket, he was concerned with trying to get the frag hand grenades out of his jacket before they, too, went off. In the process of unbuttoning his jacket and reaching in and pulling out both the grenades and the flare, he burned his hands badly and his chest. He was evacuated to the hospital by helicopter and was the first casualty within the battalion. This was also our first incident involving the use of live ammunition.

The Barrier was shaping up rapidly. The positions were

looking good, although they required constant maintenance because of rain and wear and tear from the troops' use. There was a shortage of sandbags and bridging or fortification material. This shortage continued to plague us for some time. Although the supplies might be aboard ships in the harbor, actual unloading and delivery to the user where needed was difficult. We had sufficient ammunition, clothing, and food. Fortification materials would be in short supply for some time to come.

At the beginning, on our arrival at the bivouac, it was obvious that many supplies that one could expect in a normal garrison situation would not be available. Construction equipment, such as bulldozers, graders, and other earth-moving machinery, were in short supply. Building materials, such as timber, lumber, tin, roofing, cement and nails were not readily available.

We resolved within the battalion to raise our standards of living as rapidly as possible. This was to be accomplished by scrounging or collecting from all available sources and making use of any and all types of construction material. Fortunately, most of the companies brought in considerable amounts of lumber.

It was interesting to observe the improvement within the battalion and company areas as each company commander did what he could to improve the living conditions of the troops. First priority was some kind of kitchen. This required considerable pressure and effort by Major Eberhardt, the Battalion Executive Officer; however, suitable kitchens, with cement floor, wooden frame, and tin roof, and some kind of covered dining area were soon completed.

Within Headquarters Company, priority was for construction of an S-3 Operations tent, a cement floor with a framed tent, in which the necessary communication equipment and the operations personnel could operate for the battalion. High priority was granted to the construction of an Enlisted Men's and an Officers' Club.

The Enlisted Club had first priority under the control of Sergeant Major Herbert P. McCullah. He and certain of his NCO's acquired the necessary materials to get the club going. This began first with a squad tent, simply pitched at a suitable area within the battalion. We tried to gather the maximum amount of beer and ice, which was scarce, so when troops were back in the battalion area, especially during a reserve period of one or two days, they would have a chance to rest a bit and have a few beers. American beer was scarce in the beginning, but it could be found in small quantities. Initially there was no ice, so we were forced to drink warm beer; however, if there was no ice, beer was in short supply, and you had not had any for a couple months, warm beer was a welcome luxury. There were few soft drinks. They were a premium item also.

We were able to collect some beer on the local economy in An Khe. This consisted of two types. One type was Ba Muoi Ba, which stands for No. 33; Ba Muoi Ba is the Vietnamese-language designation of the number 33. It was a good beer, but it was alleged, and I quite agreed, that it was aged by the use of formaldehyde or embalming fluid. After consuming two or three of those beers, one felt almost as if he had been embalmed. The other type beer, known as Beer La Rue, was a little lighter and more available in the small village of An Khe.

We established an Officers' Club. This began as a squad tent in the beginning with a few beers and a little whiskey available. Captain William Mozey, the Adjutant, had the task of creating an Officers' Club, supplying both design and construction. He drew up a plan for the first two-story building, a German-chateau type, to be constructed in the 1st Air Cavalry Division and probably in Vietnam. A review of the plans showed the amount of material required to be astronomical. I tried to discourage this type of construction, but Captain Mozey was insistent; and since he said he would obtain the material, I agreed to let him go ahead and build it.

Chaplain Ralph Spear, with the assistance of the Headquarters Company Commander, Captain Ramsey, had under construction a Battalion Chapel. The Chapel was to be constructed in Montagnard design or style consisting of a simple A-frame, seventy feet in length by twenty feet in width. It had a cement floor, with the frame constructed of native materials. It was possible to purchase lumber from merchants in the city of An Khe at high prices. Better yet, in the vicinity of Pleiku, large quantities of lumber were available from commercial resources at about one-third the price. In the future as Mustang convoys moved back and forth on tactical missions to Pleiku, Captain Ramsey took maximum advantage of the opportunity to purchase needed lumber.

The Chapel was to be completed with whatever materials we could find. This task was primarily that of the Chaplain. The S-4, Captain Godwin P. McLaughlin, and Mr. Samuel Rader, the Supply Officer, our finest scroungers, retrieved considerable materials. Captain Russell W. Ramsey and his crew in Headquarters Company were good at this sort of thing also. I must add, Sergeant Major McCullah was a past master at procurement. Through his various contacts with other sergeants major within the brigade and the division and adjacent units, we were doing well. Christmas was the goal for the completion of the Chapel. We did not achieve this goal, owing to tactical operations and the absence of necessary materials, but it would be completed by early spring.

Of interest was how the roof for the Chapel was to be procured. It would be constructed of a green plastic, translucent material which made it one of the most picturesque chapels within the 1st Air Cavalry Division.

Other construction priority was directed toward the improvement of some kind of supply room or tent for each company. This consisted of Connex metal containers and a framed tent, to assure that supplies and equipment were off the ground and properly secured.

The S-4 was completing similar action with his supply installations to assure that battalion supplies, including the basic load of ammunition remaining with the battalion, were properly maintained. Priority within the companies then was some kind of orderly room or command post and the construction and improvement, simultaneously, of living quarters. These would be squad tents, framed, with cement floors. A certain amount of squad tents were issued; however, issue was slow. Tents were issued on an equal basis within the brigades within the division. Captain McLaughlin and his crew gathered a number of additional tents which saw the battalion completely under canvas a few weeks later.

Materials were obtained primarily at Quin Nhon, by sending trucks to contact service units in that area and to bargain and trade for whatever they could find. It was amazing how a souvenir crossbow, a Viet Cong or NVA rifle, would bring in Quin Nhon lumber, cement, and other essentials necessary for the welfare of our troops. We also sent supply personnel to Nha Trang and Saigon; however, the problem here was in the return of materials recovered, which had to be flown in by air. This task required location of the material and equipment and also negotiations with the Air Force or the Army to fly it back to An Khe under Jumping Mustang escort and guard.

Employing all of these combinations, progress in housing and creature-comfort improvements within the Jumping Mustangs was noticeable. Initially my quarters were an improved hexagonal CP tent accommodating five men. Finally, at my own expense for the purchase of lumber and cement on the open market, Sergeant Major McCullah built a hut. The first part, a room ten feet by eight, consisted of my office, or the Battalion Command Post itself. The rear section, of similar proportions, consisted of my quarters and small living room. The Sergeant Major insisted that he was going to construct a flush toilet; however, I was satisfied for the time being with a typical outside shanty a few yards away which the S-3 and Executive Officer shared with me.

One of the priority items for creature-comfort within the battalion itself was some kind of shower. The biggest problem in war and in an area such as we were now in was sanitation. I insisted that troops keep clean-shaven and take a bath whenever possible. This meant that whenever there was a river, lake, pond, or any type of water supply available, we took full advantage of it. It meant that within the base area we created showers from any and all types of containers, mounted on a platform with improvised shower heads below. C Company had a fine shower already.

The Headquarters Company produced one, the water tank being a damaged engineer assault boat on a raised platform. A well was under construction within the Headquarters company area; however, at this point it was some twenty feet deep with nothing but red mud in the bottom. By filling the improvised boat tank each day from the nearby Song Ba River, showers were available for the men in Headquarters Company.

B Company finally completed a shower, and recently I was shown an outstanding facility constructed by A Company. There is nothing like a shower. One does not worry about whether it is hot. Simple cold water was a treasure when returning from an action or a number of days deep in the jungle under extreme physical labor.

Captain Mozey, the Adjutant, obtained a 16mm projector. These were initially allocated one to a brigade and one to each of the separate units. The one within the brigade was maintained at the Brigade Headquarters area for the benefit of the entire brigade. This meant that the Mustangs did not see movies often. Through efforts above and beyond the call of duty, Captain Mozey procured an extra projector complete with sound, from Saigon. Once we had this machine, we were able to get on the film circuit and had movies within the Jumping Mustangs Battalion almost every night. This benefited us and provided great pride within the battalion, since they knew we were the only battalion to have a machine of our own. The battalion—its staff and men—knew you must take care of yourselves over here. There were many ways to secure necessities legitimately and legally. Equipment and the supplies were available. Sometimes it just took great ingenuity and effort to find them.

My S-4 and his cohorts had an amazing faculty for coming up with additional chow. As the increased "A" rations began to be felt within the division, we not only got our share but were able to collect other luxury-type items from Quin Nhon.

We had concentrated on making our battalion base in An Khe the best possible. When back within the battalion base, we concentrated on necessary tactical missions but also found time for the improvement of our living conditions.

The two clubs, the Officers' and the Enlisted Men's, acquired beer and some ice in the little city of An Khe. We were also able to receive large quantities of American beer from Quin Nhon. Some beer was also beginning to reach the Division.

I keep referring to supplies available in Quin Nhon. Actually, most materials were abundant there. The problem was transportation to An Khe. The Division made tremendous logistic efforts however, we obtained additional stores by sending our own vehicles or, when we could borrow, one from another unit. We were not short-changing anyone else within the Division, but were simply taking advantage of available transportation to secure supplies in Quin Nhon that were there for those who wished to go and get them.

On this day a decision was made to reassign Captain Roy Martin, who had been the Assistant S-3, as commander of B Company.

The new commander, Captain Roy Martin from Pleasant Grove, Mississippi, was an old Army sergeant, an outstanding soldier, who won an OCS commission in 1959. I had confidence in whatever he did. In the coming year this company would become the finest company in the battalion, and it was to continue this outstanding performance throughout the Jumping Mustangs' tour in Vietnam.

1st Sergeant Ray E. Poynter: "After we had been cutting grass and building fences, losing machetes and tools for a week, we received word we were getting a new commander. Captain Roy Martin came down, walking softly but carrying the big stick he was known for. Regrouping and getting ready to charge was the general feeling everyone had. We were really going to get some VC's fast."

On this day we were alerted for the first major mission on the Picket Line. The battalion was assigned the majority of the brigade sector of the Picket Line, heretofore under the control of the 101st Airborne Division. Relief was to be accomplished by assuming control from a battalion of the 101st in this particular sector. The mission was to occupy the hilltops five to seven kilometers out from the Barrier and to conduct extensive and deep patrolling between the Barrier and the Picket Line and the terrain in front of the Picket Line. This would provide the opportunity to get our feet wet and the first combat action against known guerrillas in the area. It also meant the first combat air assault into the immediate area.

A young soldier: "For the rest of September, I had begun to think we had come to Vietnam to cut grass, trees, and brush and build fences. I wondered when they were bringing the cattle in. The only good thought I had at this point was that at least we could maybe have some steak instead of pancakes every day. It didn't take long to realize that we needed a Mess Sergeant that could make pancakes from any kind of mixture and make them taste like egg one time, steak another, and beans another. I figured we were going to eat pancakes all year. After that first month, I would have given fifty dollars for a big juicy steak with French fries. I also remember the first mail I got. It was just like Christmas all over again."

4

FIRST AIR ASSAULT

Picket Line, An Khe, Vietnam

On 28 September reconnaissance was completed. In order to obtain a good view of the positions occupied by the 101st, the reconnaissance was made from the command helicopter. Next came a visit to the battalion of the 101st Airborne Division that currently had the mission. Last there was final coordination with companies and units of the 101st by Mustang company commanders.

The first battalion order was issued. This was to be our first combat action. Heavy enemy action was not anticipated; however, guerrilla attacks up to possibly platoon size would no doubt occur.

The relief of the 101st Battalion proceeded smoothly. By 1600 hours in the afternoon the Jumping Mustangs were in control of one-third of the Picket Line for the entire division.

One of the most effective means of command control to evolve out of the 11th Air Assault days was the command helicopter, a UH-1D, allocated to each Infantry battalion of the 1st Air Cavalry Division. There were five of these helicopters organic to the Aviation Platoon of the brigade. One UH-1D was habitually allocated to each of the three Infantry battalion commanders. One was used by the Brigade Commander. The last bird was generally in reserve, most of the time for maintenance.

This command helicopter was normally rigged with four FM radios, using the VRC 46 receiver-transmitter, stacked two deep, side by side, in front of the rear seat. This arrangement permitted five persons to sit in a rather crowded condition across the back seat with the four FM radios and the control panels in front. Some command helicopters substituted the fourth FM radio for a UHF or single side-band radio. I preferred, under the circumstances, the four FM radios.

My airmobile command party generally consisted of the pilot and copilot, sitting in front; myself on the left side of the rear seat; Artillery Liaison Officer on the outside right seat for good observation; Battalion S-3 next to me; and probably the Air Force Liaison Officer (ALO) between the S-3 and the Artillery Liaison Officer (Arty LNO).

I monitored the Battalion Command Network on one FM radio. The Artillery Liaison Officer used one on the Fire Control Network of the direct-support artillery battalion. The Air Force Liaison Officer monitored the net with which he communicated to the Airborne Forward Air Controller (FAC), actually directing air strikes. The fourth set was used by the S-3 either to monitor the Brigade Commanders' Net, or, during an air assault, to monitor the lift frequency of the assault helicopter company or battalion.

When the fourth net was used on the assault helicopter lift frequency during an air assault, one of my radio operators sat in the right rear compartment serving as the door gunner for the right side of the bird, monitoring the Brigade Commanders' Net on his PRC-25 back-pack radio. When a call was received from the Brigade Commander or from Brigade, he called me on the intercom. I either used his radio to talk, or switched one of the four FM sets momentarily to the Brigade Net. On the left rear compartment the Crew Chief served as a door gunner for that side of the aircraft and performed his primary function of Crew Chief. In addition, often I carried my second radio operator, sitting in one of the rear compartments, when I planned to go on the ground. On the ground it was essential that I have two radios in operation, one for Battalion Net, one for Brigade. This was the usual composition of the airmobile command control party.

Each member of the command party was connected by intercom so that I could talk to all of them or to any one individually, at will. The pilots could talk to me, and I to them. Still left available were the aircraft radios, one FM radio and one UHF, which could be operated by conversing through the pilots. The UHF radio was valuable to the Air Force Liaison Officer if he wished to talk directly to the Airborne Forward Controller. He did this by simply using the pilot's headset, or better yet, by passing the plug back and connecting his own headset. When employing this system, it was necessary for the pilot to press the transmit button whenever the ALO wished to transmit.

Frequently, if I was making a reconnaissance and not actually overseeing a battle itself, I flew as one of the pilots. I flew generally from the left side in the copilot position because habitually our SOP provided for my being on the left; thus my pilots always knew which way to fly in order to give me the best view of the action. When necessary to conduct a firing mission, artillery or tactical air, priority of the aircraft was to the right so that the ALO and Arty LNO sitting on the right flank had the best observation.

A deficiency of the command helicopter was that when banking in one direction, for example to the right, occupants on the right side could see very well but those on the left saw only the sky. All had a good view forward through the plexiglas of the pilot's and copilot's windshield.

The occupation of the Picket Line was smooth. The primary actions of the units were to improve the defensive positions on top of the mountains and conduct extensive patrols.

The Recon Platoon was the first to move out to conduct a series of recon, combat, and ambush actions. The platoon was employed as an "Eagle Flight," airlifted by UH-1D helicopters in a small-scale air assault to likely enemy areas, scouting on the ground one or two hours, then retrieved by helicopter to go to another suspected area. Platoon and squad-size actions were emphasized.

Patrols were bolder each day as they tried to investigate all likely avenues of approach into the area as well as likely places where the guerrillas might be hiding.

Immediately northwest of the An Khe camp lay an area in which patrols indicated there were a number of VC. Intelligence previously gathered indicated possibly a platoon of guerrillas. It was desirable to conduct a practice air assault— actually a combat air assault—as soon as possible for companies of the battalion under conditions where they would not see a major battle and yet there was sufficient enemy to assure realism. This particular area proved to be our first air assault, first by C Company and then reinforced by B Company.

The battalion plan was formulated. First, detailed air reconnaissance of the area was made to find a suitable landing zone and to determine objectives to provide for accomplishment of this mission. The Battalion Order was issued and coordinated with all elements of the combat team that would participate.

The operation provided for the air assault by one rifle combat team, C Company, into the landing zone with a series of search-and-destroy operations to seek out the enemy and destroy weapons and foodstuffs. Reconnaissance indicated that there were people in the area, but we could not be sure whether they were simple Montagnard farmers, of whom there were many, or were guerrillas using this as their base, since it was fairly close to An Khe and provided access to essential supplies.

The operation was supported by a total of sixteen UH-1D helicopters from the 227th Assault Helicopter Battalion. The lift was initiated from a pick-up zone (PZ) within the battalion area, a large open area in which all trees had been cut down. The area was designated "Mustang" PZ for obvious reasons. A total of eight birds (helicopters) could make a pick-up simultaneously. The assault, scheduled for 1000 hours, would consist of the simultaneous lift of two rifle platoons, eight birds per platoon, followed by another pick-up of an additional rifle platoon and the weapons platoon on the second lift. The aircraft would then stand by at "Mustang" PZ with B Company if reinforcement was required. I planned to command from the command helicopter initially and then go on the ground with C Company at the first opportunity. Tube artillery from the An Khe base camp, including our own direct-support battalion, supported the operation.

The plan called for a strike by tactical aircraft commencing at H minus 45 for a total of thirty minutes until H minus 15; this to be followed by a thirteen-minute tube artillery preparation of the LZ and likely targets surrounding the area. The initial assault would be preceded by Aerial Rocket Artillery (ARA), one platoon of four birds to support the operations. The ARA were to shift their fire at the last minute to other targets, permitting helicopter gun ships from the 227th Assault Helicopter Battalion to sprint ahead and protect the final landing of the transport helicopters, knocking out any last-minute resistance. Battalion Command Post was to remain at the An Khe Base, since the distance was only two miles. Medical evacuation would be by helicopter controlled over the Medical Evacuation Net. We did not expect quite as much trouble from the VC as we did from punji-sticks, long bamboo slivers planted everywhere in the area, as well as other types of booby traps.

Planning was complete and orders were issued. The mission on the Picket Line continued, C Company was ready to go, B Company ready to reinforce. As final preparation Chaplain Spear offered a prayer.

"Our Father in Heaven, we thank You for Your Presence in our lives. As we go into combat, may we 'Mustangs' see our mission as greater than our own safety, one that encompasses the freedoms of our families, nation, and the world. Help us who would fight under the 'Mustang Banner' to have the coolness and clearness of mind to do our mission as we have been instructed and trained. Help us also to be so spiritually prepared that in the moment of crisis, our destiny might be so firm, our conviction so clear, our dedication so sincere, that we will not waver. May our victories become stairways to a spirit rededicated to live at peace with all men."

I went to sleep knowing that our first operation was well planned and we were ready. The morrow would determine the quality of our performance.

H hour was 1000 hours. I was in the air at 0845 hours because low-hanging clouds and deteriorating weather conditions might delay the operation. It was my job to make the weather decision and determine whether this operation should go as scheduled. This weather decision depended on many factors. First, would tactical air be able to operate? If not, was there sufficient other supporting fire, tube artillery and the ARA's to proceed with the mission? Perhaps the mission would have to be delayed for an hour to permit better weather so that tactical air could be employed? Second, I must be assured that the helicopters would not be seriously handicapped by bad weather, both from departure point on the Golf Course to "Mustang" PZ and finally to the LZ. In this instance, all distances were so small that local weather conditions prevailed with the same effect on all.

Weather was all right. The operation proceeded on schedule. Instructions were passed to the assault helicopter unit commander and through the Arty LNO and the ALO to the fire-power team.

C Company was standing by at the PZ; helicopters were ready. At H minus 45, two USAF A1E aircraft came in, providing a tremendous demonstration of tactical air power at its best on the LZ and surrounding target areas. These two birds were relieved a few minutes later on station by two additional birds, who continued to unload their ordnance on likely targets.

This action was the first major operation in the vicinity of An Khe, so there were many spectators, as the landing zone was so near the outer perimeter of the camp. The Air Force tactical fighters put on an outstanding display, accomplished a splendid job, and—best in my opinion—proved the coordination and effectiveness of my ALO and his ability to control, through the FAC, strikes of these fighters. If I felt that a target was not being hit properly, a quiet word from the ALO to the FAC and the pilots of the birds changed or accomplished desired results.

The air strike was completed—tube artillery picked up the fire on schedule at H minus 15. In the meantime two additional A1E's were overhead on Air Cap ready to be called in should the need arise. The beauty of this A1E prop-driven aircraft was that first, it carried a tremendous load of ordnance, and, second, it had from two to three hours' loiter time (fuel endurance) in the target area. This aircraft was ideal for the Infantry, as it provided the weapons and stay time in the air to give us what was needed when we needed it.

Artillery fire was effective. From my command aircraft I watched barrage after barrage as they fell in the vicinity of the LZ and on other likely target areas. The Air Cavalry from the 1st of the 9th Air Cavalry Squadron, a team of two of the small OH-13's supporting us, were screening the outer flanks around the objective to pick up the movement of any enemy either into or away from the area. If this "White Team" discovered anything, a quick call to the battalion to notify us of what was going on and, second, to alert their own parent unit, prepared to provide support in additional weapons ships to take care of this threat if required.

During the last few minutes of the tube artillery preparation, transport helicopters took off from "Mustang" PZ with the first two platoons of C Company. I watched their movement as they swung around to make the final approach into the LZ. The Arty LNO at the proper time lifted the artillery fire, at which time the ARA shot ahead to continue the fire, lasting for approximately one minute. The transport flight was one minute out. The Arty LNO called to the ARA's to lift their fire. A word from the S-3 over his FM net to the assault helicopter unit commander informed him fire had been lifted. The helicopter commander ordered his gun ships to sprint ahead, continuing fire on the immediate area of the LZ.

The birds were on final approach to the LZ, a few seconds out. As the gun ships completed their final pass, the door gunners in the flank transports picked up fire with their M-60 machine guns, providing continuous fire power until the actual landing of the troops. The birds were on the ground now, landing eight at a time. The Infantry from C Company made their first assault as they sprinted from the birds to the distant tree line, immediately taking over the suppressive fire of the machine guns from the transport helicopter.

The purpose of continuous fire from the minute the close air support began until the landing of the riflemen was to keep enemy heads down, return fire, and prevent reinforcement or movement or any final preparation of the enemy to inflict damage prior to troop landings. It was a continuous blast of fire, tactical air power, tube artillery, ARA's, and gun ships, and at the last, door gunners from the transport helicopters, and then finally the Infantry.

The first two platoons were on the ground. There was some shooting—the report from C Company was minimum enemy contact. Captain Smith was with the Second Platoon. The platoons fanned out rapidly to seize and secure the LZ. The birds returned to "Mustang" PZ to pick up the remaining rifle platoon and elements of the weapons platoon. They would return in a few minutes, this time escorted by both the Aerial Rocket Artillery, not firing but prepared to, and by the gun ships, which provide protection to the landing aircraft. There would be no firing this time immediately around the LZ by the ARA's, gun ships, or transport door gunners, since the LZ was now in friendly hands. All fire in the immediate vicinity of the LZ would be coordinated by Captain Smith, the company commander on the ground. If he needed help, he would call through his Artillery FO to obtain the necessary tube artillery or ARA.

The battle was progressing well—with some sniper fire. The primary enemy were the hundreds of punji-sticks scattered throughout the LZ, all around it.

The Montagnards were adept at making punji-sticks. Originally this device was used for building fences or traps to kill animals for food. These traps were easily adapted for use against human beings. The VC learned in the highlands that they could create considerable damage to helicopter-borne forces by placing thousands of inexpensive punji-sticks around likely landing zones.

Within a few minutes half a dozen men from C Company were wounded, having run into punji-sticks; stepped on, the sticks impaled a foot, piercing through the sole or leather of the shoe into the foot. The particularly vulnerable zone was the leg from knee to ankle.

Punji-sticks were serious. They caused a puncture-type wound. In addition, Montagnards and VC put poison or filth on the tips of the sticks to infect the wound. The Division experienced difficulty the first month handling the punji-stick wounds, as they had not learned exactly how to care for them.

Treating the wound as one normally would a simple puncture was not sufficient, as these wounds healed on the outside but were still badly infected inside. Medics discovered later that the best method of treatment was to lay the puncture wound completely open and let it heal from the inside out. This procedure reduced the seriousness of the wound and the length of time required in the hospital. A period of from thirty to ninety days' convalescence initially was not uncommon and in many cases caused evacuations to hospitals in Japan, Okinawa, or the Philippines after a week to ten days in our own hospital.

At this time punjis were serious and painful and accounted for our first Purple Hearts.

A few minutes after C Company secured the LZ, I decided to land and go on the ground. The bird made a low pass and landed. I jumped out with my radio operators, Ballew and Desner. Major Herman, the S-3, and Captain Wilkie, Arty LNO, remained in the aircraft to monitor over-

Purple Heart

head from the air. Because I was dealing with only one company, I joined Captain Smith and his command group. The distances were short and I could talk both to my CP at the An Khe base and to the S-3 and fire-control team in the aircraft above. They could observe better what was going on from the air and could assure control of fire power from both the tactical air power and the artillery. I could communicate anything to them that I needed.

This was my first time on the ground with the troops—our first battle. In the middle of high elephant grass which towered almost above our heads, I was separated momentarily from the other elements of C Company although I had called Captain Smith and informed him I would join up. I knew where he was on the ground, Ballew, Desner, and I started working our way through heavy growth along the right flank of the LZ. There were many punji-sticks stuck in the ground, making movement slow and deliberate.

One could smell the VC, for they were in the area. We were all jumpy, and every time a bush rustled we were observant and careful, fingers on triggers of the M-16; I even had one this time, ready for the first VC to jump out at us.

I heard the typical VC bird calls from several locations around me. These bird calls were the signals used by VC when they were separated or trying to move in or out of an area. It was strange in an area so silent, with no animal life moving anywhere, and yet to hear the repeated VC bird calls.

My first reaction on the ground was that this landing zone was extremely large. It was obvious that one company could not properly search out the objective area because of this and of the dense vegetation. A rapid call to Captain Roy Martin, B Company Commander, and the Battalion CP who was monitoring my conversation, to alert him for an airmobile assault in the eastern portion of the landing zone and to take over his preplanned mission in support of C Company. I split the sector, the western half going to C Company and the eastern half to B Company. Captain Martin had been well briefed and knew the situation. From the operation I brought him rapidly up to date on the situation. In addition, he had been monitoring the Battalion Net and knew what had been transpiring.

Captain Martin: "The company was loading for its first air assault mission. Lieutenant Robert S. Talmadge and Private First Class Lees, his radio operator, made a mad dash for the last ship on the last lift. Lees reached the helicopter two steps ahead of Lieutenant Talmadge and was in the process of scrambling into the ship when he, unknowingly, kicked Lieutenant Talmadge just above the right eye. The blow was so severe it knocked Talmadge down and broke his glasses. Lees looked back in time to see Talmadge scrambling to his feet, not knowing that he had kicked him down; and said, 'Better hurry up, Lieutenant, you will get left.'"

Landing of B Company with sixteen aircraft was to be made in much the same manner as C Company, although D Company's Recon Platoon, attached, remained in reserve at Mustang PZ.

Three rifle platoons and the weapons platoon would make the landing. Thirty minutes later B Company was on the ground and the search continued. Many more punji-sticks were found plus large quantities of rice and tobacco and a number of crossbows and arrows, along with two or three rifles, some rusty hand grenades, and a bit of small-arms ammunition. There was no question that this area had been occupied by the Montagnard guerrillas and that the area had been one of their secured redoubts. A punji-stick factory was located. Here were hundreds of punji-sticks tied in bundles. Many shavings and whittlings abounded where these sticks had been manufactured.

I finally joined up with Captain Smith's command group. In the meantime three more men in C Company had received severe punji-stick wounds, providing an opportunity to prove to the battalion the effectiveness of our Medical Evacuation Plan. When the first man was wounded, a quick call from Captain Smith to the Medical Evacuation helicopter standing by in the air on the special radio frequency, 43.0 (Medivac), brought a bird in quickly to the LZ to pick up the wounded casualty. The Medivac pilot was able to talk to the company commander or whomever he had designated on the Medical Evacuation Radio Frequency. A colored smoke grenade popped at a specific place on the LZ was the signal for the bird to come in, make its landing, and pick up the casualty. Within minutes the casualty was back at the An Khe Medical facilities and his wounds were being cared for by expert medical officers.

B Company, in the meantime, had three punji wounds, including two noncommissioned officers. Similar methods were used to evacuate these casualties quickly.

The command group was walking carefully down a trail, preceded by the C Company command group. The trail was well traveled. There were many punji-sticks positioned along the side. Moving cautiously, I was leading, followed by Corporal Ballew and then PFC Desner. We stopped. I pointed out two or three punji-sticks in the trail. I picked my way through.

From the rear came a sharp cry as Corporal Ballew, overlooking a hidden punji, swung his foot sideward in such a manner that the punji passed through his instep. He fell to the ground: the first casualty in the command group from a punji-stick. The punji-stick pulled out as Ballew fell. He had a gaping puncture through the front part of his instep and coming out near the bottom. His boot was quickly removed; he was not bleeding badly, but he was in considerable pain, though still taking it well. We had to be careful in any movement at this location, as there were other punji-sticks all around. Ballew was fortunate in that when he fell he did not impale himself on another stick and obtain a more serious wound.

A quick call was put in to the Battalion CP for a Medivac ship. One of the lift helicopters supporting us with a flight surgeon aboard was monitoring the conversation. He called to say that he could pick up Corporal Ballew. I rogered his radio transmission. The helicopter flew to our position, marked with a colored smoke grenade, and landed. The flight surgeon dashed out, followed by the medical air men with a stretcher. Within two and one half minutes after Corporal Ballew was wounded, a doctor was examining him. Ballew was placed quickly on the stretcher, loaded into the helicopter, and flown back to An Khe. The significant thing about this particular operation and wound was that here was a case where a soldier, badly wounded, received medical attention almost immediately. A flight surgeon—a doctor—was at his side within two and a half minutes, and at the expiration of eight minutes the wounded soldier was back in a hospital with excellent medical attention.

I borrowed a radio operator from Captain Smith and continued with the operation. A few minutes later the command helicopter brought in Communications Sergeant SFC Williamson, a fine NCO and Chief of the Battalion Communications Platoon, to join up temporarily as my radio operator. He wanted to be on the ground where he could observe how the communication system was working, so this served both purposes. He took Corporal Ballew's place for the rest of that operation.

B and C Companies continued their missions. Platoons fanned out and conducted a search 500 meters from the landing zone. This was a small-scale operation. The jungle growth was dense and we were making little progress.

Here we relearned the importance of machetes. They must be razor-sharp, as foot movement required enormous amounts of machete work to cut a trail through some of the search areas.

A number of huts were found and destroyed. We continued to find more rations and punjis. By 1600 hours it was clear that we were not going to find any enemy. There was no point in wasting more effort.

I decided to extract both B and C Companies and return them to the battalion area for continuance of the Picket Line mission that night. C Company was to go out first. We wound our way back to the PZ, the same open area we had landed in, and commenced extraction, a platoon at a time.

We were not aware how many enemy were in this area, and everybody, including the helicopters pilots, were leery; therefore we tried to expedite the extraction. This became another lesson relearned, that the pilots in the aircraft must not in any way try to hurry the Infantry. In this first extraction, the birds did not land according to prearranged plans, creating an excessive distance between troops and birds. Nervous pilots waving for the troops to come and join the birds caused the troops to hurry to the aircraft. They were careless with the punji-sticks and several additional men wounded as a result.

The extraction of C Company continued, followed by the extraction of B Company. At this stage I called for the command helicopter, on my smoke signal, to land and pick up the command party.

In the command ship, I continued to oversee the remaining extraction of B Company back to the battalion area. In the meantime, as we flew over the area, Captain Wilkie, the Arty LNO, was busy conducting destruction missions on huts, spotted throughout the areas outside the area of troop movement. In addition, the Air Caps overhead nearly expended their fuel. The ALO, Captain Holland, called them in on specific targets. In this manner we continued to get an excellent workout on fire power throughout the entire operation.

The operation was completed and the battalion was back in the battalion area. Congratulations were in order for both company commanders on performing a splendid job that included all of the battalion team. This had been a valuable exercise, not so much in the gain as far as destruction of the enemy went, but in polishing up air assault techniques—both

for the battalion and for supporting members of the team—
the assault helicopters, aerial rocket artillery, tube artillery,
tactical air power, and medical evacuation. Supply problems
were minor. In this case little air resupply was required
during the operation.

I was most pleased with the way the battalion team had
performed, especially the teamwork and coordination of all
elements. There were many mistakes. We conducted a short
critique immediately and the following day a more detailed
one, with all members of the battalion team present in order
to iron out any difficulties, correct problems that arose, and
determine new and better procedures.

A most interesting fact was that our fire-support plan
which we had developed through many skull sessions on the
ship in which we discussed how this system would work had
finally proven out on this first operation. This system would
continue to be the pattern for future operations of the battalion. We became quite famous for use of fire power, employing
everything that would shoot at the proper time and the
proper place.

The men were tired and weary after this operation, but
happy to finally get their feet wet—at least, to see some of
the areas where the enemy lived, even though only a few saw
an actual Viet Cong.

The battalion suffered its first wounded, although none
were killed on this operation. We knew that this year in
Vietnam was not going to be an easy thing. There were
twenty-two casualties, all the result of punji-sticks. This was
the beginning of many casualties from this deadly weapon,
including one young trooper in B Company who sat down on
one.

Soon we were back on the Picket Line ready for the
night and whatever it may bring. Picket Line operations
continued throughout the next few days with little enemy
contact, providing excellent training in patrolling and improvement in our techniques in all areas. We were becoming
thoroughly familiar with the terrain around An Khe. I made
daily flights throughout the area between the Barrier and the
Picket Line and beyond, searching the terrain for the enemy.

The most interesting fact about making a helicopter
reconnaissance flight over a piece of new enemy territory—at
a thousand feet—is that at first you see little but trees and

vegetation. As you become more familiar with the terrain and continue more passes over the area, you begin to see little clearings, to see huts through the trees and the numerous trails. Often a first look at a piece of jungle terrain seems almost hopeless. How can a landing zone ever be found in this difficult area? How can you ever get troops into this area? Even a low-level pass at treetop level often will reveal nothing the first time.

A series of passes spread over three or four days, if time is available, without arousing too much attention, will begin to highlight on the ground through your eyes the landing zones, potential enemy areas, trails, and watering points.

On the ground, men were becoming more familiar with the terrain and, most important, were improving their land navigation ability. Land navigation was a difficult problem in this area. Knowing your location on the ground so that it could be identified by coordinate and transmitted to the next higher headquarters becomes most important, often critical. With the tremendous fire power at our disposal, we had to know where our men were, where our patrols were, at all times.

We returned to occupy our position on the Barrier as our primary mission. Another battalion of the brigade had taken over the Picket Line mission for the same reasons that we ourselves had had it: to provide a training ground. Barrier duty was becoming a familiar and repetitive task that we would see many times.

Generally an Infantry battalion and a brigade spent a specific period of time on combat operations and then returned to defense at the An Khe Base. At first this mission absorbed the energies of a number of Infantry battalions. Finally the missions were reduced to a brigade of three battalions; eventually it would decrease to a single battalion. Finally, after we, the first shift, left Vietnam, the Barrier was further improved and reduced to occupation by Tenants. These permanent-party logistical and administrative troops occupied the base, defending the Barrier on the inside with an Infantry battalion conducting combat operations for a radius of five to ten kilometers outside the base.

Barrier duty was always a repetitive and somewhat unpleasant task. We were busy conducting local patrols and improving the Barrier. Improvements included the positions themselves and construction of wire entanglements. Wire supply was short—no pickets were available at the moment. Fence posts had to be cut from local jungle.

The first objective in construction of the Barrier was to establish a cow fence (six-strand barbed wire) beyond hand-grenade distance in front of fighting positions. The cow fence marked the beginning of a one-hundred-yard barrier, eventually to be cleared and constructed. Now the major task was cutting trees and finding posts. Posts were found by tearing up old bunkers and old huts scattered throughout the area, to get the necessary timber. Last was stringing the six-wire cow fence itself. The cow fence and Barrier were laid out with no interior angles, only exterior angles in straight lines, forming an octagon-type structure to permit good grazing fire from machine guns and, above all, to provide a straight line for the ARA's and gun ships to fly down, shooting anything on the enemy side of the wire without bringing fire to bear on friendly forces. The whole concept of the Barrier was the idea of General John M. Wright, Assistant Division Commander, in charge of construction of the base.

In addition, a new part of the Barrier was under construction—to include the major portion of Mustang Mountain (also known as Hong Kong Mountain). The major task was clearing the one-hundred-meter swath or "Mustang Brand" in preparation for construction. An immense number of man-hours would be devoted to this project prior to its completion. Over 1000 civilians assisted the troops in branding the mountain.

The period on the Barrier was also a time for the troops to clean up and receive necessary haircuts, to make sure that weapons and ammunition were in excellent shape, and to replenish combat equipment that had been lost or destroyed. Training was a must. Training in air assault techniques and weapon and small-unit tactics was continuous.

Supervision was one of the key jobs for every leader. Leaders were beginning to prove and disprove themselves. After two weeks in combat men able to do the job were showing themselves; the weak ones who could not were relieved.

*   *   *

C Company received a new mission. The battalion had been directed to provide one rifle company in support of an artillery battalion, deployed to the China Sea coast to provide artillery support for the Vietnamese Army. This battalion was commanded by Colonel Harry Amos. The task force naturally became known as Task Force Amos. Captain Smith flew immediately to make contact with the Task Force Commander and determine the details of his mission. A few hours later on in the day, helicopters flew the company to join the task force to provide security for the artillery battalion.

This force would range up and down the China Sea coast for a number of days to provide 105mm artillery support to the Vietnamese units scattered along the coast securing Highway 1. The howitzers were moved by Chinook helicopter.

This Chinook artillery technique was one of the excellent tactics that evolved out of the 11th Air Assault—1st Air Cavalry Division—the movement of a 105th artillery piece suspended within or beneath a Chinook helicopter. This technique provided great mobility for the artillery. When necessary to move, the Chinooks simply came in, picked up the howitzers, ammunition, and men, and moved them directly into the new location. These batteries and battalions did not use prime movers; the only vehicle employed was a quarter-ton jeep with each battery to provide electrical power for the radios necessary for fire control.

The Amos mission was a good exercise for C Company because it would put them more or less in action on an independent mission. Initially located in the vicinity of Phu Cat, C Company killed its first VC.

There had been friendly competition between Captain Danielsen's A Company and Captain Smith's C Company over who would kill the first VC. Both vowed to be first. C Company won, for the following day a patrol was able to flush out two VC trying to get away into the hills. 1st Lieutenant Charles P. Thombras killed the first VC and captured a Smith and Wesson 38-caliber pistol.

In the meantime the rest of the battalion continued its activities on the Barrier.

C Company had another change of mission and was relieved on Task Force Amos, but remained attached under

**Smith and Wesson —
.38 Cal. Revolver.**

the operational control of the 3rd Brigade at Ben Khe. Here it provided security for the 3rd Brigade Base in the Ben Khe area, the large valley a few miles east of the An Khe Pass mountain range.

The rest of the battalion was still on the Barrier.

A Company moved to relieve C Company at Ben Khe and provided the security for the Logistic Base in that area. I rotated the companies, since C Company had been away for one week, on Task Force Amos and at Ben Khe.

Then we were back on the Picket Line, having relieved one of our sister battalions. At the same time A Company returned, and the entire battalion was intact.

Picket Line operations were more pleasant than the Barrier and the men enjoyed getting out of the base. The Barrier became noted for simple, plain hard work, digging holes and stringing wire all day. This duty was not received with real enthusiasm by the troops.

Still there were advantages in being on the Barrier. At least you were back in the base camp and could enjoy some of the niceties. For example, hot meals were served, although still B-rations, for little or no fresh foods had yet been received.

Canned items could be prepared well and were quite

tasty. The battalion had a really fine crew of cooks. Instead of running one Battalion Mess, I split the Mess Section into four separate messes, with the result that each rifle company commander operated his own Mess Section. Headquarters and D Company operated jointly the mess that remained in the base itself. This was a better system; I believe the company commander should be able to exert control over his own mess, as it was one of the major morale-contributing factors within any unit.

Duty in the base camp did provide for some men a chance to sleep on their air mattress in a tent, for a few more of our companies now had squad tents. Still about three-quarters of the troops were in pup tents. Even a pup tent was a little dryer than out in a foxhole. There was also a chance for an occasional movie and a beer or two, although we received little beer at the moment and what we got was warm. Warm beer was not too bad if that was all you had.

Back to the Barrier, following another relief on the Picket Line. We shifted back and forth each five or six days between Picket Line and Barrier duty.

The Jumping Mustangs returned to the Barrier on the twentieth, for we had been alerted for an operation in Ben Khe. This would be our first operation as a battalion. The entire 1st Brigade was to cross the An Khe Pass and initiate an operation to drive the VC from mountain ranges that lined Highway 19, on both north and south. This would be a Brigade operation and would introduce a new tactic or new technique.

We were to land on the tops of the mountains—the peaks themselves—by helicopter and work down, rather than selecting landing zones at the base of the mountain and climbing up the hill. This technique had two distinct advantages. First, it was physically easier to move downhill than to climb up. Second, the Viet Cong defenses were generally oriented downhill, waiting for someone to come up toward them. The VC were so located as to cause the most destruction and damage. By landing on top and coming down, we were in their rear and could cause them havoc and destruction with fewer casualties to ourselves.

Lieutenant Colonel Harlow Clark was temporarily in command of the Brigade, since Colonel Elvey Roberts, our

Brigade Commander, had been evacuated due to a serious knee injury. The Division Commander, Major General Harry Kinnard, ordered him evacuated to the hospital in Okinawa to have the knee operated on.

Colonels Clark, Nix, and Shoemaker and I made a reconnaissance of the areas that we were to operate in, and visited Special Forces Camp at Ben Khe and obtained all the latest friendly and enemy information of the area. There were some friendly Vietnamese forces in the operational area, along with friendly Vietnamese tube-artillery support available.

Battalion sectors were worked out and allocated to each of the two battalions that would participate at the beginning of the operation. The 1st of the 12th, under Colonel Robert Shoemaker, was to remain back at the brigade area, manning the Barrier for a few days, while the 1st and 2nd of the 8th would conduct the initial phase of the operation. The Jumping Mustangs would generally operate astride Highway 19 and to the south. The 2nd of the 8th would operate farther over to the north, partly in a mountainous area.

Our mission on the Barrier continued as we conducted the planning and reconnaissance for the operation. This included issuance of the orders and the company reconnaissances.

5

BEN KHE AIR ASSAULT

On October 21 The Jumping Mustangs would be the lead battalion for the Airborne Brigade to assault into Ben Khe, twenty-five kilometers east of An Khe along Highway 19. The mission was to secure Highway 19 and clear the way for the new Rock Tiger Division due to arrive from Korea in the near future. We would organize a Picket Line similar to the one the 1st Brigade of the 101st Airborne Division established on the arrival of our own division.

The two days of waiting for the battle were spent in preparation: checking equipment, executing the reconnaissance, preparing the plan, issuing the order, and reconnaissance by the company commanders.

The past few days had been wet—troops had been wet the entire period. It rained almost continuously. The great majority of the men still lived in pup tents, sleeping on top of air mattresses. In spite of the ditching and every other precaution, the men were almost continuously soaked. What's more, clothing and equipment in duffle bags were getting damp and beginning to rot. We had one afternoon of sunshine, when the battalion area looked somewhat like a Chinese laundry. Everyone had his clothes out of bags to dry.

The battalion order was issued on the nineteenth and reconnaissance of the area was completed. It was my policy whenever possible to take the company commanders, at least the rifle company commanders, in the command helicopter and make a reconnaissance of the area, verifying the landing zone, the objectives, and other details of the entire area. This technique helped the company commanders prepare their own plans and gave them a good picture of the terrain. This proved valuable many times in the future. It reduced voice communication over the radio, because we all had been together, had identified specific terrain features, and had discussed preplanned courses of action. In the future, when communicating with one another over the radio, it was only necessary to refer to the previous conversation or to that piece of terrain previously identified or discussed, thereby easily identifying the current subject with a minimum of confusion and conversation. This system also contributed to maintaining what we were trying to do a little more secret from the enemy. It enabled us to change plans rapidly on a few minutes' notice and by issuing verbal instructions over the radio, to take advantage of a developing enemy situation.

One of the highlights of our preparation for the forthcoming battle was the visit of the Commanding General of Military Assistance Command, Vietnam, MACV, General William Westmoreland. He came to An Khe to visit the Airborne Brigade. Since the Jumping Mustangs were the only battalion in the area coiled (assembled) and preparing for combat, he spent the majority of his time with us and gave a twenty-minute pep talk to the battalion.

General Westmoreland, in speaking to the assembled troopers, complimented them on their achievements in the past and told a bit about what the future would hold for us in Vietnam and also what he expected from the 1st Air Cavalry Division in future combat. This was a highlight because the General had the opportunity to speak to the troops, which in itself was important. Many of the NCO's and officers in the battalion, including myself, had served with him on numerous occasions before, so it was also a pleasure to see him once more. He met many old friends in the battalion and left us all much inspired.

General Westmoreland had a knack for remembering names. He stood on a little mound overlooking the assembled battalion, looked down at various noncommissioned officers who had served with him during his previous tour in the 101st Airborne Division as Commanding General, and called out to them by name. This had a tremendous effect not only on the men he remembered but also on those observing and listening. His visit also aroused the old Airborne spirit, for we were still an Airborne Battalion although we had not had a chance to do anything but token jumping up to now.

Few of the men had had an opportunity to jump; however, we were covered for pay purposes for the first two or three months in Vietnam from our previous jumps at Fort Benning. We were all interested in what was going to happen, because there had been little opportunity to conduct training paratroop jumps, and we had not yet had a chance for one in combat.

The day on which the General visited us was the final day prior to our moving out. This was a chance for me later on in the day to gather the battalion together and offer congratulations on their splendid achievements individually, as well as the company's achievements; to point out deficiencies that must be corrected for the future; and also to brief them on what to expect in our next battle.

Chaplain Spear gave a Mustang Battle Prayer, customary in the battalion prior to embarking on a battle. Highlights of the prayer were:

> Our Father in Heaven, as we have slept in shelter halves and rat-infested bunkers and foxholes, securing our base by day and night, we have been reminded that our purpose in Vietnam is participation in a strange type of war, a war which has no lines, involves innocent civilians as well as the enemy, one in which a seeming friend by day becomes our enemy by night.
>
> As we continue to engage the enemy on additional fronts, may we "Jumping Mustangs" see our mission as greater than our own survival, one that includes the freedom of our families, nation, and the world. We pray for our commanders, that their decisions may be wise, their leadership confident, and their determination unending. Help us who would fight under the "Mustang Banner" to have the coolness and clearness of mind to accomplish our mission as we have been trained.

While speaking of prayers, during this two- or three-day period we had the first Memorial Ceremony for those who had been killed in action. Two troopers had been killed in action thus far. On arrival in Vietnam, Chaplain Spear and a few of the men in Headquarters Company rapidly improvised a small Chapel with an altar made of native materials. A huge cargo parachute was used as the Chapel itself. This became the Jumping Mustang Chapel. The Chapel was important for our frequent religious services while back in the base. It was the scene of this first Memorial Service.

The men in the battalion were dear to us all and, as the battalion grew closer together, the loss of any man had quite an effect on the entire group. Therefore, the Memorial Service was not so much for the individual or his family as for those of us remaining, the living, within the battalion. The service was a simple ceremony. The symbol of the soldiers who had died was a pair of highly polished jump boots placed in front of the altar. The guidons for all the companies were present. The Jumping Mustang guidon accompanied me to the ceremony. The Battalion Colors and the American Flag were both on display on both sides of the altar. Troopers gathered in the Chapel, especially those from the respective company.

A brief prayer by the Chaplain opened the memorial, and was followed by a short speech by the company commander of the unit to whom the man belonged. This was a final tribute for what he had accomplished and what he had done for us within the unit. Next a short service, if Protestant by Chaplain Spear; if Catholic, by one of the Catholic Chaplains within the brigade, in which the complete Catholic memorial services were presented.

At the conclusion of the services themselves, a Bugle and Firing Squad was assembled. The Firing Squad fired the traditional three volleys, as we all stood at attention, followed by the Bugler from the 1st Air Cavalry Band sounding Taps. This simple ceremony was effective and became the model within the battalion and was used by many units throughout the rest of the Division. When casualties from two or more companies were involved, I represented the battalion and made a short speech.

The combat operation to begin the twenty-first, actually began the night of the twentieth, with the motor movement of the Headquarters Company, D Company, and B Company by convoy overland through the An Khe Pass to the battalion base established in the vicinity of Ben Khe. Movement was completed by 2400 hours, and the movement through the An Khe Pass passed without incident. This was one of the first night movements through the Pass. The Battalion Forward Command Post and A and C Companies were scheduled for air assaults the following morning.

The weather was bad. H hour was scheduled for 0900. There were sufficient UH-1D helicopters to lift C Company to the peaks north of Highway 19, followed by A Company on the other peaks overlooking the Highway to the south. As was mentioned previously, the unusual part of this mission would be landing on top of the hills and working down, routing out the VC as we went rather than landing at the base as in the past and working up the hills against great odds.

The 1st of the 12th, our sister battalion, had recently completed an operation using the system of landing at the base and working up the hills, in which they had suffered considerable casualties. The VC emplaced on the topographical and military crest of these various slopes continued to raise havoc on the assaulting heliborne troops and also caused considerable damage to the assault helicopters.

The bad weather delayed H hour for an hour. The reason for the delay was the desire to make sure that tactical air power would be available, for the weather was clearing from the east and the birds coming from the Quin Nhon area would be able to get through later. The weather was bad back at An Khe, where the transport helicopters were based and where A and C Companies remained for pick-up. The aircraft were standing by with the troops but it was impossible to get the birds through the pass and meet an 0900 H hour. The clouds, typical for that time of the year, settled down low over the An Khe Mountain Pass. I was on the east side of the pass at Ben Khe, having flown through earlier that morning in a narrow slot on Highway 19 as it passed through the mountains. I flew down through the V where the road itself was carved in the mountain pass, into the clear valley to the east. It was difficult to bring a large number of transports in through this narrow mountain pass; therefore we waited for an improvement in the weather.

It was hard for me to realize on the east side of the pass that weather was so bad behind us. I became impatient with the Battalion Commander of the 227th Assault Helicopter Battalion who was supporting our unit. He was making every

effort to get his birds through the pass. The urgency of the
mission meant that we must execute as rapidly as we could,
because the priority of helicopters would revert to another
unit in a short period of time. It was essential that I get my
two companies in on the hilltops and the operation started,
otherwise the entire brigade operation might be delayed,
with serious consequences. If we could not land on the
hilltops, we would have to move by motor and attack up hills
to the objective. If this occurred, we were bound to suffer
severe casualties.

The Battalion Commander of the 227th did an outstanding job and by his personal reconnaissance, along with his
other leaders, was finally able to bring a portion of the
helicopters through the fogged-in pass the same way I had
come down through the An Khe Pass. The remainder of the
flight came north into a valley, around another deep river
valley, into our area of operations. This took considerable
ingenuity and initiative on the part of the aviators and the
commander of that fine helicopter unit.

H hour was 1000 hours. Tactical air power moved in
under control of the Airborne FAC, coordinated by the ALO
in my bird, who directed the strikes of the tactical aircraft.
Artillery fire commenced as close air support was shifted to
other targets. After a short preparation the first lift for C
Company approached the landing zones on the very peaks.
The ARA's picked up their usual fire. A few seconds later the
first birds began to land on the hilltops.

The major hilltop that C Company was landing on was
steep with a knife-like edge. Helicopters were able to land
actually in platoons of four each, really not touching down but
simply resting their skids on the knife edge of the hilltop or
hovering just over it as the troops rapidly bailed out onto the
crest. The ridge was so steep in this area that there was great
danger of troops actually falling down the sides of the mountain. This was vividly demonstrated when two or three equipment bundles were dumped from the helicopter on the crest
and rolled many yards down the hill, making recovery difficult.

C Company was able to complete the landing in a few
minutes. The hill was unoccupied on the crest. Captain
Smith quickly consolidated his position and began construction of two improved single-bird landing zones on the crest,
then initiated movement down the ridges to the valley toward

Highway 19 to try and destroy any Viet Cong who might still be on the hill.

The priority of aircraft shifted to A Company and similar operations were conducted on the high ground south of the base camp. Both companies were in. The search-and-destroy missions commenced. There was little enemy opposition. The major activity for the next two or three days consisted of search-and-destroy operations conducted by platoon-size combat patrols.

I was pleased with this first day's operation for a number of reasons. We had introduced a new technique, that of landing on the hilltop, successfully landing with two complete rifle companies. This meant fine teamwork on the part of both the rifle companies and the supporting assault helicopters. The airmobile assaults had been accomplished under severe weather conditions. We were beginning to fly and perform in Vietnam as we had done so many times in the 11th Air Assault days in the Carolinas.

Lieutenant Colonel Harlow Clark, the Acting Brigade Commander, came up with a new series of radio call signs in the brigade modeled after a football game.

The 1st of the 8th would now be known as "Left Half"; the 2nd of the 8th, as "Right Half"; the 1st of the 12th, as "Fullback." The Brigade Commander and the Brigade call signs would be "Quarterback"; for example, the Brigade Commander himself was "Quarterback 6."

Within the 1st of the 8th or "Left Half," our companies were further designated A Company, "Left Guard"; B Company, "Left Tackle"; and C Company, "Left End"; D Company, "Flanker Left." I would be known as "Left Half 6" and the battalion staff "Left Half 3, 4," and so on.

The new call signs led to some amusing situations, since I was not an expert football player. I was completely confused and at a loss as to my call signs about 50 per cent of the time, much to the amusement of the company commanders and the staff. Invariably I ended up calling a company commander simply "Left Half Alfa, Bravo, or Charlie," or "Mustang Alfa, Bravo, or Charlie." Every time I tried to call a company commander in the middle of some important activity, I could not remember which football play should be next. It was even worse when I tried to call one of the adjacent battalions.

I resisted this new system instigated by the Acting

Brigade Commander, Colonel Clark, but since he was the Brigade Commander and an excellent football player, he won out.

I had to learn more about football.

Search-and-destroy missions continued for A and C Companies with another air assault by B Company on a second hill mass north of where C Company landed. The weather was especially marginal in the mountains where B Company was to land. The demonstration of flying ability this day was the best example of true air assault flying yet performed by the 1st Air Cavalry Division. The aviators of the 227th Helicopter Battalion did an outstanding job.

Initially it looked as if we might have to delay H hour or not go in. We had a small lift of eight birds at a time and the distance from the pick-up zone down at the Ben Khe Base to the landing zone was only minutes away. B Company required four lifts in order to secure this hill mass once the landing began on the peaks.

I was in the command ship flying through the area trying to determine the best conditions and when the weather would permit the actual operation. Tactical Air had been able to make the strike and the tube artillery was falling; it was time to give the word to the assault helicopters a few minutes away to take off. They were standing by with the troops.

Here was where I learned that it was so easy to say, "No, we won't go today," but sometimes difficult to say, "Let's go ahead with the plan and execute it." The weather was marginal—fog and haze surrounded the peaks. I knew, owing to the priority of helicopters, that if we did not execute this mission in the next hour or so, the weather conditions would deteriorate, and the bird priority would pass to another unit in another area. Again we might be faced with tremendous physical odds in climbing the mountains from the base up— we might face unnecessary casualties.

I thought we could probably accomplish the flights, since I relied heavily on my own experience as an army aviator and the two outstanding aviators who flew the command ship. They felt as I did—that we could do it. I passed the word to Captain Roy Martin and the helicopter lift company commander to take off and execute the mission.

The first lift proceeded without great difficulty, although

the birds had to fly individually through intense haze and fog, find their target on the crest, rest the skids on the knife edge, and let the troops dismount. The second lift was also successful. Then the weather began to close in even more. At this time we had two platoons on the distant mountain. It would be impossible to reinforce them if they should encounter heavy action, in the time necessary to save them. Intelligence indicated that there might be an enemy battalion in this area.

Again I was faced with a rough decision. Should I call the operation off because the weather was bad or should we continue? The Flight Leader of the eight birds called and said that it did not look so good. I pondered a moment and told him we would try to go ahead and take off for the third lift and see if we could not get through.

The birds took off and flew through the fog. I think the gods were probably with us this day, for just as we approached the landing area, the fog cleared enough to reveal the peaks and the landing points now plainly marked with panels by the troops on the ground. The third lift went in. The weather held while the birds went back and made a fourth lift. B Company was now intact on the ground.

A full company on the ground was important. Throughout our operations the battalion policy was to always put at least one rifle company on the ground. A rifle platoon cannot take care of itself long without additional fire support and reinforcements from its parent company or battalion. A rifle company, however, was a powerful combat team. It was well able to defend itself with its mortars, artillery support, and tactical air and to provide a base for reinforcement.

I was delighted to have B Company present and know that we had completed the mission. I was extremely proud of both B Company and the aviators of A Company, 227th Assault Helicopter Battalion, and the excellent air-assault-type flying they were performing. This helicopter battalion was rapidly coming of age and approaching the peak efficiency it experienced during the 11th Air Assault days with all the original aviators. In coming to Vietnam, many of the aviators who had been here in Vietnam once before (over 50 percent) left the Division. Many of the pilots who came with the division had not yet caught on to the air-assault techniques of flying. They were learning rapidly and, from all indications exhibited in this particular operation, would soon be as proficient, if not more so, than the old 11th Air Assault pilots.

The next several days were spent in a series of company-size clearing operations, including a fine company sweep down through the valley behind A Company. A Company especially and the battalion learned much about command and control in clearing villages. This was a VC village in which few people lived, and the VC, on learning of our arrival in that area, departed. They left behind quantities of rice. We captured several VC suspects.

The three rifle-company teams continued to make sweeps throughout the battalion sector. There had been little actual enemy contact.

On this day word came from the Division Base and the Brigade that in the Pleiku area the VC or North Vietnamese Army were attacking in large numbers the Plei Mei Special Forces Camp and Pleiku itself.

The 1st Airborne Brigade was alerted to go to Pleiku immediately. The 1st of the 12th already in the Base Camp was already en route to Pleiku. The 2nd of the 8th, operating to our north, was to be pulled out immediately. The extraction was in progress now to remove and fly them directly to Pleiku.

That left the Jumping Mustangs in place to continue their mission, which had now been given to the 2nd Brigade. As of 1800 hours we came under the control of the 2nd Brigade in the Ben Khe area to continue the original mission.

The change of missions demonstrated the flexibility of the air-assault airmobile forces. Here a brigade in contact, employing two battalions, was able to extract a battalion and move it, with its own headquarters and the remaining battalion at An Khe, seventy miles to the west to engage in another operation.

The Jumping Mustangs were engaged in a battle. It would be difficult to break contact; and since the mission had not been completed, operation control could easily be transferred to another brigade. The 2nd Brigade was conducting operations in this area but further north.

The new division order left the 2nd Brigade east of the An Khe Pass to conduct the search-and-destroy mission, the 1st Airborne Brigade in action to the west of Pleiku, and the 3rd

Brigade conducting the defense of the An Khe Base and search-and-destroy missions in the vicinity of the base.

The 1st Airborne Brigade initiated the initial phases of the Plei Mei campaign, which was the first major engagement by United States forces and the North Vietnamese Army in which the North Vietnamese were to be decisively whipped in a thirty-five-day campaign.

The current operations of the Jumping Mustangs, under the 2nd Brigade, continued with company and platoon sweeps.

A two-company airmobile operation was conducted using the hammer-and-anvil tactics on the 24th of October. C Company was the anvil to A Company's hammer. C Company was established by air assault in initial blocking positions, followed by an assault landing of A Company to sweep across the river valley toward the objective, where we believed there to be at least one or two platoons of VC. On joining up, the A Company hammer against the C Company anvil, the two companies swept toward Ben Khe to search out the area and eliminate any Viet Cong that might be found.

Several unoccupied foxholes were located and a number of Viet Cong suspects detained. Quantities of 30-caliber ammunition were found and rice was confiscated. A number of huts in the area were destroyed but there was minimum enemy contact. One excellent feature of this operation, which I appreciated for training purposes, was the coordination required between the two company commanders to conduct an attack side by side and sweep the area. The control of fire in the first phase was superb when they attacked one toward the other, with a Viet Cong located in the middle trying to trick one company into firing on the other.

The coordination and control demonstrated by Captain Danielsen of A Company and Captain Smith of C Company were written up in detail by Charlie Black of the Columbus *Enquirer*, who was accompanying A Company.

We accomplished our mission. Still we had no chance to get our teeth into the elusive Viet Cong.

General Lee, the Advance Party Commanding General of the Rock Tiger Division, visited the Battalion Command Post to discuss security measures for the Rock Tiger Division and the planning and coordination for their ultimate assumption of the mission for that area.

I was impressed by the Koreans, having served with them in 1952 and 1953 when they were a fledgling force and demonstrated little military proficiency. The new Korean soldier appeared to be well trained and well disciplined and to present an excellent appearance; their equipment was well maintained and the attitude of their officers, many of whom spoke excellent English, was exceedingly professional.

General Lee and I discussed in length the turnover of operations and the enemy situation. He briefed me on his plans. His staff joined with mine to prepare the necessary details to facilitate their movement into the area.

One of their units would move in and relieve my battalion in the Ben Khe Base and then undertake tactical missions on the surrounding hills within the next few days.

A Company continued to conduct sweep operations of their area to rout out any remaining Viet Cong. B Company was operating west of the river on further search-and-destroy missions. C Company returned to the battalion base, in reserve for the next day.

I gave up control of the Jumping Mustangs at 0900 hours because of severe illness. For the past seven days I had not felt well. In the last forty-eight hours high fever reached a temperature of 105 degrees. I became irrational and did not seem to be improving. I thought at first it was malaria. Dr. Odom had me under surveillance and even tried to evacuate me two days before. I had twisted his arm a bit and remained with the battalion.

The past night with Charlie Black, my guest in the CP, I became irrational when friendly artillery was firing on enemy positions on a harassing and interdiction mission. I awoke and, owing to the fever, could have sworn that enemy incoming rounds were landing on our Medical Clearing Station which was part of the battalion base. When I was assured by Major Eberhardt that this was not the case, I decided that I had just about had it and had better get out of there and get cured. At any rate, Dr. Odom figured that I had had enough and, overriding my command prerogatives, ordered my evacuation to the Clearing Station, part of the base.

I checked into the Clearing Station at 0800 hours to see if they could take care of me. The doctors there decided that I would be evacuated to Quin Nhon, the evacuation hospital in that area. At 0900 hours, I grabbed the mike for the radios to my jeep sitting in front of the Clearing Station, called all the company commanders, and told them that they would take orders henceforth from the Battalion Executive Officer, Major Eberhardt. I radioed Major Eberhardt, in the command helicopter at the moment, and turned over command of the battalion.

I was flown to Quin Nhon to the Evacuation Hospital, where I spent the next twelve days, about seven of which I ran a fever of 105 degrees. The 105-degree fever finally broke and I began to recover. Had this temperature not broken, I would have been evacuated to the Philippines, Okinawa, or possibly even further.

As strange as this may sound to some, I did not want to leave Vietnam, because I knew that if I was gone very long, I would lose command of my battalion. Once evacuated out of Vietnam, it is difficult to get back to the same job, especially the same unit, again. Under no circumstances did I want to lose command of the Jumping Mustang Battalion. We had many things to accomplish and still had to fight our first major battle, I wanted to be there for it.

One thing that stuck firmly in my mind while in the hospital was the concern of the men of the Jumping Mustang Battalion in the hospital with me as a result of battle wounds, punji-sticks, and malaria, which was beginning to hit us quite hard. Their concern for me as their commander and a fellow Jumping Mustang was demonstrated in their many visits during the day to see me.

Two young corporals, one from A Company especially and one from C Company, came around daily to see if I needed anything; could they visit the PX for me? The trooper from A Company decided that he would keep track of all Jumping Mustangs in the hospital each day by visiting them in their wards and then came and reported to me. I greatly appreciated this evidence of morale and spirit that held the Jumping Mustangs together in what I thought was a tremendous unit. It demonstrated the concern and interest of the men for their battalion, not only by officers and NCO's, but also by the young soldiers.

I was also impressed by the daily visits from various members of the battalion staff, officers and noncommissioned officers, from the battalion base at An Khe by vehicle.

Jeep Mounted 106mm.

Sergeant Major Herbert McCullah also came frequently to visit and to keep me abreast of what was going on in the battalion.

The tactical operation continued under Major Eberhardt, Acting Battalion Commander, A Company operating to the south and B Company to the north. C Company remained in reserve.

The Reconnaissance Platoon of D Company had been conducting a series of small airmobile operations within the area to improve their proficiency and search out some of the smaller areas. The Anti-tank Platoon was also getting a good workout. We intended to use the 106 recoilless rifle for bunker busting. It was also good for mounted patrol action.

The Anti-tank Platoon and all of D Company was really an additional rifle company and I trained it as such. D Company was made up of the Reconnaissance Platoon, the Mortar Platoon, and the Anti-tank Platoon.

The Anti-tank Platoon was equipped with the eight 106 rifles mounted on a jeep. We had dismounted four of these guns and issued the extra four vehicles, three to the three rifle-company commanders and one to Headquarters Company, since vehicular transportation was so critical. The remaining four jeeps mounted the 106. In addition, we had been issued four 50-caliber machine guns, which were mounted on the hoods of gun jeeps. This plan enabled us to motorize an element of the Anti-tank Platoon for road patrols. The guns could be lifted in by helicopter and, when placed on peaks or other high ground, were good for bringing explosive fire to bear on point targets.

In addition, the Anti-tank Platoon became the Battalion Engineer Platoon. It was trained to clear landing zones; was well versed in the use of the machete, ax, and shovels; and was equipped with four power saws, gasoline-driven, which would enable them in the future to rapidly clear the landing zone and to assist the engineers, of which we were always short. The platoon was also an excellent rifle platoon.

The Reconnaissance Platoon, proficient in reconnaissance techniques, was trained as a rifle platoon. It was led by an outstanding officer, 1st Lieutenant Billy M. Onstott, and several excellent noncommissioned officers.

We had been working hard on the Mortar Platoon, which I was not satisfied with up to this time. The Mortar Platoon was in position on top of a hill where it could support A Company operations and portions of B Company to the north. They had been firing three to four hundred rounds a day, observed fire. This was an excellent workout for the gunners and fire-direction personnel, as well as for the forward observers with each rifle company. The platoon was rapidly whipping into shape. After a few more days' firing and a few more thousand rounds they should be in excellent condition.

D Company, commanded by Captain Vandoster Tabb, was a versatile company. In addition to all these things I have just described, it was capable of fighting as a rifle company, as it would soon demonstrate on a number of occasions. It would participate in one especially outstanding air assault as a rifle company with a rifle platoon attached.

On this day we received an alert that we would have to provide one company to Task Force Amos again, probably the next day. This would be C Company, which was in reserve. I hated to hear that they were on this mission again; however, since they were in reserve, the Acting Battalion Commander sent them with Task Force Amos. They would move to Tuy Hoa, forty miles south, down the coast from Quin Nhon, as security for Task Force Amos, which was providing necessary tube-artillery support to elements of the Vietnamese Army along the China Sea coast.

C Company departed at 0830, coming under operational control of Task Force Amos at Tuy Hoa at 0915 hours.

The remaining portion of the battalion continued with the search-and-destroy mission. At 1400 hours an alert was received to extract from the current mission and move by air from Ben Khe to Pleiku, and to revert to operational control of the 1st Airborne Brigade upon arrival. Operations were increasing in tempo in the Pleiku area and the 1st Airborne Brigade had been able to request and free its last remaining battalion in order to be intact.

The brigade also had one additional battalion attached from another brigade of the division, thus giving the 1st Airborne Brigade Acting Commander, Lieutenant Colonel Harlow Clark, four Infantry battalions with our arrival.

At 1800 hours B Company, the Reconnaissance Platoon, and the Forward Command Post, under Major Eberhardt, departed in the first lift by UH-1D Delta and Chinooks to Pleiku. The remainder of the battalion was extracted, relieved by elements of the 2nd Brigade, and moved by truck to the An Khe air strip; from there it was to go by air to Pleiku.

On arrival at the An Khe air strip, the air movement was cancelled owing to unavailability of transportation, and the battalion was moved by truck back to the An Khe Base Camp to revert once more to 2nd Brigade, in reserve in the An Khe Base Camp.

B Company and the Reconnaissance Platoon of D Company arrived at Pleiku and were placed under operational control of the 1st Brigade.

This meant that the Jumping Mustang Battalion, with the Headquarters and A and D Companies minus, were at An Khe. B Company and the Reconnaissance Platoon were seventy miles to the west, near the Cambodian border; C Company was seventy miles to the east on the China Sea coast with Task Force Amos. The battalion had frontage of 150 nautical miles from the left flank to the right flank—quite a large piece of real estate for one battalion.

Needless to say, I was in the hospital during this period. You can imagine my feeling as I received word that my battalion was scattered to the four winds. They were about to engage in a major combat at Pleiku and I was not with them.

The battalion received orders to relieve 2nd Battalion, 5th Cavalry, in the An Khe Pass and assume control of that pass not later than noon the next day. The relief was executed the following day and the battalion with A Company and D Company minus assumed control and security of the pass.

During this period the battalion was operating in the An Khe Pass. My jeep at about 2030 hours was driving back from the vicinity of the 1st Forward Support Element vicinity of Ben Khe to the Battalion CP. As they were passing a U-shaped turn in the road, four bullets were blasted through the right front windshield from the left rear. Two passed through the right front windshield, where I usually sit, and two through the metal frame at the top of the windshield. A hand grenade bounced off the front of the hood, thrown by Viet Cong on the high terrain overlooking the vehicle. Fortunately, as the rounds were fired through the windshield and the grenade bounced off the hood, the driver, Corporal Ballew, stepped on the gas and barrelled down the road. The grenade dropped off and exploded harmlessly behind him midway between the jeep and another vehicle following a hundred yards away. Fortunately also, the radio operator, Corporal Hill, was sitting in his customary spot in the back. There was nobody in the right front seat where normally I sat. Had there been anyone in that seat, those two rounds would have gone through him. Needless to say, the two drivers were "shook."

When I returned, I took great delight in Ballew and Hill retelling this personal war story. I left the windshield as it was and used it for the rest of my tour as Battalion Commander. It provided a wonderful topic of conversation, especially when we drove around the rear echelon back at the base camp or when in Quin Nhon at the hospital visiting some of the troopers.

*   *   *

The remainder of the mission of securing the An Khe Pass continued without incident until November 2nd. The battalion was relieved by 2nd Brigade and was moved by truck to the An Khe air strip for further movement to Pleiku.

The battalion closed on the 1st Brigade Base at the Stadium in the Pleiku area at 1830 hours. Here it received the mission of securing the Brigade Base, including the airfield. B Company and the Reconnaissance Platoon reverted to battalion control on closing the base. This left the Mustangs intact except for C Company, which was still conducting its mission with Task Force Amos on the China Sea coast. I was still in the hospital at this liaison, although beginning to improve.

This action concluded the Ben Khe operation as such and began the Plei Mei/Pleiku operation, the first big battle of the 1st Air Cavalry Division.

The Ben Khe operation was excellent in a number of respects. First of all, we operated as a battalion on a series of air assaults and search-and-destroy missions. The skill in staff planning and command-control exercise improved immeasurably. The techniques and methods of search-and-destroy and air-assault techniques within the companies were better. Both NCO's and officers became more proficient. The teamwork and coordination between the assault transport helicopters improved and further firepower refinements were completed, especially coordination of air strikes and use of artillery.

At this stage I was most pleased with the battalion team. The Artillery Liaison Officer, Captain Wilkie, was one of the finest artillerymen I ever had the pleasure of being associated with. He was a fine professional; he knew his job and did it well. He was not a "yes" type person; he was one who gave good advice and recommendations. I had to sit on him once in a while in order to obtain his compliance with my desires, sometimes a little at variance with what he thought was right or what his artillery battalion preferred. However, this was the manner in which I liked to operate and the type of personnel I liked to have working with me. It is much easier to curb an officer or NCO than to prod him.

I lost Captain Holland, the Air Force Liaison Officer, after a month in the battalion. He left to join the 1st of the 9th Cavalry. I had an equally fine replacement, Captain

Charles Corey, who was rapidly proving himself as the type of airman who made it his sole mission in life to provide Air Force fire support for the Infantry. He was not only proficient in his job as part of my command post, but did an outstanding job on the ground with his airmen, lugging his UHF radio when accompanying a rifle company in order to provide necessary tactical air support when circumstances dictated.

I was pleased with Dr. Odom. He contributed far more than he realized. I knew he would rather have been involved more in surgical-type activities, but often the Battalion Surgeon did not really realize what he contributed to his unit. He did not have the opportunity of performing the more technical and surgical-type operations that he would in a hospital, but he contributed a great deal to the battalion, not only in preventive medicine, but also in emergencies.

He refined his Battalion Aid Station to the point that the tactical portion, needed in the field, could fit on a mechanical mule to be transported overland or placed in an A-22 container, suspended from a UH-1 if making an air assault.

Dr. Odom, with his small team, accompanied the assault elements of the CP. His outstanding aide men, highly trained at this stage, were parceled out one or two to each rifle platoon throughout the battalion. We had been fortunate to receive extra aide men and we assigned them so that we had at least one with each rifle platoon and usually one or two at the company headquarters. In addition, I had several in reserve. In this war the aide men were the ones who received the larger number of casualties. Our first major hero, who would receive a Distinguished Service Cross for the Plei Mei operation, was one of these outstanding aide men.

Chaplain Ralph Spear was performing well on the religious side of the house. I liked his prebattle prayers that were now traditional in the battalion, also the simple memorial ceremonies he conducted for our dead. In addition, the construction of the new permanent-type chapel was going well.

The battalion itself performed outstandingly. Major John R. Herman, the S-3, and Captain Norm Propes, his assistant, were doing a tremendous job. I had two fireball lieutenants with the S-3 Section, Lieutenant Wendell Karoly and Lieutenant John B. Cater. They were both performing well. Their actual jobs were liaison officers establishing liaison with brigade or the other battalions as required. In free moments either of them performed as assistant S-3's.

The S-4 Section worked well under Captain Godwin P. McLaughlin. Captain Jerry Plummer, our original S-4, remained only a few weeks after arrival, having received a severe eye injury that required his evacuation to the United States and Walter Reed for surgery. Jerry would be all right and returned to the battalion later. Captain McLaughlin and Warrant Officer Samuel P. Rader, his Supply Assistant, and the men of the Supply and Service Platoon were doing a tremendous job. There was a sharp division between the "have's" and the "have not's"; the "have's" being many of the service units at locations in Quin Nhon, Nha Trang, and Saigon, and the "have not's" being the combat units. My supply people were past masters at obtaining supplies and necessary equipment from the "have's." This included critical items such as lumber and cement. The lumber was used for framing tents to put the troops into better living conditions, and the cement for cement platforms or floors for the tents to get the troops off the ground.

I was most pleased with the status of the S-1 Section. Captain William Mozey was doing an outstanding job with the administration, most important to us in Vietnam. We had few difficulties with our pay, mail, and other things of this sort which were most important.

Our S-2, Captain Charles B. Stone, performed in a Number One manner. He concentrated on developing our intelligence within the battalion—the key to success over here. Captain Stone was also in charge of the civic actions or civil affairs.

Major Guy Eberhardt, the Battalion Executive Officer, continued to perform in a fine manner also. I could not have had a better team had I deliberately set out to pick each one of them individually. It was amazing how units such as this, formed in a short period of time, with the many personnel transferred in from all over the country, had been able to assemble as such an outstanding group. For this I was thankful. It was a tribute to those back at Department of Army, Third US Army, and Fort Benning, who helped us assemble these units and prepare for Vietnam.

6

PLEI MEI/PLEIKU

On November 2nd the battalion, less C Company at Tuy Hoa, closed on Pleiku, the 1st Airborne Brigade Base, designated "the Stadium." B Company and the Reconnaissance Platoon, previously operating under 1st Brigade control, reverted to the control of the battalion.

The Battle of the Ia Drang was a long, hard campaign, the first combat action in Vietnam between major United States and North Vietnamese Army forces. A division of the North Vietnamese Army, consisting of three regiments, attacked the Special Forces Camp at Plei Mei 19 October 1965. The enemy attack was resisted initially by South Vietnamese Army forces and the Special Forces Team with its Civilian Irregular Defense Groups (CIDG). Within two days it was necessary to reinforce the Vietnamese elements with tube artillery from the 1st Air Cavalry Division.

Shortly thereafter, as the intelligence situation developed, it was obvious that this attack was a major campaign with major North Vietnamese forces involved. The 1st Air Cavalry Division was assigned the mission to move in, reinforce and take over the operations, and seek out and destroy the enemy. This was the reason for the movement of the 1st Airborne Brigade with the 1st of the 12th and 2nd of the 8th from the area east of the An Khe Pass to Pleiku a few days prior, and also the reason for our movement.

This battle lasted thirty-five days, during which the Division won a Presidential Unit Citation. The first phase in which the 1st Airborne Brigade participated ended in ten days. The enemy were driven back and scattered throughout the area on the east side of the Cambodian border. At that time, on 9 November, the 1st Airborne Brigade was relieved by the 3rd Brigade.

The 3rd Brigade's mission was to pursue the enemy, destroy his units, and capture as many weapons as possible. During this period the famous battle of the 1st of the 7th at LZ "X-ray," in which 1200 North Vietnamese were killed, took place.

On 20 November the 3rd Brigade was relieved by the 2nd Brigade and the operation continued through the end of the month. This latter phase found fewer of the enemy and consisted primarily of search-and-destroy missions.

I have not attempted to cover all of the details of the Battle of the Ia Drang and the tremendous impact this battle had on the war itself. The North Vietnamese Army was stopped cold in its tracks, thus proving that organized United States forces could fight and defeat organized North Vietnamese forces. The Jumping Mustang Battalion was in on the first phase of this action, in the early days with B Company and finally with the battalion itself. The battalion returned on 20 November as a portion of the 2nd Brigade and was the last battalion out of the Pleiku area, fighting the rear-guard or withdrawal action after the battle was terminated.

The Jumping Mustangs were the only battalion in the 1st Air Cavalry that could record participation in both the beginning and ending of the Battle of the Ia Drang. We did not participate in any major actions, with the exception of A Company, on the night of 3-4 November, although we were active and considerable energy was expended during this thirty-five-day period.

The day prior to the arrival of the battalion, B Company, operating under operational control of the 1st Brigade, conducted an airmobile assault in a landing zone in the vicinity of the Cambodian border near the Ia Drang River to reinforce B Troop of the 1st of the 9th Cavalry. B Company of the Jumping Mustangs secured the landing zone, pushed out and secured the outer perimeter, and assisted in the evacuation of the Cavalry personnel.

The Mortar Platoon of the company provided indirect fire support to elements of the 2nd of the 12th, an Infantry battalion from the 2nd Brigade, operating under operational control of the 1st Airborne Brigade. In addition, the Battalion

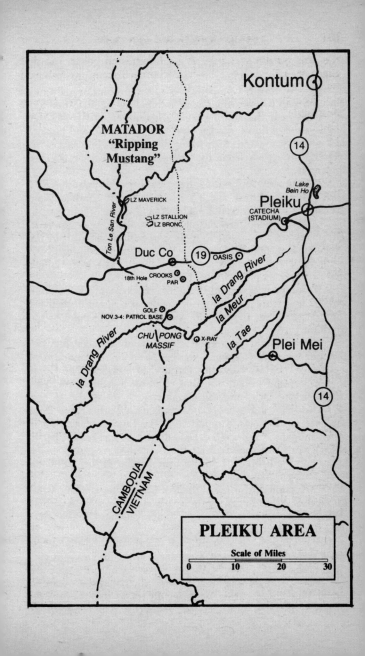

Reconnaissance Platoon worked with the 2nd of the 12th in their local area.

Patrols from B Company were sent out on the night of 1 November to recover friendly ammunition, weapons, wounded, and dead near the landing zone. In addition, a UH-1D that had been shot down was secured. All equipment and personnel were evacuated to within the landing-zone area. Six friendly stragglers from the adjacent units were recovered that night.

B Company sent out contact patrols in the morning. Two NVA were captured along with over forty bamboo hand grenades, twenty entrenching tools, and considerable quantities of enemy webbing and other miscellaneous equipment. The company continued to assist the 2nd of the 12th in the evacuation of friendly casualties and captured additional NVA equipment and medical supplies. Fifteen NVA were killed, five prisoners captured, and two NVA wounded.

B Company returned to the brigade base at the Stadium at 1600 hours; the remainder of the day was spent in securing the brigade base, the airfield, and the refueling point at the Stadium.

The battalion continued the mission of securing the Brigade Base. A Company was released to the operational control of the 1st of the 9th Cavalry, to move to Duc Co at 1815 hours and initiate the first night air assault in conjunction with the 1st of the 9th Cavalry.

The following account of this famous battle came from After Action Reports, a report from the Commanding Officer of A Company, Captain Ted Danielsen; a report from Charlie Black, War Correspondent for the Columbus *Enquirer*; and a letter and final report from the Commander of the 1st of the 9th Cavalry Squadron.

The action of the 1st of the 9th Cavalry Squadron on the Ia Drang River began with a mission from the Assistant Division Commander, Brigadier General Richard T. Knowles, directing a reconnaissance in force.

In the afternoon a patrol base was established under the command of Major Robert Zion north of the Ia Drang River, close to the Cambodian border in the area where B Company had been a few days before. It was anticipated the escaping North Vietnamese Army units would try to use the several withdrawal routes and excellent trails that paralleled the Ia

Drang River and led across into Cambodia. Three ambushes and two observation posts were set out along these likely routes.

At 2105, the south ambush was triggered by its commander, Captain Charles S. Knowlen. He then returned his ambush force to the patrol base and occupied the southern sector of the base perimeter.

Captain Danielsen in his report described the 2130 hour ambush by the Cavalry personnel:

Captain Danielsen:

> The platoon located at the ambush site heard enemy personnel approaching the kill zone. The platoon could determine that the North Vietnamese carried heavy weapons in addition to their normal combat gear, and that the unit moving through the site was much larger than the platoon lying in ambush. The ambush commander, Captain Charles S. Knowlen, watched approximately ninety personnel pass the site before triggering the ambush. The lack of security forces and the poor noise discipline indicated that the North Vietnamese in no way expected any unfriendly elements in this area so near the border. The ambush was sprung with withering M-16 automatic fire, M-79 grenade launcher, M-60 machine gun, and claymore mines. The enemy force was taken completely by surprise and all personnel in the kill zone were killed or wounded.
>
> During the confusion of the North Vietnamese force, Captain Knowlen deemed it desirable to withdraw before the superior force could react. The platoon began a withdrawal in as rapid a manner as possible, but were soon subject to 60-mortar fire. From the direction of the mortars firing, the Mortar Platoon Forward Observer from A Company determined that the enemy mortar position was at or near a previously plotted 81mm mortar concentration. He immediately called the Platoon Fire Direction Center and requested fire. The Fire Direction Center had already placed the data on the guns and the Forward Observer immediately received sup-

M-60 Machine Gun

port fire. The Forward Observer's analysis had been correct and the 60mm fire ceased shortly after the friendly fires hit the target. In addition these friendly fires served to cover the ambush platoon's withdrawal from the area as the North Vietnamese who were not caught in the kill zone were beginning to react. The ambush force returned to the landing zone to rejoin its parent unit. The Platoon Leader's report, forwarded to Duc Co, included an estimated forty-eight enemy killed with an unknown number wounded.

This report from Captain Danielsen was of interest because the 81-mortar platoon fire referred to was the Mortar Platoon from his unit, commanded by 2nd Lieutenant Stuart K. Tweedy, supporting the ambush. The platoon itself was attached to the 1st of the 9th Cavalry organization at the patrol base; thus A Company made its first contribution in the initial combat of the battle. There was more yet to come.

A Columbus *Enquirer* report recounted the first ambush engagement. He had accompanied another ambush which was located about 750 meters away on the banks of the Ia Drang.

Charlie Black:

The report was that at 2105 hours, the ambush set by Captain Knowlen was triggered, according to members of the ambush, into a North Vietnamese heavy weapons company and two Infantry platoons. Ten claymore mines and violent small arms fire were heard and the flashes observed from our position. A radio message came from Major Zion, the Patrol Base Commander, saying that the Platoon had been highly successful and was returning to the rendezvous point.

A few minutes later the enemy surrounded the ambush where Charlie Black was, and this force, too, was ordered to fight its way back to the Patrol Base.

Charlie Black:

We were moving under about a three-quarter moon. The night was clear and once out of the river cover it was not thick at all. We had as I remember seven separate contacts with the enemy, three of which were violent. I recall one kept our twenty-one men pinned down in a slight depression, less than a six-inch hollow in the ground, for twenty minutes. My equipment was ripped by tracer fire which was ricochetting from the ground six inches from my nose. The fire came from 360 degrees. The situation in which our small force was involved can be judged by the fact that we had three such fire fights before we finally were able to reach the Patrol Base perimeter at 0330 hours.

Shortly after, at 2200 hours, the first NVA attack was initiated against the patrol base. It was followed by four additional attacks at 2315, 0030, 0115, and 0330 hours. In the intervals between the attacks there was constant sniper fire. During the first attack at 2315, it was obvious to the commander on the ground that if the small force was not immediately reinforced, it would be overrun.

Colonel Stockton, the commander of the 9th Cavalry Squadron, alerted A Company for immediate employment to reinforce the Patrol Base. In addition, all remaining ambush platoons were ordered to return to the Patrol Base.

The 3rd Platoon of A Company, commanded by 1st Lieutenant John B. Hanlon, was alerted for immediate employment to be attached to the Troop Commander, Major Zion, at the Patrol Base. The platoon lifted off in UH-1D transport helicopters provided by the 1st of the 9th Cavalry Squadron escorted by armed helicopters from the squadron. The platoon made its landing at the fire-swept Patrol Base as 2345 hours.

Captain Danielsen:

It was decided to drop a flare from a C-47 aircraft which had been called on station when the ambush was executed. The flare was to illuminate the landing zone for landing, since no night landing had been attempted in that area before and none of the normal landing aids were available. The illumination served the intended purpose of providing the pilots needed visibility for the landing. However, as the lift helicopters touched down, they came under intense ground fire which hit every helicopter in the lift but did not disable any.

The 3rd Platoon immediately took moderate casualties while dismounting from the aircraft and assaulting towards the enemy positions. As they reached the southern edge of the landing zone perimeter, Lieutenant Hanlon gave the order to take up defensive positions and began reorganizing his sector, at the same time controlling the distribution of fire of his platoon. He reported at that time that he had gained the perimeter but had an estimated thirty percent casualties. His mission was one of attachment, to reinforce the existing perimeter.

This mission was completed. Wounded personnel were evacuated later on, under fire, to the middle of the landing zone to await further evacuation. Tube artillery support was not available as this area was out of range to all ground supporting tube artillery. Aerial rockets had been requested and

were scrambling to join in on the mission from bases
near the Stadium.

Charlie Black:

We heard helicopter gun ships firing, then the
noise of the 2.75 rockets distinguished from the
general battle noise over the area. Captain Oliver
told me that the helicopters actually made a landing
and had brought Captain Danielsen's men into the
vortex of the fight at the Command Post area. This
was 0030 hours as I remember. It struck me as
inconceivable that this landing could have been
accomplished and equally inconceivable that any
force put into such a situation could fight and sur-
vive. I told Captain Oliver that the platoons from A
Company were coming to a strange piece of terrain
at night, under enemy fire as close as fifty meters
(we had a running account of the fighting from
Major Zion on his Command Net), into a perimeter
which had been wiped out along its entire southeastern corner. It would be impossible for any control or for any organized fighting line to be set up
under these circumstances. At this point, to be
frank, all of us in my group had decided we were
finished and had simply resolved to fight for all
possible payment from the enemy.

At 2400 hours Major Zion reported that the situation was
still deteriorating. Colonel Stockton committed the remaining
elements of A Company. Captain Danielsen received the
mission to assault by air, reinforce the perimeter, and hold
until the enemy withdrew or reinforcements could be landed
at daylight. On landing, the already committed platoon of A
Company would revert to parent-company control.

Captain Danielsen loaded his second platoon and the
company command group on the next available lift helicopters.
The aircraft lifted off and then landed under fire at 0020 hours.

Captain Danielsen:

Although this lift was subject to heavy ground
fire from a range of less than 100 meters, none of

the ships were damaged to the point of not being flyable. This was due to the fact that this time none of the illumination was employed. The pilots stayed on the ground longer to unload troops in order to take on casualties of the already committed 3rd Platoon and evacuate them to safety. This proved to be the only method of medical evacuation for the remainder of the night. One of the ships did have to make an emergency landing enroute to Duc Co.

Back at the Patrol Base, Charlie Black crawled over to join Major Zion at his Command Post.
Major Zion:

We switched positions from one side of the anthill several times in order to get out of the enemy fire and repel assaults. The CP was actually one corner of our front line by this time. "I don't know who that Infantry captain is who came into this area in those choppers but he saved us. I had lost all control of the fight down there and it started going right when he got there. They were going to hit us hard about dawn. Maybe they'll finish us but we would have been finished two hours ago if that captain hadn't gotten his people in down there and taken over that end of the perimeter."

Charlie Black:

Major Zion gave all credit for salvaging the lower side of the perimeter to Captain Danielsen and gave him full credit for reestablishing continuity and control of the fighting there where the enemy was on the verge of pushing into his heaviest assault and overrunning the entire position.

Captain Danielsen:

The North Vietnamese probes were increasing in frequency and strength and several final protective lines had been fired in portions of the perimeter. The 81 Mortar Platoon, commanded by

Lieutenant Stuart Tweedy, did a fantastic job in firing along the edge of the perimeter, operating in the open, subject to grazing fire. They fired without firing tables or plotting boards. All corrections were made by turns of the mortar hand wheels on the traversing and elevating mechanisms. During the course of firing they fired almost two complete basic loads of ammunition without inflicting a single friendly casualty.

At daylight the next day, I measured the distance between the perimeter and the shell holes to be an average of thirteen paces along the entire perimeter. Ammunition became critical at 0130 hours and all available was being received from Duc Co and other units that could be reached by helicopter.

The helicopter pilots again landed in the perimeter under fire, dumped the ammunition, took on casualties and moved out. Aerial rocket ships from Catecha (another name for the Stadium Base) arrived on station at 0300 hours and after identifying the perimeter, did an extremely professional job of reinforcing the fires of the 81mm mortars.

It was about this time that the North Vietnamese decided to withdraw. Their tactic for breaking contact was to put snipers in the trees around the perimeter and snipe at any identifiable target. Under this fire cover others dragged casualties to the rear. It was extremely well done, emphasis of the ground fire was shifted to the trees while the casualties were being sneaked out. Its effectiveness can be judged by the fact that at daylight no enemy dead or wounded were found, although there were numerous indications. A North Vietnamese prisoner captured the next day stated that only seventeen personnel in the force attacking the perimeter withdrew without being wounded or killed.

While the battle within the perimeter was occurring, ambush elements from the north tried to reach the northern edge of the perimeter. While moving, they repeatedly came in contact with enemy units. This indicated that the North Vietnamese were trying to encircle the perimeter, but the contact outside the perimeter confused them to the point that they could not assess correctly the situation with any certainty.

At 0430 hours contact ceased with only an occasional burst of fire at suspicious targets by troops on the perimeter. Friendly personnel now moved more freely and began carrying the dead and their equipment to central locations, and for the first time to make an accurate assessment of casualties. Movement of the wounded platoon leader, Lieutenant John Hanlon, who had been seriously wounded about midnight, was still prohibited due to the lack of a litter, expected at daylight. He was better off without being moved since there was no safer place to move him.

Lieutenant Hanlon conducted himself in a heroic manner. Landing in the initial lift as the Platoon Leader of the 3rd Platoon, he was almost immediately hit with a bullet penetrating near the mid-section, alongside the spinal cord. However, since he was in command of the platoon and they were in the middle of a fire fight, he continued to direct and command his platoon for several hours. He was again wounded while crawling to and from various positions in the area to better give direction and assistance to his men. He was later evacuated back to the United States, where he is presently in the VA Hospital, Memphis, Tennessee, paralyzed from the waist down. He received a Silver Star for this outstanding heroic action, among the first Silver Stars to be awarded to the Jumping Mustang Battalion.

Another hero in the battle, within the platoon, was Spec 4 Raymond Ortiz, Medical Aide man of the platoon. He was a huge individual, a well-trained medic. He was hit almost immediately in trying to assist wounded men. In spite of the severe shoulder wound, he continued to move freely on the battlefield, receiving five or six additional hits before finally going down. He received the Distinguished Service Cross for this heroism, the first to be awarded within the Jumping Mustang Battalion.

Captain Danielsen:

At about 0400 hours I had for the first time an opportunity to consult with the CO of the 1st of the

9th Cavalry in the perimeter. An assault to the
south of the perimeter was a logical course of action.
This was agreed on and the time was designated as
first light since no personnel in A Company had
seen the terrain beyond the limit of their night
vision range.

At first light A Company assaulted from its
perimeter in a walking "Mad Minute." A "Mad
Minute," incidentally, was a technique for discouraging infiltration of enemy personnel to within effective ranges of friendly troops. It consisted of each
soldier spraying his sector of fire to include trees at
a specified time, usually just after dark or slightly
before dawn.

The assault moved several hundred meters out
and halted. Observation posts were left at the limits
of the assault and the remainder of A Company
returned to the perimeter and saw for the first time
the area.

At about thirty minutes after daylight, two companies of the 1st of the 8th landed in the landing
zone, and with that, A Company completed its
mission. It had reinforced and held the perimeter
until reinforcements landed.

Then ensued the unpleasant task of cleaning
up. Friendly casualties in A Company were 15
percent with the 3rd Platoon suffering between 40
and 50 percent. However, out of these casualties,
only two men were killed. Lieutenant Hanlon was
and still is paralyzed from the waist down.

It should be stated that this action was the first
violent attack A Company had participated in since
arrival in Vietnam. This full-scale baptism of fire
occurred in as difficult a situation as could be imag-
ined. The primary point here was not that it was
accomplished, but was the reaction of the individual
soldier. During the initial confusion on the ground,
personnel picked their own sectors of fire and tied
in left and right. Mortars were called for and used
without firing charts or plotting boards, all with
accurate results. The mission was received, plan
executed, and accomplished. This constituted mili-

tary success. This was what happened the night of 3-4 November 1965.

Charlie Black:

Captain Danielsen was described to me by one of his sergeants in the morning as laughing and joking at some phases of the fighting. Each member of his command told me how he crawled into their position during the fighting, telling them to get on up to the front line, and then acting surprised and saying, "Why, this is the front line, isn't it?" and crawling on.

I do not know what value this had as humor, but its effect on the spirits and morale of his command was obvious. He changed the attitude which, if judged from what I had undergone in my own mind, had been stubborn and fatalistic into one of aggressiveness and confidence. This aggressiveness and spirit among his troops was communicated along the badly hit positions of the original defenders and was picked up in an audible wave of taunts and invectives thrown out at the enemy along with the bullets.

Members of Captain Danielsen's command in the morning, which we reinforced, told me that this spirit and morale was directly attributable to the demeanor and actions of Captain Danielsen, assisted by Lieutenant John Hanlon [who,] badly wounded, kept command of his platoon during the action.

Just at dawn, we commenced receiving heavy fire from snipers in the trees and from the opposite end of the landing zone from the position held by Major Zion. There were two helicopters shot down in the area from the previous night's assault and they seemed to be drawing this fire in the vicinity of the command post. Mortar fire started some time previously, but a Forward Air Controller spotted the flashes of the tubes and called in a bomb attack, silencing them after thirteen rounds hit in the general area of Captain Danielsen's position.

The combined mortar attack and sniper fire

effectively pinned the defenses in my area near the anthill and was beating on the weapon positions in the center. Major Zion shouted to me, "Look at that, three of them." I looked, I saw Captain Danielsen, easily recognized by his cigar and the fact that he was an old acquaintance of mine, with an M-60 machine gun, sitting in the open, firing steadily into the trees. I saw three snipers fall from his fire out of the trees about twenty-five meters high at a close range right on the edge of the clearing. I saw Captain Danielsen shouting and then saw two of his men run to where he was motioning, and fire LAW (light anti-tank weapon) rockets into the trees. I saw him organize and advance on the run, and push his small, tired, but still enthusiastic force out into the tree line, putting heavy fire into the area and silencing the snipers.

At about 0500, the men in this perimeter did something I have never seen in combat before. Without orders, all men commenced fixing bayonets, laying out grenades and remaining ammunition, preparing for the last stand. They were the same troops Captain Danielsen led into the assault on the treeline in order to clear the area of enemy fire from the ground and tree positions so reinforcing helicopter assault could be accomplished without further opposition. His personal conduct in this final action which I witnessed, was an exhibition of individual bravery which ranked with any I observed in South Vietnam. If no other factor was considered, his use of the M-60 to return that fire from an exposed position and his constant exposure for example while getting his men to move into the assault was worthy of a high award.

Incidentally, Captain Danielsen received the Silver Star for heroism demonstrated during this battle, although it was two years late in recognition.

Colonel John Stockton, the commander of the 1st of the 9th Cavalry Squadron, provided a statement pertaining to Captain Danielsen's action.

Colonel John Stockton:

Captain Danielsen's heroism during this engagement while temporarily under my command was literally beyond belief, in view of his lack of previous combat experience under especially trying conditions and his relative youth. The leadership he demonstrated was inspirational far beyond an expected call of duty for any officer. The reinforcement action in which he was involved was the first in the history of the United States Army conducted at night by helicopters while a unit was engaged in direct fire contact with the enemy. It could have resulted disastrously. The fact that this reinforcement was not only successful, but also proved the turning point in the engagement, can be attributed almost solely and exclusively to the inspirational bravery and demonstrated leadership of Captain Theodore S. Danielsen.

The battle of 3-4 November, in which A Company of the Jumping Mustang Battalion executed the first night-combat air assault into an enemy-held landing zone under fire in the history of the United States Army was the first in Vietnam and the first in the 1st Air Cavalry Division.

The Jumping Mustang Battalion, minus C Company still at Tuy Hoa, completed its reinforcement assault into the area of action and conducted a search-and-destroy mission to find and destroy the remaining enemy who by now were rapidly retreating across the Cambodian border. Numerous bodies and large amounts of equipment were found.

By 1700 hours the mission was completed and the battalion ordered to close back to the Brigade Base to act as security for the base and to conduct security patrols out to a distance of 3600 meters. One company was placed on a thirty-minute alert status as a Brigade Reaction Force.

The account of the action 3-4 November is mostly by quotes and reports, for at this time I was back at the hospital at Quin Nhon, one hundred and fifty miles away, far removed from the battlefield.

My first indication that something serious was happening to the battalion came as rumors spread throughout the hospital, as they always do, that a major battle must be in the

offing because large numbers of 1st Air Cavalry casualties
were arriving at the hospital. Rumors of this kind spread
rapidly throughout hospital wards with more men coming in,
especially if they were badly shot up.

My first actual warning came from one of my young
soldiers, Corporal John Chard, who was keeping tabs on my
physical condition as well as that of other men of the battalion
in the hospital. He came to me early in the morning and
stated that during the past night a large number of Jumping
Mustangs from A Company had been admitted to the hospital; that many of them were seriously shot up; that there were
reports of men killed; and that at least one lieutenant,
Lieutenant Hanlon, was now in the hospital.

This information came as a surprise, for I was unaware of
the complete tactical situation and did not know what the
battalion was involved in. Rumors were rampant—there were
conflicting stories about A Company being committed into a
trap and some unusual command actions that had taken
place. This was upsetting. I was also perturbed because I was
missing a major engagement by my battalion. As all commanders do, I felt that no one could do the job quite as well
as I. I thought things would be different had I been there.

These thoughts were all flashing through my mind as I
received the various reports. Corporal Chard kept me informed the rest of the morning. About mid-morning, in my
more rational moments, the fever having subsided, I was able
to go to the Intensive Care Ward, where I talked with
Lieutenant Hanlon briefly, although he was under medication
and could say but a few intelligible words. I found two or
three other men, not wounded quite as badly, who filled me
in on small bits and pieces of the action. Later on in the day
one of my NCO's arrived from the battalion base at An Khe
and gave me further details.

These were trying moments for me personally because I
wanted to get back and join the battle. I was so sick I could
hardly move, and yet my men, seriously wounded, were
pouring into the hospital.

During the next two days I pieced together the complete
story. I could not help but view with pride the outstanding
job that had been accomplished.

I was amazed, in my visits to the seriously wounded in
the wards during the next twenty-four to forty-eight hours, at

how, in spite of the critical wounds, these men were so cheerful. When a man first came to the hospital, he was bloody, pale, and looked as though he faced the end. The tremendous job that the doctors, nurses, and medical attendants performed, cleaning the wounded, giving necessary medications, repairing the broken and torn limbs, all occurred in a short period of time.

Within twenty-four hours a casualty was usually able to talk and eager to describe his personal battle experiences. With forty-eight hours there was a complete change and they were much better off. After the forty-eighth hour, the main goal of almost every man was to recover as rapidly as possible and get back to his unit, where he could take revenge on the Viet Cong and do his share to eliminate them. This was particularly true if he knew that some of his buddies had been killed. The only way to get back at the enemy was to kill more of them.

The Jumping Mustang Battalion continued a series of airmobile assaults in search for the fleeing enemy along with other elements of the brigade. There was little enemy contact and the operation became primarily a "search and walk."

November 6th was a big day for me. I had finally talked my way out of the hospital, and ordered a vehicle to Quin Nhon to pick me up. Men from the Rear Detachment arrived with my equipment and vehicle. We spent a pleasant three hours driving back along the picturesque, winding Highway 19 to An Khe. It was wonderful to be out of the hospital again, to breathe fresh air, and to know that I would soon be back with the Mustangs.

I was extremely weak at this time, having lost thirty-five or forty pounds owing to the high temperature for so many days. I had to employ a few prevarications to escape from the hospital, but I felt fine. I had an outstanding doctor there who I think probably realized more of the situation than he indicated to me. He knew my Battalion Surgeon, Dr. Odom. Between the two of them, I would rapidly recover.

The biggest problem remaining was some kind of anemia that had developed from the drugs used against the rising fever. I had a low blood count that plagued me for the next two or three months and on several occasions threatened to cause my evacuation back to the United States. However, I was able to successfully resolve these problems and continue.

On arrival at An Khe, I spent an hour in the Battalion Base, saw what was happening, and was updated with the situation in the rear. At 1600 hours my command helicopter flew from Pleiku to the Jumping Mustang Helipad to pick me up. I arrived at the Forward Command Post at Pleiku at 1830, just prior to dark.

It was wonderful to be back with the battalion. Everybody treated me like a long-lost buddy who had returned. This gave me a good idea about the feel of the battalion and made me realize that I had succeeded thus far in welding together an outstanding fighting unit with high spirit and morale. I received an inkling of this when the young soldiers down at the hospital worried about me so much, making sure that I knew everything that went on within the battalion.

Although the battalion had been successful and had performed well under the Executive Officer, Major Eberhardt, any number of officers, NCO's and men made it their point to tell me personally how happy they were to see me back.

The tactical situation was quiet. We secured the perimeter for the night. I had little time other than to call each of the company commanders on the radio to tell them I had reassumed command and that I would give them further instructions whatever the continuing mission of the battalion might be. I settled down for a cup of C-ration coffee and a hot C-ration which had been handed to me by Corporal Ballew.

The radio from brigade sputtered into life. I was ordered to return personally to the Brigade CP at the Brigade Base immediately to receive a new mission. I climbed in the command helicopter and flew to the Brigade Base, fifteen minutes away.

There I met the Acting Brigade Commander, Lieutenant Colonel Harlow Clark, dead on his feet from the last few nights of continuous action by the 1st Airborne Brigade. He took forty-five minutes to bring me up to date on what had occurred in the battle of Plei Mei thus far, especially to commend A Company and the Jumping Mustang Battalion for their outstanding accomplishments on the night air assault of 3-4 November.

He briefed me on a new mission. My battalion was to

move out at dawn the following morning; it was detached and would again join the 2nd Brigade back at An Khe, with the mission of opening Highway 19 from An Khe to Pleiku.

I returned to my battalion and issued an alert order. The battalion prepared for movement the next morning back to An Khe and a new adventure on Highway 19.

7

HIGHWAY 19

The Jumping Mustang Battalion, with C Company still at Tuy Hoa, had closed into the Battalion Base at An Khe by 0815 the previous morning. We were required to take over immediately a portion of the Barrier with one company and the An Khe Airfield with another. The An Khe Airfield was an important fixed-wing landing field that could accommodate the C-130 aircraft that flew in the mail, troops, essential supplies, and equipment.

Since a major portion of the division was conducting combat operations in the Pleiku area to rout out the remaining elements of the North Vietnamese Division, there was a requirement for Highway 19 to be opened for the movement of supplies; therefore, we were given the mission of opening the highway the next day from An Khe to the peaks of Mang Yang Pass, where we would join with the Vietnamese Marines holding the pass to Pleiku. This meant that Highway 19 would be open from Quin Nhon to Pleiku.

To accomplish these missions, I had been given operational control of an additional rifle company rotated on a daily basis with the 2nd Brigade. I planned to use this company on the An Khe Airfield to simplify the daily exchange.

A Company was assigned a portion of the Barrier, an extensive sector which spread the company thin. Their area would be a two-battalion sector. This was simply a part of the further extension to release additional units for tactical operations as they became more proficient and as the physical structure of the Barrier improved. What was formerly held by four Infantry battalions on the Barrier eventually would be held by two and finally one battalion. At this stage the 1st Airborne Brigade was stretched thin. Two battalions held the entire An Khe area.

I designated B Company as the unit to open the highway from An Khe to Mang Yang Pass and attached to it the Reconnaissance Platoon and Anti-tank Platoon of D Company and one engineer squad. Using its jeep-mounted 106 recoilless rifles and 50-caliber machine guns, the Anti-tank Platoon would escort convoys and, in conjunction with the Engineers, reconnoiter the highway each morning prior to passage of convoys in order to detect mines, evidence of sabotage, or damage which might have been caused to the highway or bridges during the night by the Viet Cong. The Reconnaissance Platoon would be utilized in a Thunderbolt (reserve force) mission co-located with assault helicopters at a vantage point and prepared to move and quickly engage the enemy force whenever it showed itself.

The portion of Highway 19 that B Company would hold was the scene of the defeat of the famous Group Mobile 100 in 1953, when a French force of paratroopers and commandos fought its way from An Khe, a sleepy little village at that time, back over Highway 19 to Pleiku and finally to Ban Me Thout. Approaching the east side of Mang Yang Pass, they were ambushed by a highly organized force which almost completely destroyed the elite French unit. I was looking forward to the highway opening the next day and to an opportunity to drive personally along this famous road.

I was somewhat apprehensive about the highway mission because this was the second time it had been opened since the beginning of the year, when the Viet Cong had destroyed most of the bridges. Early in November, at the time of the commencement of the Plei Mei operation, the 2nd of the 8the, with the entire battalion, had opened the highway for three days. This time the same sector would be opened with only one rifle company, no reserve available, and have to be held for at least ten days. I was determined to hold this sector and, by changing our pattern of operation, avoid any serious Viet Cong attack; and to keep them off balance in developing their own plans, since the Viet Cong were slow to react, generally taking from five to seven days to scout our positions, prepare detailed plans, and complete a number of rehearsals prior to attacking.

Neither the Division nor I could afford to have any interference with the flow of supplies. I planned to hold the highway by occupying key terrain features that included bridges for which there are no available bypasses and which, if blown, would seriously impede the movement of convoys. Foot patrols of the terrain paralleling the highway, coupled with the OH-13 reconnaissance helicopters from the 1st of the 9th Cavalry Squadron screening at a greater distance, would detect enemy movement and provide early warning. Tube artillery would be positioned to provide continuous and complete coverage of the entire sector, not only in the defense of the many strong points along the highway but for the support of the airmobile platoon if committed.

During periods of actual convoy movement through the sector, I would be overhead in the command helicopter to enhance the flexibility of command and control and add assurance for the safe passage of the convoys through the area of responsibility. This type of tactical employment appeared on the surface to be one that was not within the capability of a single rifle company, but, on the contrary, it was an economy-of-force mission supplemented with the airmobile capability and aerial reconnaissance that provided the company with capability to detect the enemy early and the flexibility to move to encounter the enemy with sufficient force.

We completed relief of the units on the Barrier and the An Khe Airfield by 1200 hours. Captain Martin and I made a flight over the highway in a detailed reconnaissance to select the specific terrain features we would occupy to secure the highway and bridges, the locations of tube artillery, and locations of landing zones to be used by the Thunderbolt force. After the reconnaissance I left Captain Martin to continue his own preparations and planning.

A busy day. I took a three-hour period to fly down to Tuy Hoa to visit C Company, which was still supporting Task Force Amos in that area. I was delighted to see Captain Smith and his fine company again. They had been performing an excellent job securing the elements of the artillery task force. There had been little enemy contact and the company was a bit stale.

On my detailed tour of the company's position, a few words of admonishment were in order, but I was pleased with the attitude of the soldiers and the general condition of the

company, which reassured me that C Company would continue their mission in an outstanding manner. I would be most
happy, however, to get them back with the battalion as soon
as possible. I had continually harassed brigade and division to
relieve C Company at the earliest opportunity and return it to
my control, since I badly needed it and since a company
separated from its parent organization performing a security
mission generally deteriorates rapidly. My latest information
was that the company would not return until 14 November.

At first light the operation for the opening of Highway 19
commenced. B Company moved out by motorized convoy,
escorted by armed helicopters from the 1st of the 9th Air
Cavalry Squadron. Assault helicopters could not be employed
to position the troops. The Pleiku operation had priority for
all critical Army aviation. I supervised the movement of the
company from the command helicopter accompanied by the
command group. We watched as the convoy made its way
slowly down the highway, carefully screening for mines at
likely spots through the efforts of the engineer detachment
under the operational control of the battalion. At each critical
point, the elements to secure that terrain feature quickly
fanned out and occupied the area.

The convoy moved on. I continued to scout the area
until 0930 in the morning, when Captain Martin made contact with the Vietnamese Marine Force, atop the highest
peak of Mang Yang, where Highway 19 cuts through the
mountains. A convoy which had reached An Khe from Quin
Nhon was immediately released to proceed on through to
Pleiku. This was a hundred-truck convoy and included 35
five-thousand-gallon tankers.

I was pleased with the conduct of the operation as a
whole. B Company, under Captain Martin, had reached a
professional peak at this time. This difficult mission under
uncertain enemy conditions was accomplished smoothly, although there was no enemy contact. I felt confident that at
whatever stage the enemy might attack, the company and the
rest of the battalion were ready to react.

As soon as the highway was secured, I flew back to An
Khe to the Battalion Base. Early that afternoon, in my jeep,
and with my radio operators, I drove the entire length of

Highway 19 to the Marine sector to visit at each one of the strong points on the highway and terrain features occupied by B Company.

At one particular hilltop position, after dismounting from the jeep, I slowly climbed the seventy-five-foot winding trail and was annoyed with my own lack of physical strength. I found that I was not as strong as I thought. My knees were still weak, and in climbing that short distance I had to rest three times. I formerly had been able to breeze up a small obstacle of this sort in no time flat. In all, it was rather discouraging.

The operation was successful. The troops looked good at the An Khe Airfield, and the mission on the Barrier was being accomplished well by A Company. The battalion was in fine spirits.

The trend of operations continued for the next eight days. Considerable supervisory effort was required with the change of the one company on the airfield each day, although the procedure was simple. It was difficult to bring a new unit in, get it oriented, and have it perform in the manner which one of your own companies could do. However, all four of the companies that joined the Jumping Mustangs for the brief twenty-four-hour period performed a first-rate job, including one company which had recently returned from Pleiku and had been badly shot up.

C Company returned from Tuy Hoa on the 13th of November. The battalion was now full-strength for the first time in thirty days. The 1st of the 12th relieved the Jumping Mustangs of all portions of the Barrier and the An Khe Airfield. We were able to concentrate two companies on the highway mission, maintaining the road open to Mang Yang and leaving one company to occupy one-half of the Division's Picket Line area, a mission assumed today.

C Company received a twenty-four-hour rest. The next day they would move out and assume a portion of the B Company mission. I took Captain Smith and some of his officers on an aerial reconnaissance to show them their new sector and to complete coordination with Captain Martin of B Company. The relief was scheduled to take place tomorrow.

C Company was assigned one-half of the area previously

held by B Company on the An Khe end, which permitted
both companies to concentrate additional strength on key
terrain features and bridge positions. In the last two or three
days we had continuous sniping from time to time at three
bridge positions late in the afternoon and early in the morning. Small probes against two of the platoon positions had
occurred. As time passed, in holding this road open, the
mission would become more hazardous, because the Viet
Cong now had had sufficient time for reaction. I felt that they
were exploring and reconnoitering our positions with a view
to making an attack in the near future. If they were going to
hit us, they had had ample opportunity to feel us out, move
in, and prepare the attack. I did feel that any attack that did
come would be by small units. Although the VC might
initially give us a hard time, our tube artillery and a company
now in reserve in my own battalion would enable us to resist
anything that might come. At this stage we welcomed an attack.

The longer one is in combat without having enemy
action, the more lackadaisical one gets; thus the more the
troops longed for action and hoped that the enemy would
attack.

The mortar platoons were engaged in an excellent daily
workout, shooting a large number of rounds each night,
harassing and interdictory fire. We had an extensive H and I
program for both artillery and mortar. The targets were
selected during the day by the company commanders with
the aid of their forward observers. The Battalion Artillery
Liaison Officer coordinated the targets and prepared the final
plan. The battalion specified the number of rounds each
mortar platoon was to fire and requested a certain number of
artillery rounds from Division Artillery.

The Picket Line mission was terminated. Two-thirds of
each one of the three rifle companies were now on the
highway mission. This enabled each company to keep one
platoon back as a company reserve. In addition, I had elements of D Company as battalion reserve. There was now a
chance for the troops to clean weapons, take a shower, have a
hot meal, and generally relax a bit. We had been alerted that
probably there would be a new mission in the near future.

The following day was a quiet one. I spent most of the
morning in my command post trying to catch up on corre-

spondence and a little bit of reading. It was a beautiful day for a change, the sun shining. This type weather was most welcome to all the men of the battalion.

The battalion routine was much the same for the next few days. We had fifty percent alert at night, as there had been some probes which tended to stir everybody up and make the men lose a lot of sleep. During the day we concentrated on improving positions and maintaining equipment.

More of my time was spent in my vehicle rather than the command helicopter, since the entire battalion was stretched out along the highway. This enabled me to drop in and visit the troops on a more frequent and personal basis.

We had considerable difficulty with the local civilians, trying to keep them out of the positions. The civilians tried to join with the troops to pick up tidbits of food and to fraternize. At the same time there was, no doubt, one or two in each group of these people who might be Viet Cong agents. Therefore they were able, under the guise of civilians, to observe everything we did, seek out our positions, and at night pick up their rifles and try to do damage. In addition, it was not good for the troops to have civilians roaming around, especially the women, who were most willing to offer themselves to the troops. Some of the soldiers might be quite happy over this arrangement; however, the great bulk of these kinds of women in Vietnam were highly infected with all types of venereal diseases. I would just as soon my men were not in the hospital from that cause. Speaking of venereal disease, I think there was probably every type and kind in Vietnam and in this particular area. Some of its consequences were pretty horrible.

Large convoys continued to move over the highway daily. One day I counted over 175 trucks, including 35 five-thousand-gallon tankers. This was a lot of fuel; however, large quantities of supplies were consumed in the Pleiku area—the reason for the battalion's mission.

We had little VC contact, and the area had quieted down. I was not as concerned at this moment about the enemy situation. A bit of sniping and some proves on the bridge positions at night were the primary activity.

This period, while we had the highway mission, provided a fine opportunity to improve the Battalion Base. The platoon that was back in the base from each company was employed, among other things, to help improve and construct cement floor pads for the squad tents and to build wooden tent frames. Construction and improvement of other facilities within the battalion were progressing well.

Chapel construction was moving fast. Slowly but surely the officers' two-story chateau under Captain William Mozey was taking shape.

At 2000 hours on November 20th I received a call from the Brigade Commander alerting the battalion for an immediate move the following morning to Pleiku under operational control of the 2nd Brigade. The battalion would be relieved of its highway mission by the 1st of the 12th and would proceed by motor to Pleiku. Little was known of the actual situation in Pleiku; however, a fourth Infantry battalion was needed to continue the operation. The Jumping Mustangs were alerted for the move and plans were developed rapidly that night for execution the following morning.

One may wonder whether there was confusion and undue excitement when a sudden order such as this was received, especially at night. By this time the Jumping Mustang Battalion, as well as other battalions within the division, were used to the quick receipt of orders and their rapid and violent execution expected to be carried out in a short length of time. It became really a question of simply alerting the troops where to go and what the means of movement were.

The battalion under the Executive Officer would execute the move. The command group in the command helicopter would proceed to the scene of the operation to contact the necessary commander or personnel and would develop the plan for employment of the battalion prior to its arrival.

Thus, this move was not greeted with much excitement. There was some apprehension about going back into a vague enemy situation and back to a heavy combat area, since we all had heard rumors and some facts of the battle by the 1st of the 7th in countering the attack of the North Vietnamese. Reports of the disastrous ambush of one of our battalions in the Plei Mei area by the Viet Cong had also been received.

Rumors always magnified facts considerably. I am afraid that at this stage many of the facts were not known either to myself or to the troops. There were too many rumors floating around. This was often true in combat. In war people on the ground participating in the operation usually know less about what's going on than anyone else. The higher you go and the further away from the battle, the more everyone knows about the operation.

I think that people back home, glued to their television sets and reading their daily newspapers, often knew more about some of my individual battles and the individual actions of the Jumping Mustangs than we did ourselves.

I had great confidence in our battalion going back into action. This mission would provide a better opportunity to engage and destroy the Viet Cong and NVA. We still had a number of scores to settle within the battalion. A Company was especially anxious to again engage the Viet Cong and avenge the deaths of two young sergeants and other wounds that were suffered in the early phases of their fine night operation of 3-4 November.

C Company was anxious for a kill after spending so much time guarding the artillery. Other than the first Viet Cong whom C Company killed in the battalion some weeks past, they had had little enemy contact; therefore, most were eager to get a chance at the enemy. B Company, shaping up rapidly, had tremendous morale and spirit and had been searching long for VC. Hopefully, they would soon get their chance.

I was pleased with the progress of the battalion, its spirit, and its morale. They were a real "gung-ho" group, troops, officers, and NCO's. My staff had become exceedingly professional by this time. I was most pleased, during my absence in the hospital, to receive the verified report from a number of sources that the battalion had "driven on" without any hesitation. This was a mark of a good unit and a tribute to the men.

If a battalion or any unit was a one-man show and the individual who controlled it was lost or killed and the unit collapsed, then that commander had not performed his job very well. On the other hand, if the loss of that individual had little significant bearing on the unit; if it continued its mission—continued its successful operation—this was the goal of all military commanders, at squad, platoon, company, or battalion level.

Within a few minutes we had rapidly developed a plan for the movement of the unit to Pleiku the following day. One always tried to keep up to date on the latest situation and to make contingency plans for what one thought the mission might be. We had previously been alerted that if a battalion from the 1st Airborne Brigade had to go back to Pleiku, it would probably be us.

At this late date it had looked at though this would not take place; therefore, we had not been thinking too much about it. We had been keeping track of what was going on and made tentative plans for a return. We were familiar with the area from our previous ten days at the beginning of the campaign. During the next ten days we would support the 2nd Brigade and fight the final Division withdrawal action for the Plei Mei battle.

8

BACK TO PLEI MEI

At first light, with my command group I flew to Camp Holloway to join the 2nd Brigade. Major Guy Eberhardt assembled the battalion after being relieved by the 1st of the 12th; they moved by motor to Pleiku in four separate motor march units.

The command group included Major Herman, S-3; Captain Stone, S-2; a supply representative; Captain Wilkie, Artillery Liaison Officer; and Captain Corey, Air Force Liaison Officer. We reported to Colonel Lynch, the 2nd Brigade Commander, at Pleiku and were briefed on our new mission, to move the battalion to the Stadium, where the Brigade CP was located. Here we would spend the first night as reserve battalion to provide security for the Logistics Base of the brigade. The logistical installations were there as well as a large number of helicopters used for both tactical and resupply movements. The reserve battalion or elements of the reserve battalion were usually employed for this type of mission.

Colonel Lynch and his staff briefed the Division Commander, Major General Harry W. O. Kinnard, and the Assistant Division Commander, Brigadier General Richard T. Knowles. I renewed acquaintances with all the battalion commanders who had participated thus far in the Plei Mei action and with the Division staff to catch up quickly on what had been going on.

The tactical situation had lessened considerably from the time the 3rd Brigade had large-scale enemy contact, employing the 1st of the 7th and the 2nd of the 7th. They were relieved on the twentieth by the 2nd Brigade, with the mission of continuing to pursue fleeing Viet Cong and NVA over the entire area to the Cambodian border and to kill and capture as many as possible.

At the briefing I had a chance to talk a few minutes with General Kinnard. He was concerned with my rather emaciated condition. He said I was one of the leanest-looking battalion commanders he had ever seen. Someone had made the comment that I had always had the reputation for being one of the meanest, now I was also the leanest; this made me the typical battalion commander of the 11th Air Assault Division and 1st Air Cavalry, noted for being "lean and mean." In view of these comments, I achieved some small notoriety among the division staff and the other lieutenant colonels in the area as being "Mr. Lean and Mean" himself.

I was flattered that the General was concerned for my health. As a matter of fact, I felt better each day. I did not look it apparently, though, as one of my friends called me "Walking Death," and Colonel Lynch and General Knowles both expressed concern over my appearance and whether I could keep up with my battalion. I assured them that I could and that with the help of my Battalion Executive Officer and others within the battalion, there was no great problem.

After the briefing I made a quick helicopter reconnaissance of the area we were to occupy at the Stadium, familiar to us all, and dropped off Major Herman and Captain Stone to work out the details for the occupation of that area and for the relief of the present unit there. I contacted Major Eberhardt back at the battalion by radio to alert him for the battalion mission, then flew back to oversee the actual movement to the Stadium.

The Jumping Mustangs closed on the Stadium without incident by nightfall, dug in, and prepared to resist any attack that might come. We were alert to enemy action owing to a previous attack on this position. Shortly after the 1st Brigade occupied the Stadium, having been there ten days, the 3rd Brigade moved in and occupied the same CP and logistical base. Three days later they were attacked by two companies of Viet Cong who killed several Sky Troopers, wounded a few others, and destroyed some aviation fuel.

The attack was predicted by two or three of the local civilians, including the Frenchman at the Tea Plantation which surrounded the Stadium. This plantation was the largest tea plantation in Vietnam. It was where Catecha Tea was grown and processed. The "Stadium," as we called it, was the football name given in place of the geographical name Catecha by Lt. Col. Harlow Clark in early October.

At any rate, the local Frenchman had warned the 1st Airborne Brigade (and this had been passed to the 3rd Brigade) several days in advance that many old men and women were walking up and down the road past the Stadium as if they were going to and from various homes and little villages. These old men and women were measuring off the distances from specified geographical points so that the Viet Cong mortars would be able to provide accurate fire in a later attack on our installations.

The procedure was simple: send a half dozen women or men down the trail, plodding along as if headed from Point A to Point B; in reality, they were counting footsteps to accurately measure the distance. This provided accurate fire data to the Viet Cong. This story simply proved that you could trust no one in Vietnam—no civilian, be it a five-year-old boy or a ninety-year-old woman. Any and all of them might be sympathizers with the Viet Cong or might be forced to provide information and assistance to the Viet Cong.

We were concerned that the attack might be repeated, and we therefore used the utmost caution in laying out our defense plans, including patrols and a schedule for large quantities of artillery and mortar and interdiction fire throughout the night.

There were two or three small engagements during the night, after alleged probes of the area—perhaps simply excitement by some young soldier who saw bushes move and fired a few rounds, thus setting off a short battle. There were several snipers in the area and a few rounds whistled around through our sector. The night passed without further incident except for noise from continued outgoing artillery and mortar fire.

One factor that marked operations with the 2nd Brigade was Colonel Lynch's intense desire for maximum fire power to destroy as many of the enemy as possible and save American lives. During the next ten-day operation with Colonel Lynch and the 2nd Brigade, we really learned to employ artillery and mortars. I had always been a great believer in the use of fire power; Colonel Lynch (now Brigadier General) impressed me further and helped verify my own ideas on this important facet of military power.

Next day the battalion moved by helicopter from the Stadium to defensive positions, joining the 2nd of the 5th in defense of the area called "Crooks." This small perimeter was occupied by two airmobile Infantry battalions, including twelve 105mm howitzers. For the next twenty-four hours, "Crooks" was one of the strongest positions established.

The Battalion Commander of the 2nd of the 5th and I were hoping and praying that a couple of Viet Cong battalions would attack that night. We did not believe that the VC were aware that the 2nd of the 5th, somewhat under strength, had been reinforced by a full-strength, airborne, air-assault battalion. If the VC did attack, we would lay a lot of them low.

Company perimeters were three hundred meters in frontage. This was the smallest perimeter we ever occupied in Vietnam, and its small size enabled us to employ two rifle platoons on the line within each company, with the third platoon in a reserve position overlooking the main position where they could fire to the front. The twelve howitzers could fire direct fire if necessary, but they had the job of providing close-in defense fires for another position five miles away called "Golf." In a similar manner, the twelve howitzers in that location provided close-in defensive fires for "Crooks."

Eighty-one-millimeter mortars would fire defensive concentrations around our perimeter as well. We scheduled little patrolling that night, pulling our outposts back into the main line of resistance, hoping for the Viet Cong to hit.

We initiated, as was customary in many of the battalions of the 1st Air Cavalry at dusk, a "Mad Minute." This, mentioned previously in the A Company action in the early stages of the Ia Drang Valley, consisted in every rifleman firing a magazine from his rifle; every machine gun, twenty or thirty rounds; every trooper throwing one hand grenade if trees and vegetation permitted; the M-79 grenade launchers firing one or two rounds; and perhaps a Claymore or two being set off. In addition, the eighty-one mortars and artillery fired defensive concentrations. The "Mad Minute" was set off on a signal—usually a flare fired from a 105 artillery piece. It terminated thirty seconds later on the firing of a second flare. The amount of shot and shell thrown out was phenomenal.

105mm Howitzer

You could easily picture what might happen if an enemy were about to attack when a hail of lead cut loose.

This technique, which proved successful, had been originated by Lieutenant Colonel Hal Moore in the 1st of the 7th a few days previously when his battalion was hard-pressed by snipers and attacked by numerous North Vietnamese at LZ "X-ray."

One morning at dawn he initiated his "Mad Minute." The primary purpose was to destroy the snipers who climbed up in the trees during the night and at dawn would start shooting as our soldiers moved in the perimeter. At the first volley, half a dozen snipers fell out of the trees. Most important, a North Vietnamese rifle platoon which had sneaked in during the night to within a hundred yards of the friendly positions was ready to attack at the most opportune moment.

They thought they had been discovered and opened up themselves, giving away their position, resulting in their almost total annihilation. From that time on, that battalion—and as soon as the word spread to others, all of us—initiated "Mad Minutes" morning and night when we were on a defensive position.

This technique was useful for other reasons. It permitted a positive check on the functioning of weapons; it rotated old ammunition by firing it; and, most important, it gave each soldier a psychological uplift and rise in morale by firing, thus expending his anger and personal frustration against the enemy as well as inspiring confidence in the vivid demonstrating of his unit's unity of effort. Patrols always moved out immediately following the "Mad Minute" to check out the area.

The "Mad Minute" proved successful for B Company, the 1st of the 8th, a few months later down at Tuy Hoa, when they initiated a "Mad Minute" under similar conditions and precipitated an NVA company-size attack, minutes from executing a final assault. This splendid action resulted in total destruction of one enemy company and the capture of the company commander by a single American rifle company with no friendly deaths and only six wounded in the United States company.

Nothing happened this night, and all of us were discouraged that it did not. The din and roar of the tube artillery and mortars throughout the night was continuous. It was amazing to lie there within a hundred yards of exploding artillery and mortar rounds and still sleep. If the cannons stopped roaring, you woke up.

Many of the men received excellent introductions to how close one could get to tube artillery and mortar fire without being hurt. We purposely moved the concentrations in close, and fragments of hot metal fanned out through the battalion area, spent portions landing near the feet of many young troopers. This was an excellent lesson because it proved how close in fire could be brought without hurting your own troops when conditions were rough. It also provided great faith in the battalion, because here every soldier could see what his whole battalion looked like when it was massed in a small area and how it functioned as a team—in this case, how it functioned in coordination with another battalion. The troopers could see and hear the tube artillery firing all night and could hear or see other members of the combat team participating.

Another idea initiated that night that we continued to follow as a Battalion SOP was placing flare pots at each of the respective corners or furthermost point outside the perimeter surrounding the battalion. These cans of liquid napalm or gasoline and sand were wired with an incendiary device as trip flares so that they could be set off at will. If under attack, the flares were set off to mark the outer perimeter of the battalion, enabling the Air Force fighters, aerial rocket ships, or gunships from our own forces to come in and destroy anything on the outside of that illuminated line.

The nights in Vietnam were dark. There was no light or any type of artificial lighting to assist in identifying a position out in the jungle. The flare-pot technique was the only way we could definitely mark our positions and it provided for effective nighttime use of close air support and aerial rockets. The technique worked two or three times with one of the other battalions under actual enemy assault conditions and soon became part of the Battalion and Division SOP.

Plans for the next day required the battalion to continue to hold "Crooks" while the 2nd of the 5th moved overland to occupy another objective area six kilometers away designated "Par." At the end of the day when "Par" was secured, the Mustangs were to move by helicopter to that area and secure it, relieving the 2nd of the 5th to come back by helicopter to the area we now occupied. The purpose of this play was to position the Mustangs on "Par" to attack the following morning, in an overland offensive action to a position called the "18th Hole."

The objectives in this phase of the operation all referred to the game of golf. Colonel Lynch was a great golfer; therefore, in marking out the objectives and plans on his battle map, he designated each of the appropriate control measures something pertaining to the game of golf. As with the football plays, if I continued around here much longer, I was going to become a master of the terminology used in both football and golf.

The 2nd of the 5th moved out early on their overland attack to "Par." The Jumping Mustangs provided supporting mortar fire and were prepared to assist our comrades if en route they ran into anything they could not handle. Otherwise we spent most of the day preparing for helicopter movement to "Par" and preparing plans for the attack of the "18th Hole." We made a helicopter reconnaissance of the area around "Par" and the "18th Hole" with the command group. This operation would require a difficult overland foot movement in extremely heavy, thick, jungle-like terrain.

During the day the battalion continued preparation for the movement to "Par" late in the afternoon. The company commanders conducted a helicopter reconnaissance of "Par" and for the forthcoming battle the next day at "18th Hole." The Battalion Order was issued and the troops were ready.

In a tragic, unexpected instance, an 81mm mortar round exploded ten meters from the tube, causing thirteen casualties in D Company. Two men later died. The incident had a serious effect on the battalion, causing lack of confidence in the mortars. The explosion was apparently caused by faulty ammunition and was unavoidable. In war one accepts the inevitable—an occasional short round; a malfunctioning shell; always something you hated because of the results it could create, but something you learned to expect. You wondered what that ammo technician was doing back in the states at that factory when he forgot to install a pin or left out other vital portions of the fuse.

The Battalion Base was installed at Camp Holloway, north of Pleiku, where the S-4 installations and the Executive Officer would operate from. The vehicles were assembled along with all portions of the battalion not needed out in the forward position. The battalion was traveling light. The Forward Command Post consisted primarily of the one Hex tent for the S-3's night and wet-weather operation, plus a small tent for use of the doctor and the Battalion Aide Station.

All food was prepared back at the Battalion Base and flown forward to the troops by helicopter. We were trying to serve hot breakfast and hot supper with a C-ration lunch. Whenever we were in a static position, and the helicopters were available, hot chow was served.

The highlight of the evening, when the ice and the beer were available, was cold beer flown in with hot chow. Beer served to the troops as they went through the chow line was opened, so they had to consume it in that area; therefore they could not hold it until later and it could not possibly interfere with combat operations. We provided soft drinks for those who did not care for beer. No whiskey of any type was permitted in the battalion and beer was served only on my order when it was available, either in the forward area with chow or back at the Battalion Base at An Khe at our Enlisted, NCO, and Officers' Club. We received little beer at this time, as the supply had not yet begun to arrive as it would later. Ice was extremely scarce.

At 1600 hours the battalion initiated the heliborne move in eleven UH-1 Deltas from "Crooks" to "Par" to relieve the 2nd of the 5th. This was a mutual exchange, with the same helicopters that were taking my troops to "Par" picking up the 2nd of the 5th troops to bring them back to "Crooks." I maintained command of "Crooks" until less than 50 percent of the Mustangs were at that location; the Commander of the 2nd of the 5th maintained command of "Par" until one-half of his troops were gone. Then we switched command: I assumed command of "Par" and he of "Crooks" and the remaining troops there. The lift was completed by dark, except for two or three loads of equipment that we did not need for the night.

Supply was delayed owing to the lack of helicopters and the priority for exchange of the two battalions. It was necessary to resupply ammunition and other critical items at "Par" during hours of darkness. Usually we tried to complete all such activities prior to dark, because bringing helicopters into small landing zones at night created many problems, both for us and for the aviators. In addition, if there were any Viet Cong in the area, they felt more secure about firing at the helicopters at night than daytime when more rapid retaliation might occur.

At any rate, it was necessary to obtain night logistical runs. This worked well, employing the Pathfinder Team from the 11th Aviation Group attached to the battalion. Under my personal supervision we talked the pilots down into the small landing zone, marked with appropriate lights. The first time or two the helicopters missed, being unable to pinpoint the postage-stamp landing zone. In spite of flares to mark the LZ, it was like finding a needle in a haystack.

"Par" was deep within the jungle. There were no lights of any kind around and the pilots flew an azimuth or radio beam until a specified time distance elapsed, when hopefully they were over position "Par." There was activity going on in other parts of the sector; therefore our flares were sometimes confused with those of other units.

After two or three tries and with the cooperation of the Pathfinders, we talked the UH-1D's in and unloaded necessary ammunition and water needed for the next day's operation. Resupply was completed by 2030 hours.

With the arrival of the battalion elements at "Par," I made a rapid tour of our perimeter. "Par" was an overgrown clearing in the jungle 300 meters in diameter. Foot movement in the perimeter was difficult owing to the dense vegetation. Jungle trees reached a height of 120 feet around us. This was a difficult position to occupy so late in the evening and with such little detailed reconnaissance on the ground.

The three rifle companies rapidly moved into position and by late dusk I completed a walk of the perimeter with the company commanders, observed the rapid progress as fields of fire were cleared and positions dug in for the night.

Registrations were completed late by tube artillery and mortars and we were finally ready for what might come. There was a Viet Cong battalion estimated to be in the area, located somewhere between the positions "Par" and "18th Hole." Several automatic weapons were known to be in the "Par" area and there had been considerable activity throughout the day.

The day before, on a reconnaissance by helicopter, a high-explosive shell had burst a few yards from my helicopter— probably a 60mm mortar, fused as an anti-aircraft round. This explosion caused considerable confusion throughout the area and we were heroes for being shot at with what was first thought might be an anti-aircraft gun. There was a characteristic puff of black smoke often connected with an anti-aircraft round. We heard that there were anti-aircraft weapons other than machine guns in the area but had no visible proof of them prior to this time.

We expected trouble this night and were not in as good a position or condition as we would have liked to be. However, the troops were prepared and ready.

The night passed quietly without further enemy contact or incidents other than a little sniping. Friendly mortar and tube artillery fire continued to fall close to our positions throughout the night as defensive concentrations were fired to prevent or discourage any enemy from bothering us.

The Jumping Mustangs initiated the attack, a large sweep with B and C Companies abreast and A and D Companies trailing. Tight formation was maintained to provide mutual support between all companies. We moved as a rectangle or square. Control was maintained from the heliborne command post with a supplementary command post on the ground. Major Eberhardt, the Battalion Executive Officer, commanded the operation on the ground. I maintained command from the helicopter. With me was Major Herman, the Battalion S-3, the Artillery Liaison Officer, and Captain Corey, ALO.

I was still too weak to make it on the ground, where I normally would have been and would like to have been under the circumstances; hence the switch between the Executive Officer and myself. This operation would be a complete overland movement with the only helicopter support being aerial rockets, the command helicopter, and, finally, extraction by bird later on in the day.

Progress was slow, as the area was secondary growth twenty or thirty feet in height. It was necessary for the battalion to move on a series of short paths or trails hacked out of the heavy jungle growth.

A new system was initiated employing tube artillery in two ways. First it was used to maintain direction by firing preplanned tube-artillery concentrations (single round) every two or three hundred meters on the previously planned route. The commander on the ground or I could call for a specified concentration to be fired with a second round 300 meters greater range in the direction of the attack. These rounds could be distinguished easily on the ground and helped establish direction to supplement the use of a compass. In addition, from the air in the heliborne command post, we could often see elements of the troops on the ground. If we could not observe troops, the lead elements identified themselves on order with a specific colored smoke, which enabled us to match the smoke position on the ground with that on the map, inform the commander on the ground by coded information what his location was, and thus guide him.

The second use of tube artillery was to form a rectangle around the battalion, firing on likely avenues of approach into our position or likely areas where an ambush might occur, as we moved forward. In effect, artillery was used to screen the advance, to protect the flanks, and to provide rear security. In this manner we were able to minimize troop outguards and points and to move as rapidly as we could through the jungle. The enemy could hear us coming, because of the hacking with machetes to clear trails; thus there was little to be gained in maintaining silence. The artillery did not reveal anything specifically, as it was similar to a rolling barrage directed toward the enemy.

The attack was to be preceded by B-52's on "18th Hole" and was set to go off before we were within a specified number of kilometers from the target. At the last minute we learned that the B-52 strike was cancelled. It was a disappointment because this would have been one of the few opportunities in which B-52's were used to blast a known enemy target, with a troop unit following in to see what the actual results were within a few minutes or an hour after the attack. We were disappointed also as this meant less fire support on the estimated enemy battalion in the area. Lack of B-52 support was partially compensated for by additional quantities of Air Force A1E fighters available to conduct strikes on the objective and other targets of opportunity.

During this operation, Captain Charles J. Corey, our Air Force Liaison Officer, performed in an exceptionally heroic manner. He developed a case of scrub typhus which reached its most severe peak while in the command helicopter. He should have been in the hospital. He was running a temperature of 103-104 degrees and out of his head from time to time.

He stayed with the battalion because he was so conscientious and because there was no other Forward Air Controller available. In spite of my insistence that he go to the hospital, he was equally firm that he wanted to accomplish his job. He felt so badly at times that he lapsed into unconsciousness in the air. When we were ready to fire a mission, or the fighter aircraft came in, we punched him to wake him up. He talked to the pilots or Airborne Forward Air Controller in order to direct the mission.

I have never seen an individual perform more dedicated

service under such adverse conditions of illness and sickness
as he demonstrated that day. This soon became well known
within the battalion, and Captain Corey, although wearing
the blue suit of a sister service, was truly a Jumping Mustang
and a Combat Infantryman. He stayed with us the rest of his
tour in Vietnam and continued to perform in his demonstrated outstanding manner.

Captain Roy Martin: "You recall how you insisted on Six
to Six communications (commander to commander). During
the long, hot drive, we were crossing a stream on a foot log
when you called. PFC Robert Brown, my radio operator,
handed me the radio hand set. In the process of reaching for
it I lost my balance and fell eight feet into a small stream.
There were quite a few chuckles up and down the line of
troopers while I scrambled up the other bank where Brown
was waiting with not even a grin. He was one of the most
emotionally capable men in the company."

The movement to "18th Hole" became a walk through
the jungle. There was no enemy contact and either any
enemy in that area moved out or intelligence reports were
false. By midafternoon, it was obvious that we were in a dry
hole—that there would be few results. Unless we used
helicopters to extract and make an assault on "18th Hole" by
air, we would never reach the objective prior to dark.

Time was running out in the Battle of Plei Mei and the
Brigade Commander was desirous of continuing certain other
operations the next day, including another offensive overland
search-and-destroy mission in a different direction from position "Crooks." At 1600 hours he ordered the extraction of the
battalion; provided a minimum number of helicopters with
orders to extract and move back to position "Crooks"; and
ordered us to be prepared to continue the attack toward the
burned-out Montagnard villages to the northwest the following day.

The word to extract came late. Because of the small
number of available helicopters and the lack of landing zones
in the area, we had a difficult task in extracting the battalion.
D Company was assigned a new mission, once I learned that
we might have to extract. I stopped them en route to "18th
Hole" at a previously selected area where they began clearing
a potential pickup zone. When the Brigade Commander gave
the final word for the extraction, the battalion backtracked

two kilometers to the newly prepared PZ and commenced extraction. In the meantime, the few elements that remained on "Par," secured by a sister company from "Crooks," closed out and evacuated back to "Crooks."

Extraction from the pickup zone en route to "18th Hole" and from "Par" was completed without further difficulty. Both the 1st of the 8th and the 2nd of the 5th again assembled on "Crooks" in a defensive position. The following morning the 2nd of the 5th, with equipment, was scheduled to move back to Camp Holloway and ultimately to An Khe.

The Jumping Mustangs were scheduled for an attack to the "19th Hole," then to continue the operation in that area and to be the last battalion to extract and move back to An Khe. We had been designated rear guard for the 2nd Brigade and for the 1st Air Cavalry Division.

The defensive position at "Crooks" was established again that night. We were careful to fire in defensive fires, both tube artillery and mortars, and to make sure that we had an intensive H and I program during the night. It was quite possible with all the activity indicating a withdrawal from the Pleiku area, that the enemy might try to pounce on a small United States unit of battalion size to cause a local victory and create additional casualties. The Division Commander had been careful to screen the movement or withdrawal from the Pleiku area and make it look like a continuation of offensive operations. This was part of the reason for the original movement to "18th Hole" and the scheduled movement to "19th Hole" for the following day.

During the evening word came from Colonel Lynch that the attack on "19th Hole" for the following day was cancelled, the battalion would continue to maintain position "Crooks," and would maintain rear guard for the evacuation of the 2nd of the 5th, as well as other evacuations and withdrawals going on within the Pleiku area.

The final evacuation of the Jumping Mustangs from position "Crooks" was scheduled for the morning of the twenty-sixth.

On November 25 the 2nd of the 5th commenced extraction, including the movement of six of the 105 howitzers. This left the Mustangs intact with six 105 howitzers, plus tube-artillery support from an adjacent position.

The extraction of the 2nd of the 5th was smooth, and by midafternoon the operation was completed. There was initial delay in movement of the artillery, since the battery was not familiar with the use of the Chinook helicopter in the lifting and rigging of the 105 artillery pieces.

However, the artillery finally was completed and the Jumping Mustangs were the sole possessors of the position "Crooks" by 1800 hours. The defensive perimeter was reorganized, with all four companies, including D Company, on the line. The remaining mortars were shifted to defend that portion of the position formerly under the control of 2nd of the 5th and were fired in.

We spent a quiet night although there was an increase in our own defensive fire, both on the adjacent position supporting us as well as their fire in support of us as we tried to maintain the same tempo of fire, with a reduced number of howitzers and mortars, as we had the night before. The plan was to make the Viet Cong believe we were continuing the attack rather than executing withdrawal. As a result, the night was violently noisy.

We received one or two incoming rounds during the night; however, they proved to be short 81-mortar rounds, fired by A Company. Although Captain Danielsen denied it, I am quite convinced that's where they came from.

The following day we extracted and displaced to Camp Holloway. There were twenty-three UH-1 Delta's available to the battalion plus 2 CH-47's. The plan was to lift out the tube artillery first, followed by the Infantry. In the meantime the position supporting us, "Golf," was gone. We were the only combat troops left in the Pleiku operational area now. Instead of tube-artillery support, we depended upon aerial rockets with Air Force fighters overhead ready to shoot if necessary.

The battle was more upon our own shoulders now in the event we should be attacked during the extraction. It was pretty obvious to the enemy at this stage that the 1st Air Cavalry was withdrawing from the area of operation. The reason for ending the battle was that the Viet Cong and the North Vietnamese had moved back across the Cambodian border where they were safe for the time being. There was nothing left in the area except a few scattered individuals. Another mission was pending for the 1st Air Cavalry Division

CH-47

over to the east along the China Sea coast in the Bong Son area. Therefore no more time could be afforded for this operation, since the payoff was less and less.

The artillery extraction moved slowly during the morning and finally was completed by 1300 hours. I organized the battalion lift into four elements. The first lift was to depart at 1250 hours and according to schedule, the last lift should arrive at Camp Holloway by 1520 hours. B Company was assigned the mission of covering the extraction.

The helicopters came in and the first unit, A Company, moved out to Holloway, commencing the extraction. As each company departed, B Company rearranged its element to secure that area and tried to maintain the perimeter in the original size that we had before. In some cases they pulled in the perimeter a bit to make it smaller; however, the large landing-zone area required for the use of twenty-five helicopters required that we maintain most of the entire position.

I was on the ground at the Battalion Forward CP with the command helicopter and command group. The second and third lifts continued, with C and D Company out. Finally Captain Martin suggested to me that he would be much happier if I also left the area now because he was concerned with my safety, since it was the most opportune time for an enemy attack.

One had the feeling that the NVA or Viet Cong were closing in as we extracted, reducing our force to a smaller size, thus increasing our vulnerability. Our fire power was reduced and the situation became more critical.

Understanding Captain Martin's feelings and worry, I took off in the command helicopter and supervised the remainder of the extraction from the air.

Aerial-rocket helicopters were flying around the camp in contact both with the Artillery Liaison Officer in the command helicopter and with the Forward Observer with B Company. Finally the birds came in and picked up all but the last platoon of B Company, who remained to cover the last extraction. This was the most critical point in time. Everything proceeded on schedule without any enemy contact. I breathed a great sigh of relief as the last helicopter lift came in and picked up the remaining platoon, and B Company successfully completed its evacuation.

I made a low pass over position "Crooks" to make sure there were no friendly troops left in the area. I've always had the feeling, as I flew out of an area of extraction, that nothing could be more horrible than to see the enemy assaulting the position and one or two troopers there left behind, forgotten in the haste of withdrawal.

As soon as I gave the word, the aerial-rocket artillery began to blast every likely avenue of approach into the area and any place the enemy might possibly be. The gunships escorting the transport helicopters wanted to get a few last rounds in, and they were given permission to fire also.

I finally bade farewell to "Crooks" and flew back to Camp Holloway, having observed the successful extraction of the Jumping Mustangs from the area of operations and seen the conclusion of the Plei Mei Campaign.

I was interested to learn later that I was not by myself in the air, although sometimes I felt that I was. General Kinnard told me that he was also airborne listening in on my radio nets, observing the extraction. He was worried that the enemy commander might take the opportunity to hit us during this critical last stage. Since my battalion was the only one left, we would be the target.

General Knowles was also standing by in the air. I had

no idea that either general was there. They had not interrupted or interfered with the operation, but were standing by in case I needed help. Another Infantry battalion was available at Camp Holloway had there been an attack. An attack would have pinpointed or located the enemy forces, and if of any size at all, the 1st Air Cavalry would have launched again back into the area to destroy this force. It was reassuring to know that others were ready to help the Jumping Mustangs.

I flew back to Camp Holloway and landed. Our mission was general security of the overall area and a breathing spell for the next couple of days, assembly of equipment, and preparation for the convoy movement of the battalion to An Khe on 28 November.

One bitter taste remained in our mouth at Camp Holloway. Some of the rear echelon commandos at this station were unhappy because the combat troops—the Infantry, or "Grunts" —were drinking their cold beer and going to their NCO's and Officers' Clubs to eat hamburgers and other little knick-knacks and were buying some of their goodies from the PX. This was an unusual feeling for an installation of this type, for most everywhere in Vietnam that the Infantry goes, they are greeted with open arms. Anything that a unit might have, be it PX, beer, or food, is always shared with the Infantry.

Most of the military personnel in Vietnam knew that the Infantry soldiers, or the "Grunts," as they were sometimes both derogatorily and affectionately called, were the men who were actually doing the fighting and were winning this war in Vietnam. It was everybody else's job to serve the Infantry and support them. I was sorry to say that this small segment of the unenlightened at Camp Holloway had not yet learned this vivid and well-known truth.

The motor movement to An Khe began with 145 vehicles in the convoy—a sixty-five-minute time length. A series of five-march units were employed under the command of various commanders, in both the battalion and the attached elements. The Delta Troop or ground troop of the 1st of the 9th Cavalry provided the advance and rear guard. Two artillery batteries moved with the battalion, as well as the last remaining elements from the Division Logistics Base.

There was a possibility of an enemy ambush and attack en route. This possibility could never be discounted, and, since we were the last major convoy to move back to An Khe, at the end of which the road would be closed, there was a good possibility that, if it were to happen, it would happen to us.

In addition, the Division had worked out a series of exercises in which, after clearing Mang Yang Pass, and well within the security of the An Khe Base, there would be a simulated ambush of the convoy to test troop reaction. Except for Division personnel, I was the only member of the battalion who knew where the ambush would take place. I would trigger the ambush. Thus, everybody was alert on the movement to An Khe, first, to participate in the exercise and, second, in view of a possible enemy attack.

The return march was smooth, with minimum mechanical breakdowns en route. On the highway, at the proper point, in the vicinity of the ambush of Group Mobile 100 of the French Army in 1953, in which this regiment-size unit was badly torn up by the Vietnamese, I triggered an ambush of C Company.

The counter-ambush or reaction was professionally accomplished. C Company mortars were in action immediately. Word was passed and the tube artillery quickly went into position and commenced actual firing on the designated enemy location.

The entire action was monitored by personnel from Division Headquarters. I later learned that ours was the most outstanding counter-ambush demonstrated by any of the returning battalions. The ambush was also observed by General Knowles, Assistant Division Commander.

I came back in my jeep as part of the convoy. On arrival, I parked near the entrance to the division area to return the salute of the arriving elements of the convoy. The battalion closed into An Khe by 1710 hours and reverted to 1st Airborne Brigade control.

I was most pleased when the movement was completed, as it marked a successful combat motor movement and the successful completion of the first major campaign in the history of the 1st Air Cavalry Division and the Jumping Mustang Battalion.

On arrival back in the battalion area at 1715 hours, I was greeted by a call from General Kinnard's headquarters asking me to join the General for dinner at 1800. I quickly showered,

changed clothes, and arrived at the General's Mess to join
him, the Assistant Division Commander, his staff, and Colonel Lynch.

I was pleased that Colonel Lynch and I were the only
guests, in honor of our being the last brigade and the last
battalion out of the famous Pleiku/Plei Mei action.

At this dinner the Jumping Mustangs received several
comments I was happy to hear. First, our withdrawal from
"Crooks," the rear-guard action for the division, had been
skillfully and professionally accomplished. This from General
Knowles. Second, the battalion was complimented for the
skillful counter-action on the ambush. Third, the excellent
motor movement was observed by several others, and, finally,
commendatory remarks were made by Colonel William R.
Lynch for the outstanding performance in support of his
brigade. He stated that the Jumping Mustang Battalion was
welcome to join the 2nd Brigade at any time. This was quite a
compliment coming from another brigade commander. I re-
plied that we were most happy to work with the 2nd Brigade
at any time and would look forward to it in the future. If he
were in trouble, the Jumping Mustangs would come to his
rescue at a gallop.

As an indication of the accomplishments and the ability
of the battalion, I issued the following letter on 30 November
1965:

Subject: A Job Well Done

The participation of the Jumping Mustangs with
the 2nd Brigade in the final stages and conclusion of
the Plei Mei Campaign merited high praise of our
battalion from senior commanders.

The rear guard action and withdrawal of the
division and final defense of LZ "Crooks" evoked
high praise from Brigadier General Richard Knowles,
Assistant Division Commander, as an outstanding
professional job under potentially dangerous conditions and anticipated Viet Cong attack. The Commanding General reaffirmed these comments. Special
merit goes to B Company for their action as final
rear guard and an excellent extraction.

The battalion tactical motor movement from

Pleiku to An Khe on 28 November with 145 vehicles merited comment from Brigadier Richard Knowles as the best yet in the division.

The simulated ambush on the return to An Khe on 28 November merited praise from Brigadier General Knowles and Colonel William R. Lynch, Commanding Officer, 2nd Brigade, as the best of all battalions participating, Special merit to C Company, especially the Weapons Platoon, for their effective mortar fire. Artillery was outstanding, especially rapid and effective.

Colonel William R. Lynch thanked the battalion for an outstanding job and gave an invitation to join his brigade at any time. He also stated that we were the only battalion that knew how to properly employ artillery, both offensively and in defense of LZ "Crooks."

I wish to add my own congratulations for an outstanding job in every respect. We are becoming more professional in every way. I want to especially commend our exceptional communications and outstanding logistics support. Mess personnel performed a phenomenal job in preparing the excellent Thanksgiving dinner, served the evening 28 November. We all owe them a vote of thanks.

To each and every one of you, well done. Keep up the good work. Drive on—all the way.

Thus concluded the Plei Mei Campaign and the actions of the Jumping Mustang Battalion in that famous campaign.

A recap of the results of the total 1st Air Cavalry Division operation in the Plei Mei Campaign was as follows:

1,447 Viet Cong killed in action by actual body count
1,998 Viet Cong estimated killed in action
43 Viet Cong wounded in action
1,008 Viet Cong estimated wounded in action
136 Viet Cong captives
497 individual weapons, including pistols and rifles
126 crew-served weapons

This was a severe blow and almost the complete destruction of one North Vietnamese Division consisting of at least three regiments. These units did not show their faces again on the field of battle for several months.

9

THE BATTLE OF AN KHE SOUTH

The next twenty-four hours at the base in An Khe were spent cleaning up troops and equipment, re-equipping, eating a hot meal, and getting ready for the next routine and customary mission on the Barrier, Picket Line and An Khe Air Field.

When you came back from a combat operation, there was little time to rest and relax. You were fortunate indeed if you had twenty-four hours. The accelerated pace within the 1st Air Cavalry Division was rapid. The Division was responsible for the entire II Corps Tactical Zone. This zone extended from the China Sea coast, 150 nautical miles west to the Cambodian border, and 200 miles in length, 100 miles north and south of Highway 19.

There were at least two North Vietnamese divisions in this area plus one or two separate regiments and a number of Viet Cong battalions and smaller, lesser units. Therefore the demand for the airmobile combat capability of the Air Cavalry Division was unrelenting. As one battle was finished and the enemy solidly trounced in a portion of the battle zone, a need would then arise for the Sky Troopers somewhere else. The ability of the Air Cavalry to move rapidly from area to area meant continuous deployment.

The twenty-four hours were a welcome change, and along with the forty-eight hours at Pleiku (Camp Holloway) prior to the motor movement eastward enabled us to get rapidly back on our feet and ready to go again.

The mission for the next eight or ten days involved one company on the Barrier, one company on the Picket Line, and one company at the An Khe Air Field. These company missions were rotated every forty-eight hours to provide a change for the companies and to keep maximum elements back in the battalion base area. We would have only a few days on this particular task and had already been alerted, in conjunction with the 1st of the 12th, a sister battalion, for an operation ten to fifteen clicks south of An Khe.

The proposed operational area had not been touched in a number of years and was astride one of the major avenues for troop movements from the Pleiku area southeast into Quin Nhon and further south to Tuy Hoa. The Division had had a requirement to send troops into this area for some time. It looked like the Jumping Mustangs would have the job in the near future. Plans were in progress, reconnaissance had been conducted, and orders would be issued.

A Company had been selected to be the basis of a story to be filmed by ABC Television depicting the life of a rifle company in combat in Vietnam, actually the life of its company commander. A team headed by Mr. John Hughes from the American Broadcasting Company arrived with one photographer, a sound man, and a writer. During the next six weeks this team filmed hundreds of feet of the actions of A Company and of the Jumping Mustang Battalion, with background from the 1st Air Cavalry Division. The one-hour TV documentary was scheduled for release in the United States during the month of March, 1966. Mr. Hughes and his crew were a fine group. They were willing to do whatever was necessary—to go wherever the troops were. They were living with us now in the battalion area. They carried their equipment in battle and actually participated where the men were.

At first we were all self-conscious to have a group of photographers in the battalion, filming and listening to everything that took place. You never knew when your speech was being transcribed on tape, including radio conversations. Also, you might in effect be on "Candid Camera" at any time within the battalion area or during an operation. We were all proud that A Company and our battalion were to be the basis for this spectacular. It would not only provide the American people with a good idea of what goes on in Vietnam, but would give some desirable publicity to the Jumping Mustangs.

*   *   *

Plans were completed for a seven-day operation, twenty clicks south of the Division Base. This was to be the ultimate in air assault—an operation into rough terrain with mountainous jungle growth. Lift was to be by Huey and included the use of the operational Chinook ladder for the first time.

The operation was to consist of a series of company and battalion air assaults as we employed hammer-and-anvil tactics in likely areas where we expected the enemy to be. Included would be a search of the An My River valley, which we knew to be an east-west throughway or route for passage of Viet Cong troops. Intelligence indicated that there were many way stations or rest stops. These we would seek out and destroy, and hopefully would capture or kill a number of Viet Cong.

In the past day reconnaissance had been completed at battalion level, the plan completed, and the order issued. I had taken the company commanders for a heliborne reconnaissance. They completed planning and issued necessary orders. The operation was to begin on 9 December 1965.

The Chinook ladder was a flexible ladder lowered from the aft section of the Chinook which permitted troops to clamber up and down the ladder as the Chinook hovered above the obstacle at a distance up to 120 feet. This was a technique developed back at Fort Benning, Georgia, with the 11th Air Assault Division, primarily through the untiring efforts of Lieutenant Colonel Harlow Clark of the 1st Airborne Brigade. He developed a rough, flexible ladder which was tried by a rifle squad a few days prior to departure from Fort Benning. A demonstration was conducted for General Hamilton Howze when he came to visit the Division, specifically the 1st Airborne Brigade and its battalions.

I remember being present along with the company commanders at this demonstration when Colonel Clark explained and put a squad through its paces to show how this technique could be used for entry into and exit from an inaccessible area. General Howze gave us a pep talk on the use of the air assault, or airmobile, techniques. He felt that we really had a new weapons system, one that had been proven in the 11th Air Assault in maneuvers, and one that had proven itself with the 1st Air Cavalry in Vietnam.

At that time there were many doubters concerning the

capability and effectiveness of such a division—doubters not only in the Army, but also in the Air Force. General Howze mentioned that the only reason airmobile techniques could fail would be because its leaders at the lower levels—the captains, majors, and lieutenant colonels—would not have the mental agility to employ the full capability available in this remarkable new weapons system.

The Chinook ladder had not yet been used in Vietnam, although we had talked about it considerably. The old improvised ladder that Colonel Clark first developed had been refined in conjunction with Vertol, the producer of the Chinook helicopters. The later version of the Chinook ladder was narrow enough to be employed from both the aft end and the center cargo well, or cargo compartment, midship of the bird. This technique provided two ladders and permitted simultaneous movement of two streams of troops either up or down.

We decided to attempt this method of putting troops into the area because there was almost complete absence of landing zones within the proposed area of operation. The few available landing zones were of one- and two-bird size. We would have to take full advantage of river beds. Owing to the absence of suitable LZ's, the Chinooks would come in handy. We had little time for practice or training in using the Chinook ladder. Since ours was an Airborne battalion, and paratroopers were accustomed to doing the difficult and dangerous, I did not believe there would be a great problem. I was proved correct later on in the afternoon.

The operation commenced with the movement of A Company and B Company by assault helicopter to a landing zone designated LZ "Bull." The companies landed, with no enemy resistance, and began an overland drive, pushing against estimated enemy positions in the vicinity of another objective which would be C Company's mission, called LZ "Rope." This was the landing zone in which the initial landing would be by Chinook helicopter. The area was one of secondary jungle growth. Movement was painfully slow. Every inch of progress was chopped out by a soldier with a swinging machete. At this stage one of the most important soldierly abilities was how to use a machete correctly.

Late in the morning two Chinook helicopters were flown to Mustang Landing Zone. Here C Company was assembled for a demonstration of how a combat soldier with equipment climbed up and down the trooper ladder. One squad was selected by the Acting Company Commander, Lieutenant Frank Spiers, since Captain William Smith was absent on "R and R" in Hong Kong. The rifle squad, with some feeling of misgiving and apprehension, commenced climbing the dangling ladder suspended from the Chinook hovering sixty feet in the air.

This ladder was one of the first models in Vietnam, was quite wide, having been designed to accommodate two troopers, climbing simultaneously. It flapped much like a string or rope dangling from an object overhead. It was necessary to anchor or hang on to the bottom of the ladder and try to stretch it as tight as possible. The helicopter pilot had to hold his bird almost motionless at sixty feet in the air. This was quite a feat in any helicopter and required the utmost in professional competence. Any movement of the helicopter in a lateral plane, left to right, forward or rearward, was translated to the ground and made it difficult for troops to hold the ladder and difficult for those climbing.

The squad started out with little difficulty. The climb became harder as the soldiers continued to struggle upward, rung by rung. We were concerned about the difficulty that the squad seemed to be having. Since this was a new technique, if one man should fall, no doubt he would be seriously injured or perhaps killed. This would have had a bad effect on the initiation of such a new technique, not only from the Division view, but from the morale view, in discouraging other troopers against using the equipment. I was also concerned that should one of the top men on the ladder fall, he might wipe everyone else from the ladder, resulting in the injury and possible death of most or all of the squad. The squad continued to climb on up and finally reached the top of the ladder and climbed into the bird, demonstrating how it was possible to make an extraction from a confined area by simply climbing up the ladder.

The effect on the observing paratroopers was interesting. As you looked at their faces and into the eyes, nowhere could you see enthusiasm for this new technique. There seemed to be nothing but doubt. This was also true among my advisors, especially one member of my staff, who was extremely concerned that we should stop this operation immediately. I knew we could never go ahead with the proposed operation to the south unless we could employ the ladder technique. I knew also that it as a valuable technique and that we might just as well be the ones to test it now.

After a few minutes' rest, the squad started back down the ladder. Movement was much easier except when the ladder was not firmly held at the bottom; then a man could end up on the reverse, or inner, side of the ladder as it rotated 180 degrees. If the trooper was not careful, he might dangle entirely by his hands, his feet free from the rungs themselves. The best way to picture the scene was to visualize a ladder propped against a building; instead of climbing up the normal side, you climb up the inside.

The squad reached the ground, blowing a bit, but glowing with pride and confidence. I picked out the youngest trooper in the squad, a young lad about seventeen years of age but appearing more like fifteen. In front of the company, I asked him what he thought of the technique, and was it difficult? His answer sold the entire mission, because, as most paratroopers do since, he had succeeded; he passed it off as being of little difficulty—easier than a parachute jump. With this and a few words to the company, we decided to go ahead with the operation. The first actual use of this ladder by every other soldier would be a combat climb down into the enemy position a few hours later.

At 1300 hours, C Company and the command group (I had decided to go with C Company and would also climb down the ladder with Captain Charles Stone, the S-2, plus my radio operators) were picked up and we made the short flight to LZ "Rope."

Prior to the landing at LZ "Rope," it was necessary to secure the LZ—by employing the UH-1D and the rappel technique, which had been standardized within the 11th Air Assault and the 1st Air Cavalry Division. In this technique, a UH-1D helicopter hovered above the treetops. Four ropes were dropped to the ground. The troopers climbed down the ropes, rappelling in a manner like that you would use off a cliff, ranger style.

A platoon made up of troopers from both the Reconnaissance Platoon and C Company rapidly rappelled from eight hovering UH-1D helicopters to secure LZ "Rope" and ascertain that there were no enemy in the immediate vicinity prior to our bringing in the Chinooks. The area was secured successfully in the first combat rappel in Vietnam and the first one in the 1st Air Cavalry Division. The Chinooks came in and the troopers commenced the first combat ladder technique method of entry into an LZ, quickly climbing down the single ladder suspended from the aft section of each bird.

The troops were quickly on the ground without incident. The unloading of thirty-five troops from the bird to the ground took ten minutes. The time was excessive because it meant that a bird had to hover in the treetops for an excessive length of time. We were able to refine and cut this time by two-thirds later when we initiated a double-ladder technique. Employing two ladders and at the minimum distance above the obstacle, a platoon of troops could climb up or down within a matter of three or four minutes.

The helicopters went back after disgorging their troops, picked up the remainder of C Company, and brought them back rapidly to the LZ. I came in with the second lift. I found no difficulty in climbing down the ladder, along with Jordan, Culbertson, and Captain Stone. Private First Class Jerry Culbertson was the replacement radio operator while Corporal Ballew was in the hospital recovering from his punji-stick wounds. Culbertson was a sharp, aggressive young man of eighteen years who performed well in this demanding task.

Our landing on the ground was a surprise. We came down in a Montagnard animal trap, a small inclosure surrounded by slivers and bamboo three feet in height designed to capture animals and keep them confined until the Montagnard could come and kill them for food. At first we thought it was a Viet Cong man-trap and were apprehensive that we were in the middle of a number of these fiendish devices which the Viet Cong had adapted for killing the enemy. This proved to be untrue. We were soon on the ground and continued the improvement of LZ "Rope" into a permanent landing zone for helicopters.

Next began the third phase of the "Air Assault Day." The first was the combat rappel, the second was the combat Chinook trooper ladder, and the third was the carving of postage-stamp-type landing zones in the vicinity of "Rope" to accommodate the landing of both UH-1D and Chinook helicopters later on in the day. All of the terrain in the vicinity of

LZ "Rope" consisted of high shrubs and trees, the tallest forty feet, plus bamboo growth—all difficult for the attached engineers and the riflemen of C Company to cut with machetes and axes to clear a way and create a landing zone.

In three hours the first stage was completed, permitting the landing of one bird. To test the new LZ, one of the transport helicopters providing support from the 227 Assault Helicopter Battalion came in and after one pass was able to land. Improvement of the LZ continued so that two birds could land side by side. By the end of the day a Chinook was able to set down.

In the initial stages, landing required a high degree of air assault professional flying such as we had accomplished in the days of the 11th Air Assault in the Carolinas and at Fort Benning, Georgia. This action closed the third phase of our Air Assault Day.

By this time A and B Companies drove overland through the heavy vegetation (secondary jungle growth) with little or no enemy contact and finally reached the phase line, where they remained for the night. They established a perimeter, and the first day's operation ended with A and B Companies three kilometers from LZ "Rope" in one perimeter and C Company with the recently arrived D Company and the Battalion CP at LZ "Rope." Thus the battalion at least was positioned for the first day's operation, had completed the first successful air assaults, and was ready to continue the mission.

I was pleased with C Company and their first combat use of the Chinook ladder technique and also proud of elements of the Reconnaissance Platoon of D Company and those of C Company that had made the first combat rappel preceding the Chinook ladder employment.

At first light the following day A and B Companies continued their overland drive from the previous night's position to join up with the remaining elements of the battalion at LZ "Rope." In the meantime C Company conducted search-and-destroy missions within the vicinity of LZ "Rope." D Company was primarily concerned with improvement of the landing zone, which by the end of the day was able to accommodate two Chinook helicopters landing simultaneously. The command helicopter was temporarily disabled, having landed on a stump in the postage-stamp LZ at "Rope," causing a broken skid and a flight back to An Khe for immediate repairs. I switched over to an OH-13 helicopter for a flight out of LZ "Rope" to the vicinity of A and B Companies to see what progress they were making with their difficult overland movement.

The day was hot, the obstacles high. As was easy to do in an OH-13 helicopter after flying a Huey where the RPM control was automatic, we took off, losing RPM slightly. Loss of RPM in an OH-13 meant that the helicopter was going down. The only way to recover RPM was to lose altitude. Fortunately for me, as we flew off the LZ, located on top of a little hill with a deep valley below us, I simply nosed the helicopter over, dropped down the valley, rapidly picked up RPM, gained throttle control, and flew on. The Artillery Liaison Officer, Captain Dave Wilkey, who was with me, was not even aware of any particular problem. The observers of the CP at the landing zone were given a scare, thinking we were lost as we disappeared from view over the knob. Realizing what had happened, one of the pilots who had been flying with me simply closed his eyes and said "Farewell." They were quite relieved when the helicopter reappeared again a few seconds later above the horizon.

I did not learn of this reaction until I arrived back at the CP. I was kidded considerably by some of my staff, all good-naturedly, because I think they were glad that we did not auger in. Captain Wilkie was considerably shaken when they told him later what had happened.

By the afternoon it was obvious that A and B Companies were in a dry hole and were not likely to make contact. They would not be able to join up at LZ "Rope" owing to slow movement through the difficult terrain. Since aerial surveillance by scout helicopters from the Cavalry Squadron had indicated that there was nothing in the immediate area, I decided to break off this phase, reassemble the battalion, and proceed with the second phase further south.

To accomplish this change in mission, Chinook helicopters were employed with the trooper ladder to retrieve both A and B Companies. Both companies were directed to establish a pickup zone in their immediate area and prepare for extraction by Chinook helicopter employing the trooper-ladder technique. For the extraction a small, grassy area was found in a stream bed, an easily prepared pickup point for the Chinook-ladder technique. Using two Chinooks, the companies were rapidly retrieved from this area in forty-five minutes.

With this extraction to LZ "Rope," the entire battalion was assembled, ready for the next day's operation.

Each of the rifle companies had made either one up or down, employing the Chinook ladder technique. C Company had made a "down," as I call it, and A and B Companies had executed an "up." The significant fact was that the ladder technique had been proven, in climbing both up and down, in combat. I think back how easy it would have been to call the effort off. I'm glad we made the right decision. I shall never forget how much the young private in the earlier demonstration on the trooper ladder back at An Khe influenced my decision.

Two days' efforts had produced little enemy contact or damage to the enemy, but it had provided excellent air assault training for the battalion. We relearned and requalified in the rappel and were proficient in the trooper ladder. The use of the trooper ladder would become standard within the 1st Air Cavalry Division. All Infantry battalions would be required to practice and train for the employment of this system, for both assault landings and extractions.

I took pride in the knowledge that the Jumping Mustangs again pioneered the way for a new tactic. It was also a splendid tribute to Lieutenant Colonel Harlow Clark, who originated the idea and had seen it progress into actual combat use on a large scale.

The Division had sufficient ladders for all of the Chinooks. The system could be adapted and we had the equipment available for the UH-1D helicopter; however, the small ladder used one on either side was limited to four troops and thus had limited practical application. It was useful for small patrols and would prove valuable in the future for long-range patrols and smaller numbers of men who were to be inserted into or extracted from an area of operation.

A battalion air assault launched from LZ "Rope" would take two companies, B and C, to the east up the river astride the major avenues of approach of the enemy, who were infiltrating from the west. They would land at LZ "Gater," one company on either side of the river for a movement to the southwest. The two companies were to move abreast of one another, to drive against the anvil formed at LZ "Corral" four kilometers west along the river occupied by A Company. A Company executed an air assault into LZ "Corral," followed a few minutes later by the remaining elements of D Company and the Battalion Forward Command Post. LZ "Rope" was abandoned, that phase of the operation being completed.

Little enemy contact was made at LZ "Gater" by either B or C Company as they initiated their foot movement toward LZ "Corral." A Company received enemy contact from half a dozen snipers or guerrillas on the initial landing. The landing was made on the sloping side of a hill, and in short order four stairstep-type earth platforms were carved out of the side of the hill as the landing zone.

The movement of B and C down the river was most interesting. I joined B Company on the ground with Jordan and Culbertson and continued throughout the operation to join up with A Company.

A series of Viet Cong way stations or rest areas were located. These ranged from small groups of huts complete with rice, narcotics in the form of poppy seeds, tobacco, to a variety of shelters. One camp consisted of eighteen large bamboo huts, each one twenty feet long by ten feet wide, solidly constructed with wooden floors; the whole structure was built high, two feet off the ground. The huts were placed in two rows of nine which permitted the housing of a large unit at least a company or more in size.

There was little evidence that these facilities had been occupied in the last few days. It was obvious from the trails along the river and the large number of such installations, as well as large quantities of rice found, that both sides of this river valley were a major avenue for the movement of troops from the west, probably Pleiku.

B and C Companies continued up the river searching each area that had been previously located through the use of infrared photos taken a few days prior. These infrared photos had pinpointed the cooking fires built by troops living temporarily in the way stations. The infrared evidence or intelligence proved to be accurate. We actually found an enemy hut for each location pinpointed on the photo.

The two companies continued on, receiving fire from distant snipers along the way; by dark they had rejoined A

Company at LZ "Corral," where the entire battalion spent the night.

There was little contact during the night, except for continued sniper activity. An intensive H and I program, both artillery and mortars, was conducted and a tight battalion perimeter established.

The ABC team under Mr. Hughes was getting some good footage. The landing of A Company under fire at LZ "Corral" would be documented and shown in the final TV production, "I Am a Soldier."

Resupply techniques were working well. I was most pleased with the whole operation, especially with regard to the employment of the helicopter. We had been given a total of eight UH-1D's which supported the battalion for this operation. Chinook helicopters were available on call if we had occasion to use a Chinook ladder technique or employ the Chinook in a movement role.

The battalion was supported by tube artillery from a position to the east. Artillery support was excellent.

The battalion continued on a series of search-and-destroy operations within this vicinity. Each company was on an individual search within two or three kilometers radius, B Company to the north, C Company to the east, and A Company to the south. Reconnaissance Platoon was exercised to the west. Anti-tank Platoon with D Company was responsible for security at LZ "Corral."

Search-and-destroy operations continued until midafternoon on the thirteenth, at which time we commenced a movement further southwest down the river to search out possible enemy locations and enemy base camps. C Company initiated an assault by UH-1D. The birds came to a hover in the river bed, on top of the high rocks. The troops jumped from the skids of the hovering helicopter to the river bed and soon secured the area. They were followed by A and B Companies, by Chinook trooper ladder, A Company to land in the same river that C Company did; B Company landing on a Montagnard field on the steep side of a hill to the west. Both companies executed their landings without difficulty and continued to screen the area, search out, and secure for the night. The operation in this area would be continued for one more day.

D Company, less Reconnaissance Platoon on a mission back at the An Khe base camp, moved by helicopter to LZ "Saddle," where the artillery battery supporting this operation was located. The Infantry elements formerly supporting the artillery were moved out; the security now came under my control. Captain Tabb, in charge of Task Force Flanker, as it was designated, executed a heliborne landing to secure LZ "Saddle."

Later on in the afternoon the battalion closed in on LZ "Saddle," moving by Chinook and Huey to assemble the entire battalion in that area. Our mission now was to secure the tube artillery supporting not only our own battalion but other forces in the area, and to continue search-and-destroy operations within this area.

It was obvious that few enemy remained as the operation reached its seventh day, little to be gained by remaining in the area. Knowing that we had a new mission coming up in the near future, the Brigade Commander terminated the operation and ordered our return to An Khe.

A night extraction of the entire battalion, including the artillery, was planned for that night. This would be the first time a night extraction of a battalion combat team had been attempted. The aviators of both assault helicopter battalions had been practicing night operations extensively. The Infantry was accustomed to operating at night, but there had been few combined helicopter-Infantry night extractions except for the famous operation conducted by A Company and the 1st of the 9th Cavalry on 3-4 November.

LZ's were carefully selected and procedures worked out in detail with the supporting aviation units. The battalion was set for the extraction commencing at 2200 hours. Various degrees of night illumination were to be tried, employing mortars, artillery, and a flare ship from the Air Force.

Later in the afternoon the weather began to close in. It became obvious that it would not be possible to conduct the operation at night on a practice basis without incurring casualties caused by the bad weather conditions being forecast. If this were an actual operation, there would have been no question about it going, but since this was a practice, both for the Infantry and the supporting aviation, there was no point in pushing our luck too far at this time.

The night portion of this operation was called off and the afternoon extraction of the battalion and the tube artillery began. Extraction techniques had been refined since our last major operation at "Crooks." This extraction was executed smoothly, although not under fire and with remote possibility of any enemy attack. All precautions were taken with the extraction in the exact reverse of an air assault; all elements of the company or the battalion were constantly prepared and ready to fight. Security was maintained to the last, fire power was always available, in the form of either mortars or tube artillery, and there were aerial rockets plus the close air support on "air cap" overhead.

In an extraction just as in an actual air assault, the aerial rockets overhead and the tactical air power from the Navy and Air Force birds provided rapid and effective fire power during the vulnerable periods.

The extraction was swift and by 1700 hours it was completed with the battalion and the artillery battery both back at An Khe. I made a final sweep over the landing zone in the command helicopter to make sure that we had not left any young soldier behind, then headed for An Khe Base and the conclusion of a seven-day combat operation in the area, called An Khe South.

In recapping the operation, we did not achieve a great deal in the destruction of the enemy. We did verify intelligence concerning the value of the area as a way station and found evidence of the enemy, including their installations. All of these installations were destroyed.

The greatest benefit came to the battalion in the form of an air assault training exercise. In these seven days we did everything we had practiced in the Air Assault Days at Fort Benning and in the Carolinas. We made the first combat rappel from Huey helicopters; executed the first combat use of the Chinook trooper ladder; and lastly, concentrated on air assault techniques in the use of postage-stamp LZ's, cutting new LZ's, along with all of the techniques that go with them. We would have made the first mass battalion combat extraction at night had the weather conditions not prohibited; however, the practice and coordination between both the aviation and the Infantry were extremely valuable even though this operation was not executed.

I was proud of the battalion and the way it had performed as a team. I was convinced now that we were ready for whatever might come. I knew I could rely on every officer and man within the battalion and especially the members of my efficient staff.

I did not realize that in a few days we would vividly demonstrate our combat ability, for on 18 December 1965 the battalion embarked on its first major combat action in the vicinity of Ben Khe, Vietnam, where a battalion air assault was executed, landing on top of one enemy main force VC battalion.

10

FIRST BLOOD

Operation Scalping Mustang, a search-and-destroy mission, was to be conducted in the Binh Dinh area, vicinity of Ben Khe, commencing 18 December. The Jumping Mustang Battalion was under operational control of the 3rd Brigade, part of a four-battalion operation to search out and destroy the VC. The Jumping Mustang Battalion would be working with the 3rd Brigade for a period of three days, after which time it was to be withdrawn, returning to the 1st Airborne Brigade for further operations.

The weather was extremely bad. The planning for the operation was in progress. Air reconnaissance was impossible. Our major mission was to plan for the movement of the battalion by motor and air to a staging area east of the An Khe mountains. We would complete the battle plan on the seventeenth and conduct a heliborne air assault into an area eight miles north of Highway 19 on the eighteenth.

The normal battalion attachments were with us, including one platoon from C Company of the 8th Engineer Battalion, a light reconnaissance team, and two OH-13's from the 1st of the 9th Cavalry, called the White Team, fine for scouting. We would be supported initially by a total of thirty UH-1D aircraft, escorted by gunships. After the landing of the battalion, two platoons would continue with the battalion for the remainder of the operation. The helicopters were from the 229th Assault Helicopter Battalion. The plan called for the battalion to land by helicopter on two LZ's designated "Tonto" and "Trigger" at H hour, 0900. The landing was to be preceded by thirty minutes' tube-artillery preparation and, weather permitting, a thirty-minute prestrike by the Air Force.

Our intelligence indicated that at least one main-force Viet Cong battalion was probably in the immediate area and that there were elements of a possible second and third battalion, plus one or two companies. It was anticipated that the main force would attempt to withdraw from the area under cover of delaying actions by local-force units. Only if main-force arms and food caches were threatened would the main force stand and fight.

The mission was to conduct a search-and-destroy operation within the assigned sector; execute an airmobile assault; evacuate captured rice where possible, destroying it if necessity dictated; destroy all Viet Cong structures or defensive positions; and control and evacuate all male personnel of military age.

The plans were completed and the orders issued. The reconnaissance was primarily by map and the use of an excellent photo, taken a few days previous, which detailed the entire area. This was one of the finest photos that I had seen up to this time. It was to prove most useful and would supplement the helicopter reconnaissance the next day for the final confirmation of plans.

The initial objective area was a small hill, rising fifty to sixty feet above the flat rice-paddy area that characterized the eastern coast along Highway 19, adjacent to Highway 1. The hill was covered with vegetation extending to a height of thirty to forty feet. The many rice' paddies had numerous dikes running between them, with some vegetation growing in and around the dikes not unlike the hedgerows of Europe. Selection of landing zones would not present a problem, since there were ride paddies generally all around the objective area. The final selection was two LZ's that lay immediately north of the objective.

The plan called for an initial assault by C Company to seize Landing Zones "Tonto" and "Trigger." The birds would then return to the PZ, thirteen minutes away, to pick up B Company. The second lift would make its landing in the same landing zone, followed by a third and fourth lift with A Company and D Company. D Company was designated the "Thunderbolt Force" and consisted of the Anti-tank Platoon and the Reconnaissance Platoon. The Mortar Platoon had been split, and there were elements with each of the three rifle company lifts. A skeleton battalion headquarters was to accompany C Company, including Captain Corey, the Air Force Liaison Officer, who was to remain on the ground with his UHF radio and accompany C Company on their initial assault.

Weather was expected to be a problem. Ceilings were forecast to be 200 to 300 feet, with visibility down to less than one mile. These conditions would not delay or interfere with the lift of the helicopters, but would probably deny the use of the Air Force support and possibly hinder the use of the ARA's.

Our Chaplain offered this prayer to the troops as we gathered together in a last battalion formation for a short pep talk:

> Our Father in Heaven, as we approach the Christmas season, we are reminded that the festive spirit of giving is meant as a response to the great gift we have been given in the Christ Child.
>
> May our foxholes, shelter halves, and ponchos become such places of meditation, faith, and courage that in effect Christ would be born anew in spite of the "strange cradles," then our hearts will become His cradle. May he also be born to Vietnam, that they might know a new life and peace.
>
> As we "Mustang troopers" approach the battlefield once more, may we feel Thy comfort, even as the shepherds felt Thy intangible presence so many years ago. Amen.

The morning hours of the 17th were devoted to final preparation of the battalion, checking equipment and making sure that we were ready to go. The mission appeared to be another normal exercise, similar to a number that we had previously carried out. The weather continued to be bad; rain fell continuously and clouds both handicapped visibility and created low ceilings.

In the afternoon the battalion commenced a motor movement to the east side of the An Khe Pass to the Battalion Base co-located with the 3rd Brigade Base. The Forward Command Post was established further to the east, in the vicinity of the 3rd Brigade CP, co-located with a South Korean unit. By 2100 hours that evening the battalion had completed its move; the CP was in operation with all communications established.

Approximately one hour prior to dark, I made a pass over the proposed landing zone with the command helicopter at 1500 feet, flying from south to north as if simply flying toward the Bong Son area. I was accompanied by one other aircraft with the Battalion Commander and Flight Leader from the 229th Assault Helicopter Battalion. With me in my bird were the three rifle-company commanders and D Company Commander. We were able to get a quick look at the objective area and confirmed the photo selection of the landing zones. The landing zones were former rice paddies unused for a considerable length of time. They were large enough to take up to thirty helicopters landing simultaneously in formation. We were unable, at the altitude we were flying, to detect any recent enemy activity. One more pass and a return trip were made over the area to try to pin the routes and get an idea of the terrain to the south, where we would be continuing our search-and-destroy mission after the initial landing on and seizure of the first objective.

The company commanders were returned to their units at the Brigade Base and I returned to the Command Post with the 3rd Brigade. It was still raining, the weather miserable. Everybody was wet. However, the battalion was in good spirits. Little did we know that next morning would be the first major battle of the battalion and our "first blooding," so to speak.

A cold C-ration and hot coffee sufficed for the evening meal. Colonel Hal Moore, the Brigade Commander of the 3rd Brigade, dropped by for a short visit prior to my turning in.

The operation was on schedule. The initial assault began to the west of the Jumping Mustang area, with priority of fires and aircraft to a sister battalion of the 3rd Brigade, who made the initial assault into that area. Our H Hour was 0900.

The birds were on time; however, weather precluded the tactical air prestrike we had hoped for. I took off in the command helicopter with the command party, including Major Propes, S-3, Captain Wilkie, Artillery Liaison Officer,

Captain Stone, S-2, and PSG Johnson, S-3 Sergeant. It was my intention to observe the initial landing of C Company and then, owing to the requirement for replenishing fuel, the bird would have to return for refueling. I intended to go on the ground with Captain Stone and PSG Johnson and my radio operators, join C Company, and direct the activities of the remainder of the assault from the vicinity of the landing zone.

It was difficult to judge the effectiveness of the artillery preparation because there was a minimum of artillery firing in support of the Jumping Mustangs, since artillery must also support actions of the adjacent battalion. Although the preparation was timed for sufficient length, there were insufficient rounds, we learned later, and the artillery preparation had little effect on the landing zone.

C Company, the assault company, loaded up back at the Brigade Base, was en route to the landing zone. From a position overhead I observed the area of operation and the last few minutes of artillery preparation. Captain Wilkie lifted the artillery fire on my order, permitting the Aerial Rocket Artillery to close in and conduct a final preparation on the landing zone. A call to the assault helicopter company commander informed him that the ARA was lifted. One minute out, the gunships escorting the thirty UH-1D Helicopters sprinted ahead to cover the landing.

C Company received small arms and 60mm mortar fire from the southeast of LZ "Tonto" upon landing. Fire was immediately returned and platoons were deployed to clear the landing zone, to continue contact with the Viet Cong. The landing was made on time at 0900. The birds returned to pick up B Company. It appeared from the initial reports from Captain Smith and my own observations overhead that the assault was proceeding as planned against minimum enemy contact.

At 0920 hours, Captain Smith reported a gunship shot down south of the objective, approximately 1000 meters from his landing zone. The gunship had crashed in the area where there appeared to be a number of Viet Cong. The Division SOP as well as common sense dictated that the crew be rescued. Time was precious. I flew to the vicinity of the gunship and spotted it and the nearby Viet Cong. In the meantime, the battalion commander of the 229th Assault Helicopter Battalion, Lieutenant Colonel Robert Kellar, was making an approach to land accompanied by another aircraft, to pick up the wounded crew. Captain Martin's Company was seven minutes away en route to the landing zone. I decided to divert him. I quickly called him on the Battalion Command Net; informed him that there was a change of plans and that he was to land on the rice paddy to the south of the objective, near the downed gunship; rescue the crew of the helicopter; and continue to attack to the north in a double envelopment in conjunction with C Company. Similar instructions were passed to the commander of the support helicopter unit, monitoring the battalion command net. The order was substantially: "You have a change of mission and landing zone. You will land south of the objective, secure the gunship, and attack to the north. I will mark the landing zone."

This change of mission was an excellent example of the flexibility of airmobility, in execution and in the mental agility of its commanders. Both the Infantry and the aviation commanders were able to accept and execute this new order within the limited time available to them.

I directed the command helicopter on a low pass to the west of the proposed landing zone to make sure that it was satisfactory and to mark it. The approaching helicopter flight was two minutes out. Timing was excellent, for as I flew in the direction of the approaching flight, fifty feet above the ground, and dropped the yellow smoke grenade, the flight leader indicated that he had spotted the smoke and was homing on the target.

The helicopters touched down in the big, open rice paddy which was the new landing zone. Bravo dismounted on the run and moved off rapidly to engage the enemy, coming under heavy automatic weapons' sniper fire at the very beginning. All the empty helicopters flew out, leaving a number of men wounded almost immediately as elements of B Company were pinned down for the time being. It was obvious that the VC had expected the arriving force to come into the first landing zone, "Tonto," where C Company had landed. We had caught them by surprise and now had them trapped between two rifle companies, Captain Smith to the north and Captain Martin in the south.

Captain Martin of B Company later reported that he had been able to readily spot the yellow smoke, marking the LZ, from the air and had obtained an excellent view of the downed helicopter, the terrain, and the enemy. When he was at 300 feet and a minute outbound, a heavy volume of fire was directed at the landing flight.

The fire seemed to be coming from the high ground to the northwest of the LZ. This estimate was confirmed on landing. Incidentally, almost every helicopter in the flight was hit at least once, but not enough to put it out of action for the remaining flights.

I knew that there were some enemy at that location, for as I flew in to mark the landing zone, we had made a turn over the edge of the woods, where I could see fifteen to twenty Viet Cong with rifles and automatic weapons firing from foxholes. As later reconstructed, it all seemed unreal. All of us concentrated on operating the radios and making sure that the important mission of dropping the smoke grenade was executed correctly. I was busy as I tried to guide my pilot, indicating a few degrees' course change and a lower altitude. At the same time I could see out of the corner of my eye the Viet Cong firing at us. Captain Wilkie remarked over the intercom, "We are being fired at." At about the same time my left doorgunner, at that time PFC Jordan, opened up with his M-16.

We continued the flight, marked the landing zone, and observed the landing of B Company. B Company had arrived at the proper time and in a race beat the Viet Cong to the downed gunship. In the meantime Colonel Kellar, landed, retrieved the wounded crew, and transferred them to his aircraft and one other.

I continued to watch the actions of B Company for a few moments, and then, being low on fuel, informed the Battalion Forward Command Post that I would land and control the battalion from the ground. I called Captain Smith and told him I was coming in to LZ "Tonto."

Upon landing, the command ship immediately came under heavy fire by the same VC who had been shooting at C Company in their initial landing. The bird remained on the ground a few seconds while a wounded man a hundred yards away was carried to the ship.

It was this time that heavy fire was directed toward the command ship. I had immediately jumped out of the bird upon landing and dashed over to a piece of nearby high ground where I intended to establish a Command Post. Supposedly I was followed by my radio operators; however, as I looked back, I saw that they were flat on the ground, having taken cover from the increased fire directed at the bird. In addition, Captain Stone and Sergeant Johnson, who were to accompany me, were assisting, along with the crew chief, the loading of the casualty into the helicopter.

I dashed back, grabbed the radio operators, ordered them to accompany me on the run to the piece of ground where the Command Post was to be located. In the meantime the crew chief ran around to the other side of the bird to assist the wounded man. He was immediately cut down by VC fire and became a second casualty. Captain Stone and Sergeant Johnson assisted in putting both the wounded crew chief and the C Company casualty aboard the helicopter, at which time it took off.

The pilot and the copilot, Warrant Officer Robert Merkel and Ronald Emman, performed an exceptional job in holding the bird on the ground during all this firing. After the bird took off, Captain Stone and Sergeant Johnson made their way across the fire-swept LZ and arrived at the CP location.

When the bird returned to the Battalion Base, it was found that there were more than twenty-two hits on the aircraft, one in the compression chamber of the engine. The bird could not fly again until it had been repaired. It was a miracle that the bird actually got off the ground and that during all the firing no one was hit.

The loss of the bird caused quite a problem, since it was unable to return to the battle until the following day. In the aircraft were Major Propes, S-3, and Captain Wilkie, the Artillery Liaison Officer, who were going to maintain radio contact with me and conduct and supervise artillery fire and tactical air from the bird. The loss of the bird denied the use of the S-3 and the Artillery Liaison Officer until hours later when they finally joined the battalion that afternoon.

The two pilots were each recommended for a Distinguished Flying Cross; Captain Stone and Sergeant Johnson were each recommended for a Bronze Star for their heroic actions in trying to rescue the Crew Chief. Unfortunately, the Crew Chief died prior to the bird's reaching the Battalion Base.

Action at the objective continued, with both B and C

Companies heavily engaged. Heavy 60mm mortar fire landed on the LZ. I personally observed some thirty to forty rounds. The entire landing zone was continuously swept by fire, from both rifle and automatic weapons. C Company had a difficult task routing the snipers and machine-gun nests.

A Company landed thirty minutes later on LZ "Tonto." Upon landing, Captain Danielsen was given the mission of attacking, to the northeast, a piece of high ground that overlooked the landing zone and would assist in reducing the enemy fire coming from the main objective. A Company demonstrated a skillful display of fire and maneuver, including their employment of friendly tube artillery as they moved to capture this high ground.

All three rifle companies were joined in a coordinated battle. A Company attacked toward the high ground to the north, B and C Companies attacked toward one another to reduce the primary objective. The action continued until 1530 hours in the afternoon before the enemy were finally killed or destroyed and the remainder broke off the battle and withdrew to the northeast.

At 1220 hours, the Thunderbolt Force, D Company minus the Mortar Platoon, was committed to LZ "Tonto" with a mission of securing that landing zone in order to release the remaining elements of C Company so that they could continue their attack. The Thunderbolt Force, under Captain Tabb, executed a landing under sniper fire, the mission being completed successfully.

The first major problem concerning the entire battalion was medical evacuation. C Company had a number of casualties in the beginning who had to be evacuated as soon as possible. A medical evacuation ship was called in, escorted by a gunship. The bird attempted to land near the Command Post, which was still under sniper fire. The Viet Cong waited until the bird touched down, then opened up with at least one machine gun and several rifles. The co-pilot was killed immediately. The pilot took off and returned to the air. It became obvious that medical evacuation in this area was going to be difficult as long as the enemy were still on the objective. The battle continued to destroy these enemy, but it was essential that medical evacuation be initiated in the meantime.

Contacting the helicopter lift commander of the aircraft

that remained to support the battalion, a plan was developed in which the lift ships would come in and land in a small depressed area north of the landing zone. A dry wash ran through the area; aircraft, by making an approach from north to south into this depressed area, received protection from the enemy in the objective area. At the same time, Captain Smith of C Company initiated a mass of rifle, automatic weapons, mortar and artillery on the enemy. In this manner we were able to successfully bring in the lift ships to pick up casualties. The casualties were hand-carried to this pickup zone to the rear of the Battalion Command Post. I devoted considerable effort toward coordination of the fire of C Company and the landing transport helicopters in order to take care of this essential evacuation mission.

At this point I was impressed by the tremendous spirit and morale of the wounded. This action was the first major battle in which the entire battalion was engaged. The men knew this and the only concern of the wounded was that they were not able to help. The quiet courage demonstrated by each man as he lay there bleeding on the sand, perhaps on a stretcher, waiting for the evacuation helicopter to come in, was something inspiring to behold. If some of our civilian comrades in the United States could only see the dedication and the motivation of these men, their soldiers, they could not help but be inspired and know that we have a wonderful group of men in this present, much maligned generation.

I talked to a number of the wounded and tried to comfort them. Even though some were badly wounded, they were still cheerful and concerned only with the progress of the unit, asking how we were doing, how the battle was proceeding.

The success in evacuation of casualties using this method of coordinating the landing of the helicopters with the fire power worked so well with C Company that the same system was employed to the south where B Company was continuing its action. Captain Martin coordinated the fire, the landing zone was marked by smoke, the birds came in, and all casualties were soon evacuated from B Company.

There were more difficulties within the A Company area in evacuating casualties, since this area was more exposed. Casualties received when A Company came under assault on their hill objective had to be evacuated, under sniper fire, back for a few hundred meters to an appropriate landing zone. This took longer and required more difficult coordination. Captain Danielsen handled the evacuation in a fine manner.

Evacuation of casualties was an important factor in any battle. I had assured the battalion that a wounded man would be evacuated, and that he would immediately receive medical attention. We would always retrieve the bodies of those killed. This action was the first major test of my promise. I was most pleased to see evacuation work well in C Company initially, later in B Company, and lastly A Company. The successful evacuation was positive proof to all of the officers and men of the battalion that we had a going organization and that it would look after its own. I was convinced that this vivid demonstration later contributed to the increased morale, motivation, and dedication of the battalion in future battles.

A soldier is ready to do whatever is required; will not worry too much about being wounded; is willing to risk his life if he knows that if wounded he will receive prompt medical attention, that somebody will look after him, and, as funny as it may sound to some, if he is killed that his body will be retrieved. This promise was carried out within the battalion.

In the meantime the battle continued vigorously, especially with B Company. On landing, the 2nd Platoon of B Company had assaulted and carried the first two strong points, killing eight Viet Cong. The 1st Platoon assaulted and secured the hill overlooking the downed helicopter and the ground occupied by the bird itself. In accomplishing this, five Viet Cong were killed. The 3rd Platoon took the hill to the east without contact. At 1100 hours, the Viet Cong counterattacked against both the 1st and 2nd Platoons. By 1130 the counterattacks had been successfully repelled with thirty Viet Cong killed and one captured.

One of the platoon leaders of B Company in later describing the landing and the battle stated the following:

"The new landing zone was hot. Captain Martin in the lead helicopter landed close to the stricken gunship. Heavy enemy fire caused the other lift ships to scatter over a wider area than originally planned. The company commander had not been able to inform me of the change in mission. On landing I saw where he had set up his Command Post next to the downed gunship. He was serving as the focal point for the reorganizaton and assembling of scattered elements of the company. The 2nd Platoon had walked into a trap and was receiving heavy volumes of mortar and small-arms fire from three sides. The fire from the enemy was effective, causing several casualties and pinning a portion of the platoon to the ground. My platoon was not engaged in a fire fight initially, so I was committed to maneuver around the south flank against the Viet Cong positions. The first attempt I made was unsuccessful because of the thick jungle growth, which made movement difficult. I had one man badly wounded, who was carried to the Company CP. I launched a second assault, which was successful in relieving the pressure on the partially pinned-down platoon."

Another platoon leader of B Company reported the battle: "Few units have an intuition as to their destiny. Our company was not any different. We had little indication that fateful morning that the coming action would be different than any of a dozen previous ones. We had a report that C Company received fire and was engaged; thus we were forewarned to expect trouble. We lifted off from pickup zone en route to the objective. About seven minutes out the company commander called to give me a change in the company mission. Two minutes out our assault helicopter received fire. We could hear small arms and automatic weapons popping all around us. Before the ships could settle to the water-filled rice paddies, the troops jumped out in a hail of small-arms fire, including explosions I assumed to be sixty-millimeter mortar. Men scattered everywhere. The initiative of the air assault landing was partially spoiled by the retaliating enemy force."

First Sergeant Ray Poynter another view of B Co's battles described:

> We made our first real contact 18 December 1965. The plan sounded good. Captain Martin seemed real informed and seemed to have the situation well in hand. Of course no one thought of the mission changing. It was real combat now and the feeling

came back like in World War II, that crack close to your ear would be a bullet. Makes more noise coming than going. Then they used machine guns, sixty-millimeter mortars, and there I was out in the middle of the rice paddy, pinned down in two feet of water. Of course someone had opened the spigot again and it was really coming down. Bullets were hitting all around us. My first thought was to dig. I did, but before I finished, seven men tried to get into my incomplete foxhole.

Charles was getting close, too close for comfort. We had to move somewhere. Then we heard we were needed as soon as possible, 800 meters forward, to the front where the action was. Just then I saw a black pajama-clad individual moving to our rear. I immediately realized he could get into position with a machine gun and this must have been just what he was doing. I fired about three magazines and everyone else there was trying to hit him, but he was out of range. This worried me, so it was time to get while the getting was good. The getting place wasn't so good, though. We moved through about five hundred to eight hundred meters of open terrain with Charlie looking down our throat. He used what he had and caused some casualties. One of our twins, Benny May, was hit bad. We got him out and then the bad news came that several troopers were dead. This was war; we were really in the middle of it. I'll never forget the feeling when I finally thought I was under cover.

After I caught my breath from the long run up to within six hundred meters of where Charlie was, I discovered someone else—a Charlie. He fired a burst, the last round six inches away. He had that machine gun set up to our rear. Now we called in an air strike and he quit firing. We took the position. Charlie was quiet, but now the real problem of resupply was at hand. I called in my resupply and was waiting to receive it, but first the ships had to evacuate the dead and wounded. Charlie had taken some of B Company out, but we had taken our share of Charlie.

We saw this the next day, as we searched the valley; when the battle was over.

At 1030 hours it was obvious that resupply would be necessary because large amounts of rifle and machine-gun ammunition, hand grenades, and mortar rounds were being expended. A resupply mission was called for and a platoon of four birds from the assault helicopter battalion arrived, using the same techniques by which we had coordinated the medical evacuation. The four birds landed and received sporadic sniper fire, a round of which damaged the control system of one aircraft after it was on the ground. The crew immediately jumped out, ran to a sister ship, and departed with the flight of three. Ammunition was left on the bird sitting in the center of the landing zone. The other three aircraft crews had dumped the ammunition out of the doors prior to takeoff.

A similar resupply mission was successfully concluded for B Company using two birds in their particular area. I remember how funny it seemed, even in the battle, to look out there and see that single helicopter sitting in the landing zone. Although the engine had died, the rotor was still turning for a few minutes afterward. This was one of the incongruous situations of the battle that stick on one's mind, remembered for many months.

Later on in the afternoon, a CH-47 Chinook came in and with a maintenance crew evacuated the downed helicopter successfully back to its base. Fortunately none of the crew were wounded.

By 1400 hours, five hours after the initial landing, the situation was well under control. D Company was securing the landing zone. A Company was on its objective, silencing the mortar and machine-gun fire coming from that area. C and B Companies were rapidly converging on the main objective, destroying any remaining enemy. Limited tactical air support was in progress, along with extensive use of the aerial-rocket artillery and the improved tube-artillery support by this time.

All casualties were being evacuated within minutes after being hit. Resupply of critically needed ammunition was satisfactorily maintained. Members of the Battalion Headquarters, that portion of the Medical Platoon not forward, and the Supply Platoon, all located at the Battalion Base twelve minutes away, under direction of the Battalion Executive Officer, Major Herman, performed in a herculean manner to assist the 3rd Brigade Forward Support Element, part of the Division Support Command, in caring for the casualties as they were returned to that point and in handling the additional ammunition resupply requested.

Since artillery and tactical air support were limited, phenomenal quantities of 81 mortar, 40mm grenade launcher, and hand grenades were used. The urgent call for resupply complicated matters at the Forward Support Elements, for they had not anticipated heavy enemy contact and an early request for resupply. In addition, a portion of the Forward Supply Element, including elements of the Medical Clearing Company, had not yet reached the Brigade Base owing to weather conditions and a shortage of trucks. Had it not been for the excellent work of the Jumping Mustangs at the Brigade Base, the medical evacuation and the resupply would not have been as efficient and as satisfactory as it proved to be. The Battalion Medical Platoon, including Dr. Odom, were the ones who unloaded the helicopters, cared for the patients, and saw to it that they received emergency medical aid and that the more critical casualties were loaded aboard medivac helicopters and flown to the 2nd Evacuation Hospital, located at Quin Nhon, fifteen minutes away.

By 1530 hours, B and C Companies had cleared their objective, linked up, and established a defensive perimeter. A Company was secure on its objective; thus the battalion was formed into three tight perimeters mutually supporting each other by fire support and patrols. Resupply of ammunition and rations was completed. Defensive concentrations were fired in by tube artillery and mortars. All enemy had been killed or driven from the area, escaping apparently through a small draw to the northeast of the objective.

Colonel Hal Moore, the 3rd Brigade Commander, and Colonel Elvey Roberts, 1st Brigade Commander, arrived at 1600 hours for a short visit to the Battalion Command Post and a walk through the objective area of B and C Companies. A change of orders was received. We would secure for the night and, instead of being prepared to continue the mission to the south as planned, would from our present locations attack to the west. This attack would be a continuation of the present search-and-destroy mission. The former mission south of our objective area was being assumed by the South Korean unit working with the Division. Since the enemy had moved into their area, it was better for coordination purposes that they try to rout them out.

It was instructive, looking in detail at the objective area and the installations, and then recapping the situation. Upon looking back at the initial landing of B Company, it was obvious that a VC main-force battalion was in the area. Its strength was estimated at approximately 250 men. The Viet Cong that had initially been observed along the southern end of the landing zone, from which they brought fire to bear on C Company, wore black pajamas and pistol belts and carried individual weapons.

From B Company's area a number of Viet Cong were observed in khaki uniform, wearing the standard pith helmets. In both areas Viet Cong tactics were characterized by sniper fire and delaying tactics, except in the vicinity of the canebrake, near the downed gunship, where B Company had threatened to cut off their escape route. Here the battle was most intense.

The weather and terrain favored the Viet Cong. The village south of the landing zone was characterized by hedgerows and thick underbrush. Fighting positions, foxholes, and spider holes were concealed all along the hedgerows. In the area in the vicinity of the canebreak, tunnels were extensive.

The critical terrain features in the area were the hill mass, seized by B and C Companies, and the hill later seized by A Company. The piece of high terrain seized by A Company, from a study of maps and the photo, had not appeared to be as dominating as it later proved to be on the ground, thus necessitating the change of plans.

Numerous documents were found in the objective area and evacuated back to the Brigade Base. No additional Viet Cong units were identified.

A Vietnamese civilian in the area stated that a Viet Cong battalion had been working on the tunnels in the area during the three preceding nights, arriving just after dark and leaving before first light. Where the Viet Cong went during the day was not known. Probably they were holed up to avoid detection. The tunnels were scattered in lines throughout the objective area. Each tunnel entrance was a hole approximately six feet square and twenty to thirty feet deep. Bamboo ladders were in place, obviously used to ascend from and descend into the holes.

All of the holes had some sort of a digging rig located nearby, a bamboo tripod, a primitive pulley, and ropes and baskets used to pull the earth out. The objective of the holes was to dig some twenty to thirty feet straight down and then move laterally, creating long tunnels at the bottom, well beneath the surface. These tunnels provided a storage place for ammunition and weapons and shelters for troops.

A tremendous amount of work had been accomplished in the two or three days. The fortificatons were about one-third finished. The spoil or earth had been removed from the tunnels and scattered under vegetation throughout the area in order to avoid detection from the air. Even though extensive digging had gone on for two or three days, it was impossible to foretell this from either photos or the limited visual reconnaissance prior to the operation. Had this task been completed, the fortifications would have defied the heaviest guns available in this area, as well as serial bombardment.

It was obvious that the Viet Cong expected the Jumping Mustangs to land at LZ "Tonto," where C Company made the initial landing. The enemy were well dug in around the entire hill mass of the objective. They began to move against C Company when the first landing was completed. They either did not anticipate additional forces coming in, or believed that if they did, reinforcements would land on the same landing zone. Thus they moved to the high and dominating terrain overlooking the landing zone and attempted to destroy C Company. They also were prepared to destroy as many helicopters as arrived should there be another lift.

The gunship that was shot down minutes after the initial landing of C Company caused a change of plans. The aircraft going down to the south side of the objective in the edge, shot down by the few personnel remaining with the rear guard, changed the whole complexion of the battle. The fact that the next rifle company, B Company, almost seven minutes out, could be diverted into a new landing zone to the south near the gunship was something not anticipated by the Viet Cong. The fact that this mission was carried out put the Viet Cong in the middle, with one airmobile rifle company in the south and one in the north. It caught the Viet Cong "with their pants down." It caused them to split their forces and fight in two directions. I am certain that they were greatly surprised by the landing of B Company.

The change of mission for B Company was another splendid example of the flexibility and the agility of the airmobile concept. A rifle-company commander, inbound only seven minutes out, on a preplanned assault, received a change of mission and a change of landing zone in a short period of time, yet successfully executed the change. It was further demonstrated by the flexibility with which the assault helicopter commander received a change in landing zone and mission and executed the landing. This was difficult for both commanders. The new order meant a new situation to be grasped mentally, a change of plans to be quickly formulated, and a rapid issuance of orders, followed by violent execution by both the troops of the rifle company and the individual pilots flying the mission.

The helicopter commander readily picked up the yellow smoke grenade marking the LZ. The LZ was adequate in size. The word passed to him giving him a direction of landing was sufficient so that the flight had merely to alter course thirty degrees and land using the same formation on the new landing zone.

The most difficult portion of the task was with the Infantry. Although leaders were aware of the change, many of the men were not quite sure what had happened. This state of mind was customary in the airmobile concept in airmobile battles. A few quick directions from the leaders, plus enemy fire coming from the edge of the woods, made it obvious where the enemy was. The troopers in each individual heli-copter had been given the word on landing that the objective was to the right. This simplified knowledge as to where the enemy were, even though they had not been fired upon, was a matter of standard procedure within the airmobile battal-ions, especially the Jumping Mustangs.

The same airmobile flexibility was demonstrated by A Company. Although they landed on the preplanned landing zone, their initial mission of continuing with C Company to seize the objective was altered so that they attacked in a different direction to seize a different objective. The company commander, his platoon leaders, and the troops were able to receive this order, rapidly readjust their thinking, make plans, issue orders, and execute the new direction of attack to seize the new objective. The successful use of fire power by A and B Companies demonstrated that rapid changes of plans could be executed effectively by both the tube artillery and the Aerial Rocket Artillery.

Fire power in this battle was limited initially so far as artillery was concerned, owing to priorities to other units. Tactical air power was limited by the weather until later stages. As the weather lifted later on in the morning, the battalion was able to employ tactical air power successfully. However, air power was not available at the critical time.

M-79

The absence of adequate tube artillery and essential tactical air power required the battalion and the companies to rely primarily on organic weapons. This they did in an excellent manner, using the 81mm mortars and 40mm grenade launcher as well as smaller weapons, resulting in a call for ammunition resupply, catching supply personnel slightly off base. Supply men could not anticipate or understand how the tremendous quantities of ammunition were being used.

This action constituted the first time since the Ia Drang,

and probably the first time in the history of the Air Cavalry, that one airmobile battalion had landed physically on top of a Viet Cong battalion. In skull sessions and in previous training we had discussed what happened and what you did if you landed on top of an enemy battalion. Many argued both ways whether this course of action was desirable or whether it was not. In this case it proved desirable and provided the successful destruction of a Viet Cong main-force battalion.

A recap of the entire situation, friendly and enemy, indicated that the battalion had landed on both sides of the main-force Viet Cong battalion. The VC were armed with at least two or more 60mm mortars and at least five machineguns, including the two that shot down the gunship in the initial phase. The landing of B Company on the south side of the objective caused the Viet Cong to fight in two directions. The outcome in numbers of friendly casualties and in success of the mission might have been far different had the original landing plan been followed. The Jumping Mustang Battalion fought a coordinated action with each one of the company commanders buying a piece of the pie.

All portions of the Battalion Combat Team functioned smoothly and had a part in the battle. Supporting Army aviation units performed professionally, without regard to the low ceiling and the poor visibility. The teamwork demonstrated in this first major engagement proved that the battalion's long, hard training had not been in vain. It proved every trooper's confidence, not only in himself, but in his platoon, his company, and his battalion. The Jumping Mustangs had been blooded as a unit. They had killed a confirmed 105 Viet Cong by body count, and probably many more, while suffering only 11 dead of their own, plus 58 wounded. Most of the wounded were quickly returned to duty.

Several lessons were learned from this battle and became important additions to the Mustang SOP.

First, be prepared for changes and ready to take advantage of any situation that might arise suddenly in combat. Changes should be expected as a matter of course.

Second, responsive tube-artillery support was a must. Every battalion in a brigade operation must have tube-artillery support, even though another battalion might be enjoying priority of fire. With regard to this tube-artillery support, it was interesting to note the relationship that an

Infantry battalion had with its own direct-support artillery battalion. In this case a strange artillery unit was supporting us. No matter how well they might carry out their job, they would never be able to perform quite as well as our own artillery battalion could, at least in our minds.

Supply personnel should anticipate resupply needs and medical clearing at the Forward Support Element and be prepared for the worst. A battalion's basic load of ammunition does not last long for a unit heavily engaged.

Evacuation of casualties from the battlefield without delay was of utmost importance. At times a considerable portion of a battalion's efforts may be required, coordinated against the enemy in order to accomplish the evacuation mission successfully. This fact was most important to a soldier's morale and well-being. A man would give his all if he knew someone would do the same for him if he were hit.

Last, this "first blood" proved that an airmobile force could operate in all conditions of weather. Monsoons, including heavy rain with the accompanying low ceiling and visibility, need not prevent the mission from being carried out. This was especially true in a unit that was determined to accomplish the job. The battalion motto changed slightly after this battle in view of this point and became simply: "Drive on—all the way."

The battalion spent a quiet night, although a wet night. It had been raining continuously, beginning with the operation that morning and, with the exception of a few minutes, had continued throughout the day. All troops were wet during the day and of course during the night. When soaked, wearing the normal fatigues and boots we were wearing at that time, even with a rain jacket you soon were wet all the way through from the rain on the outside and the perspiration from the inside. The first night was not quite so bad: though chilled and uncomfortable, we were able to sleep, especially if tired, even though extremely wet. It was interesting the second night, however, being wet all the way through, how difficult it was to stay warm, how impossible to be dry, and how difficult to sleep.

We expected a possible counterattack during the night in view of the fact that the objective area had extensive fortifications and evidence of extensive effort expended. It was obvious that this area was important to the Viet Cong, so they might try to retake it. We were disposed fairly well, the companies tied in to each other by fire and patrols, though the perimeter was not as tight as one would like in a night engagement in Vietnam. B and C Companies did have tight perimeters, but A Company, although a small perimeter itself, was tied in only by fire power and patrols joining B Company. D Company, the Thunderbolt Force, protected the remainder of the landing zone and the Command Post and completed the tie-in between A Company on its left and C Company on its right.

8" Howitzer M110

A program of H and I fires, both tube artillery and mortar, was initiated and included the extensive use of the eight-inch howitzers on the route which we thought perhaps the Viet Cong had attempted to move out by and perhaps even the location they had gone to.

I spent a sleepless, wet night, still at the location where we had initially established a Command Post near LZ "Tonto." We dug in in the soft sand, using foxholes to assure maximum cover and protection for all personnel.

It was interesting to look back at some of the episodes that occurred during the day which were somewhat amusing. The first one that came to mind was when the command helicopter landed and I jumped out and went bounding across the forty or fifty yards of sand to the newly selected Command Post. I expected my two radio operators, PFC Jordan and PFC Culbertson, to be at my heels as they usually were.

It took a few seconds for them to get out of the bird with their equipment, and when the sniper fire picked up, they both hit the ground. This was the reason I dashed back to pick them up. They watched, as one of them explained to me later, as I ran toward the Command Post location. The dirt was kicked up at my heels by a machine gun firing from the high ground overlooking the landing zone.

I came back, chewed them both out, and told them to get the heck along with me. I took off again. PFC Jordan told me that he decided this was it—this was where he was going to die. But I had told him to go, and go he would. He closed his eyes and blindly charged toward the Command Post location, making it safely, as did PFC Culbertson seconds later.

They quickly unloaded their two radios—one for the battalion and one for the brigade—and put on their long antennas so that I could have the necessary communications both with the companies and with the brigade.

I had to chew out both PFC Culbertson and PFC Jordan about five times because they were prone to stick their heads above the little mound to see what was going on. The minute any one of us showed his head, the snipers, having our position under surveillance, popped a round in our direction. I finally got them to keep their heads down and concentrate on operating the radios and digging foxholes.

In looking back at the landing, I marvel at the tremendous job that both helicopter pilots performed in the command helicopter as they held the bird on the ground. It seemed an eternity as Captain Stone and Sergeant Johnson and the crew chief attempted to put the casualty from C Company aboard and then, after the crew chief was hit, as Captain Stone and Sergeant Johnson were getting the crew chief on board as well. Captain Wilkie, who was in the aircraft, had the dubious honor of receiving a Purple Heart that day as well as one the following day. He was sitting on the right side of the helicopter in his customary position monitoring the radios, continuing the direction of fire. A round from a sniper whistled in, barely nicking him as it passed between a portion of his armored vest and his flesh. Had he not been wearing the armored vest, he probably would have been seriously wounded.

There were many examples of individual heroism that day. One in particular was 1st Sergeant Grady Trainor from C Company. On the landing zone with his company, he demonstrated outstanding courage and devotion to duty as he arranged casualty evacuation back to the pickup point and resupplied his troops with ammunition. It was necessary to carry the casualties across the exposed fire-swept landing zone for a distance of two or three hundred meters. I watched 1st Sergeant Trainor time and time again personally carry casualties, with another man or two assisting, to the pickup zone and then go back for more. The last time I observed him, he had discarded weapons, harness, and everything else and was wearing only his helmet in order to facilitate carrying wounded men.

When the ammunition resupply arrived in the four helicopters, one of which had been damaged by fire, 1st Sergeant Trainor, with two or three of his men, grabbed the ammunition, broke it down, and made distribution to the platoons within C Company. He certainly showed vividly this day that he was one of the outstanding professionals of the United States Army, a true soldier, and dedicated to his battalion, his company, and his men. He provided positive proof again of the excellence of his company. He was later awarded the Silver Star for this heroic action.

All three rifle-company commanders demonstrated outstanding professional abilities and were the real heroes of the battle, along with their platoon leaders and the many of their men. Their moving freely on the battlefield, without regard to snipers and incoming mortar rounds, in order to accomplish their job, was an inspiration to all. Captain Martin of B Company had the most difficult job and demonstrated his heroism several times. All three company commanders were recommended for the Silver Star; however, these recommendations for decorations were later downgraded by higher headquarters to Bronze Stars with a "V" for valor.

Communications were good throughout the battle, both from the Forward Command Post location to the Battalion CP co-located with the 3rd Brigade CP and also to the Battalion Base. Occasionally it was necessary to relay through one of the two CP's. Although I had good communication with my own elements, including my Command Post at the Brigade Command Post, I had difficulty contacting Brigade throughout the morning. However, by relay from the Battalion Command Post to the Brigade, I was able to keep the Brigade Commander informed.

The absence of the command helicopter handicapped the battalion considerably, because this denied us the eyes necessary for the closer and more effective coordination and control of the companies. It had been my plan to remain on the ground as I did, but to keep airborne the helicopter command post with the S-3 and the artillery officer to assure more effective fire support and to keep me informed as to progress of the enemy and the progress of the battle itself. I had to rely entirely on reports from the company commanders, reinforced by word from some of the supporting gunships or aerial-rocket artillery working with the battalion.

Captain Corey, the Air Force Liaison Officer, was with C Company and in position to use tactical air power when it was available. He was able to obtain certain information through his Air Force channels from the supporting fighters.

Captain Stone became S-3 and my primary staff officer during this battle. Sergeant Johnson, the Operations Sergeant, performed in an excellent manner, and between the two of them, they were able to assist in the control of the battalion. This included acting as pathfinders to operate the landing zone, although we received much assistance from two of the pathfinders from the 11th Aviation Group, who came in on one of the later lifts and set up their communications at the CP location.

Medical evacuation was coordinated by Captain Stone. He also established coordination with the incoming helicopters for supply. Both Sergeant Johnson and Captain Stone assisted on coordinating artillery support; however, in general, the artillery was controlled by the company commanders through their forward observers for each of their respective battles.

The battalion mortars were not too effective initially. Since the entire battalion planned to land on one LZ, the mortars had been split throughout the three rifle-company lifts in order to fill up aircraft. This was something we resolved never to do again, because when B Company was diverted, a portion of the Mortar Platoon was with that unit; therefore, the platoon operated as a split unit, part supporting B Company and part supporting the rest of the battalion. On the arrival of Captain Tabb with the Thunderbolt Force, he soon had the platoon organized and functioning effectively in support of the entire battalion. The mortars throughout, both in the companies and in the battalion, did a tremendous job in view of the curtailment of tube artillery and tactical air, and rewarded the many hours of effort expended by the gunners and crews, forward observers and leaders, to become more effective in their work.

The battalion was preparing to move out to continue the attack to the west. Before we were able to move, however, we had one additional mission: to assure the evacuation of the downed helicopter gunship. Later in the afternoon before there had been an attempt to evacuate the downed bird, however, the enemy situation was still vague and this mission could not be accomplished. Coordination was completed for the arrival of the evacuation Chinook the following morning.

At 0900 hours the Chinook arrived, preceded by a UH-1D helicopter and a maintenance crew to rig the bird with slings for the evacuation. During this time B Company cleared the entire area and kept a hail of mortar and artillery fire on the surrounding hills to the south to assure no interference with the maintenance-evacuation mission.

I joined Captain Martin at the location of the downed ship. The bird was badly damaged, several pieces being scattered throughout the area. It was amazing that the crew, having ridden the ship down, were still alive. Although one pilot was seriously wounded, he would live.

The bird was rigged with slings, the pieces were picked up, and in a few minutes the Chinook arrived, made the hook-up, and attempted the first pickup. The bird was damaged to the extent that on pickup a portion of it broke off. The load had to be re-rigged. The Chinook then successfully moved the broken fuselage from the area. The UH-1D helicopter with the maintenance crew picked up the remaining pieces and departed from the area. Scraps of no use were destroyed in place to assure that the Viet Cong would not be able to retrieve any portion for their own use.

Police of the battlefield in Vietnam was important. I

think at first the soldiers felt that their purpose was simply in the Army tradition, to tidy things up. However, the Viet Cong used almost anything that was discarded by American soldiers. Old batteries from the radios could be taken apart, since they still had sufficient power to electronically detonate mines. Any kind of metal tube could be used as a gun barrel. Metal itself was valuable and could be used to improvise mines and booby traps. Almost anything could be used in some way to support the Viet Cong effort. They were past masters at improvising. Therefore, it was customary that every item of equipment that was to be discarded, such as batteries and C-ration components, were all destroyed in some manner or removed from the area.

A tragic incident occurred back at the Command Post a few minutes after I departed to join B Company. The supporting artillery fired a mission with the rounds passing directly over the Command Post at a greater range some 1500 meters distant. A change of mission to bring the fire to the left at a shorter range was requested. The guns shifted and reduced the charge on the rounds, with the exception of a single gun, which for some reason left the direction the same, however reducing the range as directed.

On firing, a single 105 artillery shell fell in the middle of the Battalion Command Post. It struck in the foxhole which the Artillery Reconnaissance Sergeant and his radio operator, part of the liaison party for the Artillery Liaison Officer, were occupying. The Artillery Liaison Officer himself was standing outside the hole, talking on the radio. Captain Propes, the S-3, had rejoined the battalion. Several personnel from Operations and Supply standing by were there when the round hit.

When the shell exploded, the Reconnaissance Sergeant and his radio operator were killed. Captain Wilkie was severely wounded, accounting for his second Purple Heart in two days. Several men standing nearby were blown from their feet. Fortunately, the soft sand partially shielded the blast from this highly explosive round. Minor wounds were received by two other men; however, the Pathfinder NCO standing nearby was killed and the radio operator for the Air Force Liaison Officer, standing near the artilleryman, was badly wounded.

This single round, a short round, was destined by fate, owing to an error on the guns, to fall into the Artillery Officer's foxhole. Most of the men killed and wounded were artillerymen. Needless to say, both I and the Battalion Headquarters were upset over these needless casualties. It was always bad to have men die or be wounded in combat; it was doubly bad when this happened from your own efforts, although in this case it was certainly not any of our fault, and probably not that of the artillerymen.

It was interesting to note that had I been there with my radio operators, I probably would have been near the Artillery Officer, because the primary activity in progress at that time was the direction of artillery and mortar fire to make sure that the maintenance evacuation mission was not disturbed. This reinforced my own belief that in war or in combat one should not worry about when he was going to be wounded or killed, because if it was not intended to happen, it probably would not. This feeling was reinforced a number of times throughout the remainder of my tour in Vietnam.

The helicopter gunship having been evacuated, the Battalion Command Post quickly reorganized. The Artillery Liaison Officer was replaced by the senior forward observer in the battalion from C Company. We were ready to move out on our new mission to the west to reconnoiter and drive out any Viet Cong within the area. The battalion assembled and the movement commenced with B and C Companies leading, two companies abreast in widely spread-out company columns. A and D Companies followed with the battalion moving in a box formation, two up and two back.

Movement continued through the rice paddies and the hedgerows, by the many villages, throughout the rest of the afternoon. There was no enemy contact whatsoever, but there was extensive evidence that the Viet Cong had been in this area. These were obviously Viet Cong homes. Many signs on the houses indicated that Americans should get out; signs by the Viet Cong demonstrated for their cause.

The terrain was characterized by series of rice paddies, all full of water, with narrow dikes or footpaths. There was also some vegetation—the whole thing difficult for movement, especially for a unit in a fighting posture. The command helicopter was in the air, with Captain Stone and

Captain Corey plus the Artillery Reconnaissance Sergeant, ready to assist in directing artillery and tactical air power if required.

A tentative battalion location had been spotted for the night, that we would try to reach. The battalion moved toward this area, arriving just prior to dark. The perimeter was set up, resupply had been coordinated to include the little ammunition required plus C-rations and, especially important, hot coffee. Hot coffee was most important for the chilled troops, who by now had stopped moving and were beginning to feel the effect of the cool weather and our own wet condition.

I took the command helicopter and got a good look at the terrain, searched for possible enemy avenues of approach, and evaluated the general situation. I landed and then went on a tour of each of the company perimeters, visiting with the company commander and a maximum number of troops to assure a tie-in and that we were secure for the night. The mortar and artillery fired in defensive concentrations and an extensive H and I program was coordinated by the Artillery Liaison Officer for the night.

Plans were discussed for movement out the next day, this time to swing back in a northerly direction to continue the search-and-destroy mission. It was planned that we would reach a landing zone late in the afternoon, to be extracted and moved back to the Brigade Base and possibly to An Khe to continue another mission with the 1st Airborne Brigade.

The night was quiet, again with no enemy contact. The basic problem was the weather: the continued rain, fighting off the chill from the wet clothes and the dampness of the night. At 0200 I was unable to sleep, after having fought the battle of the air mattress and poncho, which for some reason seemed to collect more and more water so that, instead of getting drier, I got wetter and wetter. I got up and found some coffee still remaining in one of the marmite cans from the evening meal. Although only lukewarm, that seemed one of the finest cups of coffee that I had ever had. It was funny how your perspective changed with a particular situation.

The operation today was one primarily of movement, with much reconnaissance and searching. It would appear that the next day's mission would be the same. Before dark, the new Artillery Liaison Officer arrived from the 2nd of the

19th Artillery, Captain Harry W. Wolfsenholme, along with a complete new artillery liaison party to replace the casualties from this morning's CP episode. The pathfinder had been replaced, as well as the Air Force radio operator.

Reports from Major Herman, the Executive Officer, who had flown up with the resupply helicopter, assured me that everything was in good order at both the Battalion Base and the Battalion Command Post. He informed me of the status of the casualties and the condition of some of the more serious ones. His words confirmed the feeling of pride that I had had in the battalion since yesterday's operation—not only for their tremendous job under adverse conditions, but also for the fine manner in which the wounded conducted themselves and the way the entire battalion, including the headquarters, supply, and medical evacuation personnel back at the Base, performed. The battalion was a functioning team.

Ben Khe, Vietnam

The battalion moved out the following morning shortly after daylight to continue its search-and-destroy mission to the west. This was a repetition of the preceding day's action with no enemy contact and, again, the same type of terrain, rice paddies, villages, and hedgerows. A tentative pickup zone was located by elements of the battalion staff in the command helicopter and the battalion reached this location by midafternoon.

Coordination with the 3rd Brigade headquarters indicated that helicopters, both Chinooks and UH-1D's, would be available at 1600 hours to pick up the battalion. The move would take place back to the base and to An Khe.

The weather had broken somewhat for the afternoon and the first sunshine revealed itself as we assembled on the pickup zone. This was a chance to check equipment, eat a C-ration, and try to dry out a bit. The pickup zone was secure, with troops on the perimeter. The plan for extraction would leave A Company until last to secure the battalion's departure.

A news reporter, Mr. Bob Poos, had been with us for the last three days. He did not observe the action of the battalion in the forward area the first day but did see what had been going on back at the base with regard to the casualties and had been with us on this third day. He wrote an excellent article concerning both the casualties and a second one concerning one of my radio operators, PFC Culbertson. This latter article, appearing in all the leading newspapers, pertained to "what happiness is." Over here, for PFC Culbertson, happiness was just being alive. It was a hot cup of coffee, a dry pair of socks. Incidentally, the battalion was beginning to get considerable publicity in this operation, as well as some from the Battle of the Ia Drang, for A Company. This led to the greatest publicity we received when on the first of the year we reached the Cambodian border.

The first helicopters were in and B Company was extracted to move directly back to An Khe. This was followed by successive lifts of C and D Companies, with A Company eventually lifted back to another location to secure an artillery battery and then back to An Khe, by truck, by 2200 hours.

This ended the Battle of Ben Khe, the first major engagement by all elements of the battalion. One hundred twenty-five enemy were killed by body count, an estimated 100 wounded, and one captured. Friendly losses included 11 killed and 58 wounded.

On arrival back at An Khe, a new order was waiting for us. We would remain in An Khe for only two days, and then were to move to Pleiku. Movement would be by motor convoy and we were able to be there on the twenty-third of December. We would be established as a Division Reserve Force in the Pleiku area for the II Corps Tactical Zone.

We began to refer to An Khe as the "An Khe Way Station," for this was the name given to the rest stops by the Viet Cong. It seemed that every time we got back to An Khe, we were there only for a day or so before moving out on another mission, thus the name "An Khe Way Station."

11

CHRISTMAS, VIETNAM—1965

A motor movement of the entire battalion was being made to Pleiku to relieve the 2nd Battalion, 8th Cavalry, as a reserve battalion to provide security for the United States elements in that area. The battalion was now a Battalion Task Force. It included an artillery battery, an engineer platoon, two Chinooks, eight UH-1D helicopters from the 227th Assault Helicopter Battalion, and a troop of the 1st of the 9th Cavalry Squadron.

The motor movement was smooth up Highway 19 to Pleiku. Major Herman, the Executive Officer, was leading the convoy on the ground. I was in the command helicopter, flying overhead to oversee the movement. The battalion closed 1500 hours that afternoon. The relief of the 2nd of the 8th was completed and we were soon the owners of Lake Pleiku, a beautiful lake situated two miles west of Pleiku City.

A bivouac was established with pup tents for the men, squad tents for kitchens, and our regular CP installation. All vehicles were here, as well as the equipment for the Battalion Task Force. The rest of the day was spent establishing the bivouac and organizing security in the form of a battalion perimeter. This period would be a chance to relax a bit and to carry out some essential training for future missions, especially more training on the Chinook ladder, rappelling, and perhaps a parachute jump.

Detailed preparations had gone into the Task Force's stay up here. Captain Mozey, the S-1, went all out to assure a good recreational program, including swimming and boating on the lake. Since the battalion was bivouacked on the lake, there was an excellent opportunity for swimming. Two smooth, sandy beaches were kept in operation during the day. In addition we had a branch of the PX with adequate beer and soft drinks available for off-duty men. A movie was shown every evening, since light discipline was not observed owing to the security of the area. A chapel was established, employing a large cargo parachute. Chaplain Spear worked hard to provide a bit of Christmas spirit and atmosphere.

The battalion began to receive large quantities of Christmas packages which had started arriving during the month of November but had been held during our combat days until we had a chance to receive them. These were packages not only from family and friends to specific individuals, but also large number of packages simply addressed to a company, or perhaps the battalion; or our share of those sent to the division as a whole.

The beatnik activities going on in the Fall resulted in a real repercussion in the form of many civilians in the United States wanting to do something for the soldiers in Vietnam. This resulted in hundreds of letters from a cross section of America. Several civilian organizations adopted companies and battalions. For example, C Company was adopted by Captain Smith's home town. This resulted in large numbers of packages and letters for C Company. The University of Chicago adopted the battalion as a whole. We were receiving large numbers of letters and packages.

When these letters arrived, simply addressed to a soldier, they were parcelled out equally to the companies and to the platoons. The bachelors in the units, especially the sergeants and lieutenants, quickly looked for letters with a return address showing "Miss" and liberally sprinkled with the best perfume. These were the ones they answered themselves.

We answered every letter that came, even though it might be only a short note. I selected two or three that I answered, including one from a twelve-year-old boy in Chicago, with whom I have had an interesting correspondence for a number of months.

The packages consisted of items that for the most part could be used by the troops: candies, gums, toilet articles, books of various types, and other reading materials. Receipt of these small gifts had a tremendous effect on the troops because it was vivid appreciation and proof that the American public did care for the men over here and were proud and aware of what these men were accomplishing and sacrificing in Vietnam. Every day brought its loads of packages, newspapers, and bundles of letters.

Coupled with this had been a drive on the part of Captain Mozey to encourage anyone in the United States connected with the word "Mustang" to remember our battalion. This resulted in letters from a ski organization in Florida who manufactured a Mustang-type ski and the promise of several pairs of water skis, although I was not sure where we could use them, although at the moment we could. It brought us a Mustang radio phonograph from a certain maker of that product. I was expecting a Mustang Ford in the mail, but thus far none had come through.

We received large quantities of such things as model airplanes and other models for the troops to build, and games from various game manufacturers, including cards from other sporting-goods companies. I was informed that we also had a letter from a certain manufacturer of a Scotch product from outside the United States, who assured us that a case of his best product was en route to Vietnam from Australia. Incidentally, this case never arrived. I assume that it was waylaid by some well-meaning soul.

Of interest also was the desire and the assistance from the Monsanto Chemical Company, who volunteered to provide the battalion with the roofing for the Chapel. I mentioned previously the fine chapel under construction by the battalion back at An Khe. A letter was received from this company, after some publicity received on the project, in which they volunteered to provide the roof from plastic, a product they manufactured. Difficulty developed in trying to arrange shipment to Vietnam. The company itself shipped it to San Francisco; from there we made arrangements for the Army to ship to Vietnam. We know that it arrived in Vietnam, but unfortunately it was never received by the Mustangs. I assume someone else has a nice green plastic roof somewhere in the country. I was always on the lookout from the air for a green roof for which the owner could not properly identify the source.

*   *   *

More relaxation and further establishment of the camp. Word was received that the Chief of Staff, General Johnson, would visit on Christmas Day. He was in Vietnam and had expressed a desire to visit his old regiment, the 8th Cavalry, which he commanded in Korea. The 2nd of the 8th was back at An Khe, in not too good a position for such a visit, the 1st of the 8th all assembled. It was decided that the General would eat Christmas dinner with us. I gave the mission to Captain Roy Martin of B Company to provide the Christmas dinner.

Today and the following day were a fine example of scrounging and working together by the battalion, plus assistance from any and all sources in order to provide a typical Christmas dinner within B Company for the General. A squad tent was located for a dining hall and tables were manufactured by the men of B Company from empty ammunition boxes. Tablecloths were borrowed in the form of sheets from one of the hospitals. All of the available silverware and dishes throughout the battalion and within the Pleiku area were assembled. The plan was to have representatives from each of the companies and the battalion Headquarters join General Johnson for dinner. This would include the company commanders, the 1st Sergeants, and two soldiers from each company, as well as key members of the staff: Sergeant Major Herbert P. McCullah, my Battalion Sergeant Major, and myself. The Brigade Commander, Colonel Elvey B. Roberts, would be present, as would General Harry W. O. Kinnard, the Division Commander, and General Jack Wright, the Assistant Division Commander. General Johnson was to be accompanied by one aide or escort, a small party.

The battalion was thrilled that the Chief of Staff would be with us. This was going to be a highlight of this Christmas and a major historical event of the Jumping Mustang Battalion.

Plans were completed to initiate training after Christmas. Training would include every man becoming rappel- and Chinook ladder-qualified and executing one parachute jump. A number of replacements had been received who were not up to date on the use of the rappel method and the Chinook ladder.

Since we did not have towers available and had limited time, we planned to initiate the rappel the first time from the aircraft. We would accomplish this after completing the ground training, where the men learned how to handle the ropes and the rappel techniques. They would make the first rappel from a helicopter hovering twenty feet in the air. Using a double rope, one the control rope, it was almost impossible for a man to be injured seriously, even if he fell from the rope. The only way he could fall was to let go. If he did, he probably would suffer nothing more serious than a broken bone. The second rappel would be from a hovering helicopter at sixty feet.

Training on the Chinook ladder would be relatively simple, hovering a Chinook helicopter at sixty feet, with the troops climbing up the ladder and then back down three times.

We were refreshing our memory on parachute training, especially parachute landing, falls, and techniques for exiting from the aircraft. Our jumps would be made from UH-1D helicopters with the pickup zone and the drop zone adjacent to the battalion area, thereby simplifying the entire matter.

A second battalion mission, that of security—actually the primary reason we were up here—would entail continued reconnaissance by the staff, company commander, and myself of the entire area within a radius of fifty miles of Pleiku.

The officers and men assigned at Pleiku to the various United States installations had been jumpy since the Battle of the Ia Drang. The Battle of the Ia Drang saw the defeat of one North Vietnamese division formerly in this area. Although the NVA had been driven back across the border, the rumors were still strong that the Viet Cong or the NVA would make an attempt to do some damage to the Pleiku area, especially during Christmas.

Within the battalion this was quite a joke. We believed that the Viet Cong and NVA, particularly from the shattered enemy division, were pretty well defeated, and we did not expect to receive any trouble from them for quite some time. It was also interesting to see the attitude of the "Brave Soldiers" in the Pleiku area who were certain that there was a Viet Cong or an NVA regiment behind every bush. This was in part contributed by the South Vietnamese, who had much the same feeling, owing to the shortage of troops in the area, both Vietnamese and United States. There had been little friendly patrolling other than by our own battalion and our predecessor, who remained here after the Battle of the Ia

Drang. At any rate, we were busy on recons, searching out the area, and making all possible plans for commitment of the battalion in defense of the Pleiku area, in the event there should be an attack.

In addition, we would run a series of search-and-destroy missions in the vicinity of Kontum. These exercises were primarily the movement of artillery batteries or artillery pieces into areas in the vicinity of the Special Forces Camp designed to provide additional artillery or fire support where there had not been this type of support in the past. A rifle company accompanied each one of the batteries. This project had been under the command of the commander of the Air Cavalry Troop from the 1st of the 9th Cavalry Squadron, now working with the battalion. I had gone on several recons with the 1st of the 9th Cavalry, who were very familiar with the area. These exercises and movements of a company with the artillery out to the various areas were excellent training, both for the artillery and for our own battalion.

A third mission had been given us, to secure the arrival of the 3rd Brigade, 25th Division, who were to commence landing at the new Pleiku Airfield beginning a day or so after Christmas. The advance party was already here, including commander of the brigade. The leader was looking over the area. The bivouac area that the new brigade would occupy was adjacent to the new Pleiku Airfield, between our battalion location and the airfield. We were assisting the advance party in plans and preparations for laying out their bivouac. Our mission was to secure the bivouac for the first two weeks, secure the landing of the aircraft at the airfield, and assure the uninterrupted movement of the new unit from the new Pleiku Airfield by vehicle to the bivouac nearby.

This was Christmas Eve. The pre-Christmas religious services were conducted by Chaplain Spear in the parachute-silk chapel, with many of the men present.

Christmas finally arrived, and with it at 1100 hours came the Chief of Staff, General Johnson. B Company cooks and many others worked all night to make sure that the Christmas dinner would be first-rate. Christmas dinner was one of our first real A-ration meals. The supply of the Christmas dinner to the units had been good. There was turkey, cranberry sauce, ice cream, and all the fresh vegetables that go with it—a complete Army Christmas dinner. Our hat was off to the Division Quartermaster, who had been able to assure that these nice Christmas foods arrived in time and in good condition in the forward area.

Colonel Elvey B. Roberts flew in and was quickly shown throughout the area. In about thirty minutes, General Kinnard and General Wright arrived for a similar look. We all met General Johnson when he flew in. General Johnson made a quick tour through each of the companies and talked to as many men as possible prior to dinner. He had a friendly manner. It was most interesting to watch him as he spoke with the troopers. This was a real highlight for the troops, not only to see their Chief of Staff, but to be able to get a chance to talk with him.

The battalion staff, the commanders, and the senior NCO's were drawn up in front of the temporary mess tent for the General to meet them prior to lunch. He passed down the line, visiting with each man momentarily. We then went in to dinner and were served a fine Christmas dinner by Captain Martin's men. The General was most complimentary about the dinner and about the battalion. At the conclusion of dinner, he made a short tour of the remainder of the battalion area, especially to the Chapel, where he talked with Chaplain Spear. He was most impressed with the temporary chapel and the efforts of Chaplain Spear to provide a Christmas atmosphere.

As he departed from the Chapel, Captain Mozey, the Adjutant, arranged for the presentation of a Montagnard crossbow with arrows to the General. With the photographers present, I presented this bow to General Johnson, and he accepted for the United States Army. This was a memento of the battalion and of the 2nd Corps Tactical Zone, where there were so many Montagnards, as well as of Vietnam itself. The General made a short speech to us and after a few minutes departed to visit other Army units belonging to the 1st Air Cavalry in An Khe.

The rest of the day was spent quietly, most men relaxing, getting ready for whatever might come the first of the year.

A sergeant in B Company:

No one can convince me that being at Pleiku was an R and R except for the first day when I did go swimming. We had more security, more guards, and more patrols.

Then Bravo got some real news. The General was coming! The General! There were about seven of them and we didn't even have a table. Wow, yet Bravo came through. I'll never realize how so much happened so fast and preparations could go so smooth. Yes, it was Captain Martin. Seemed like everything good was Captain Martin. That was the general feeling of everyone in Bravo Company now. It was true, too. By now he was father, mother, and generally our hero at this point. He kept us going when the rough got rougher. I'll never forget Christmas night when he and I and several others sat down in the CP and had a C-ration together. It was the best C-ration I had ever eaten. He ate a C-ration by the numbers, not wasting even the peanut butter.

Training began in earnest on the 26th, with the companies taking turns at rappelling and the Chinook ladder and conducting patrols throughout the area, as well as performing the escort missions of the artillery in the Kontum area. The helicopter reconnaissance of the entire area continued with the staff and myself, including the other elements of Task Force, in order to get thoroughly familiar with the area. We received a tentative warning of a forthcoming operation beginning the early part of January along the Cambodian border. The Jumping Mustang Battalion had been assigned a large area of operation extending along the Cambodian border for about twenty miles. Each day in the course of the reconnoitering of the entire Pleiku area to carry out my current mission, I flew over this new area to make the recon for and preparation of the final plan for our assault on 5 January and the search-and-destroy operation accompanying it.

The first flight over this area was rather shocking, because one saw nothing but jungle growth; whether from the higher level or on making a low-level flight on the treetops, it was equally bad. Some trees rose up to 150 or 200 feet, and the jungle was dense. Other places, the trees varied from scrub twenty to thirty feet high up to fifty- or sixty-foot trees. It appeared that landing zones would be difficult to find.

After a second, third, and fourth flight throughout the area, though, my opinion began to change. As one looked over an area, it became more familiar and things not seen in the first pass began to show themselves. First, little clearings on the ground, trails, huts, or little villages semi-hidden in the trees popped into view. After the fourth day, you could see landing zones everywhere. Maybe they were only one-bird, or two-bird, or maybe five-bird. Within a short period of time the staff and I had prepared our plan and issued the necessary orders for the battalion's new mission.

A highlight of these recons, according to the company commanders, was a flight in the command helicopter with me as the pilot. You must either be high in the air at about 2500 feet above the ground to avoid snipers, or else down in the treetops. One of the company commanders was not too enthused about seeing the tops of the trees brushing the skids of the helicopter as we flitted in and out through the valleys, contouring in order to get a quick look at the landing zones and the terrain itself. I found that Captain Corey, an Air Force type, my Air Force Liaison Officer, did not like low-level flying either. However, this was a major way to accomplish a recon of this type, and both the company commanders and the Air Force Liaison Officer were going to have to learn to live with it, which they did.

We began jump training, making parachute jumps from UH-1D helicopters. Every man was able to get his first and only jump in Vietnam. Jumps were initiated back at the An Khe area, where we were able to jump one-third of the battalion. We were able on this day and the following day to finish off the rest of the battalion. This really aroused the old Airborne spirit within the battalion. A group of paratroopers knows nothing better than to jump, and sometimes low morale and spirit could be revitalized easily by a parachute jump. Therefore, the Airborne spirit was running high in the battalion at this time.

The Chinook-ladder training was completed and also the rappel from the helicopter. I made my first rappel from a UH-1D. It was similar to the rappel made off the cliffs as was done in Ranger training at Fort Benning, Georgia, and in the mountains of Dahlonega, Georgia. My radio operators and I successfully qualified at this skill we would need in the event that the command group had to use this method of entry into combat.

The mission of the securing the 3rd Brigade, 25th Division, was working satisfactorily. The Brigade arrived by C-141 aircraft direct from CONUS. They landed at the New Pleiku Airfield and were moved rapidly to their bivouacs. My mission was to assist them in any way we could, and specifically to care for the security aspects. The first night, two companies of their troops were on the perimeter. In coordination with the commander of the unit, I made certain that these new troops did not have ammunition in their weapons, that they stayed in their holes and did no shooting, even though there were some snipers or an attack on the perimeter. It was always best for new troops not to have to protect themselves the first night, because they were all jumpy and trigger-happy. There might be disastrous consequences if this principle was not used. This system worked extremely well, and on the second or third night the new troopers of the 3rd Brigade, 25th Division, were able to join on the perimeter under our control and accomplished a credible job. At the same time we included them in recon missions and patrols with our own patrols to get familiar with the area. We were performing for the 3rd Brigade, 25th Division, a mission similar to that which the 1st Brigade, 101st Airborne Division, had performed on the arrival of the 1st Air Cavalry at An Khe.

Preparations continued for the forthcoming mission on the Cambodian border. We had two or three minor enemy alerts within the area that proved to be false alarms. There had been reports of repeated sighting of an enemy battalion within three or four miles of Pleiku City; however, after investigation when reconnaissance elements moved in to search out the area, negative results were obtained. However, we did stay on the alert and each one of these threats was investigated quickly, either by the Air Cavalry troops from the 1st of the 9th Squadron under my control, or by moving a platoon or company of our own battalion into the area to search it out. An intensive fire-support program was maintained throughout Pleiku, employing all of the tube artillery within the area, to assure an effective H and I program on potential enemy targets.

On this day General Westmoreland came for a visit to

the battalion, spent a few minutes with the troops, and observed our parachute training. It was at this time that he announced that a new rule would be in effect within Vietnam in the near future. Owing to the shortage of aircraft, parachute jumps would no longer be necessary beginning 1 December in order for the qualified paratroopers assigned to Airborne units to draw their jump pay. I was glad that we had been able to get one jump for the battalion, for it looked as if there would not be additional training jumps unless we were going to have an actual Airborne mission. This had a bad effect in one way in that we would not be able to maintain a high degree of jump proficiency, but it did assure jump pay for all the troopers, one of the primary incentives and a major morale factor.

During this entire period while at the lake, the troops had a chance to relax, catch up on sleep a little bit more than they normally had, and enjoy swimming at the lake. Each afternoon, accompanied by my radio operators, I went down for a swim and a beer from the concessions operated by the civilians along the lake shore. This was a beautiful area and the water was clean. It was good to see the troopers relaxing. It reminded one of one of the resort beaches back in the United States.

A highlight this day was a memorial service for the eleven Jumping Mustangs killed at Ben Khe in the battle of 18 December. General Harry W. O. Kinnard was invited to this memorial service. The battalion, less those essential for carrying out the missions in progress, was assembled on the side of the hill overlooking the beautiful lake. Chaplain Spear established an altar on the side of a hill. The chapel was the blue sky itself.

A single pair of highly polished jump boots stood in front of the Altar, representing the eleven troopers killed in battle. The ceremony started with a short remembrance by Chaplain Spear, followed by a few minutes' speech from each of the company commanders whose men had been killed. When they finished I said a few words about the tremendous job the battalion had accomplished and the outstanding job that these men had performed. I was followed by Chaplain Spear with the Protestant service for those who were Protestant; then the 1st Airborne Brigade Chaplain conducted the Catholic portion of the service. This was a simple but touching service. At the end, after the firing of the Rifle Squad and the sounding of Taps by the Bugler, there was a lump in our throats, with a feeling of pride in the battalion and in what these men had died for.

The last day of December brought with it the conclusion of our Pleiku operation. The next few days were devoted to wrapping up the final mission with the 3rd Brigade of the 25th and preparations for the new assault on the Cambodian border. Reconnaissance was intensified by the battalion, including the company commanders and supporting commanders working with us for this battle.

I was concerned over the initial landing zones which had been selected. We planned to use two: one for the battalion minus, and the other for a company. The one company LZ was to position an artillery battery to support the battalion as well as other units.

The movement of artillery into the area of operation became a principle of our airmobile operations. This was accomplished thus: a rifle company made an air assault to seize the LZ, the artillery battery moved in, and then the assault was continued within range of the artillery. The first landing zone would take one company and the artillery. The second landing zone, the battalion minus. From then on we would conduct a series of search-and-destroy operations, leapfrogging every day by air assault to a new base and continuing search-and-destroy operations.

While at the lake, and during our parachute jump, one young soldier in jumping from the helicopter caught his parachute harness on the skid. He must have been embarrassed and astonished as he slid out of the door, began his count, and then received what he thought was the opening shock; when he opened his eyes, he found himself dangling from the helicopter skid. This happened rarely, and in this case one of the safety men in the helicopter reached out and helped hold him as the helicopter flew rapidly back for a landing and touched down to a hover, where a man on the ground removed the trooper from the skid. We were concerned he might be worried about his next jump. Therefore I had him go right back up in another helicopter and perform his scheduled parachute jump. This he did easily and without any problem.

One captain came in for his share of humor, especially concerning his operations down at the lake. I found that during his establishment of recreation activities, he planned to let some of the young ladies who were not concessionaires come into the recreation area to ply their wares on the beach. He had what he called "Boom-boom Parlors," a common name referring to prostitution in Vietnam. I was horrified when I learned that I was about to be operating an establishment of this kind, and quickly gave him pointed instructions, much to the disappointment of the troops, I am certain, to remove any and all such people from the premises. This he did, but from then on the recreation area at the lake was referred to jokingly by the Jumping Mustangs as the "Boom-boom" area.

Sergeant Major Herbert P. McCullah, the Battalion Sergeant Major, was still grumbling and griping about the fact that when he was on Rest and Recuperation (R and R), the Battalion had its major battle on 18 December. He had departed the day before for Hong Kong on the scheduled R and R, little knowing that we would be in for what became the battalion's first major battle and one of the biggest participated in. He still had not lived it down, not only in kidding from the other NCO's, but in his own feelings, because he felt he missed an important battle during which he would have been of great help and service to the battalion.

The ABC Team under Mr. John Hughes was still with us, shooting valuable footage about the battalion and the Task Force while we were in the Pleiku area which would be a part of his TV spectacular. He and his crew performed outstandingly with the Jumping Mustangs. This day in the afternoon we had a simple ceremony with a token element from each of the companies: a decoration ceremony for the battalion in which I awarded medals to the various heroes within the companies. At the same time, a Battalion Crest was awarded to each of Mr. Hughes' four members, making them "Jumping Mustangs" and entitling them to a free drink from any Jumping Mustang anywhere in the world.

These four civilian photographers and writers endeared themselves to the battalion in the way they lived and worked with us to record our story, asking no special privileges and requiring only what any other soldier required. In the movement and in the various battles, they additionally had to carry their heavy equipment with them: tape machines and cameras, which made their movement even doubly more severe than some of our own.

Unfortunately, they had not anticipated the battle of 18 December either, and had gone to Saigon to process film; thus they returned at the end of the battle and missed this most interesting episode, not only of the battalion but for A Company, the main heroes of the TV spectacular. At any rate, on this date we made them all Jumping Mustangs at the ceremony.

The ceremony also gave me an excellent opportunity to again congratulate the battalion for the tremendous job that they had performed heretofore and to give them a little idea of what the future held, especially the forthcoming battle. I was sure that our new campaign would be equally successful.

The "Year of the Snake" for the Chinese calendar ended on this date. The year 1966, beginning the next day, was the "Year of the Horse." This was symbolic of the 1st Air Cavalry Division with its great horse's head on the patch and of the Jumping Mustang Battalion with the White Stallion rearing on the Jumping Mustang guidon. We were convinced that 1966 would truly be the "Year of the Horse," in which not only the 1st Air Cavalry Division, but our own battalion would play a major role.

12

ON THE CAMBODIAN BORDER

The operation on the Cambodian border, designated "Matador" by the Airborne Brigade and the Division and "Ripping Mustang" by the Jumping Mustangs, was the most publicized battle for the Jumping Mustang Battalion.

Time magazine, 21 January 1966, ran the following article.

No sanctuary. That was remedied last week in a massive assault called Operation Matador. Swooping down onto the Vietnamese side of the Ton Le San River which forms the border with Cambodia went four sizeable units of the 1st Air Cavalry Division. Planes and rocket-firing helicopters first softened the river bank landing zone with shells and napalm and the "First Team" rode in on their choppers. In some places the brush was too thick and high for proper landings, so that the troops leaped fifteen feet to the snake-infested ground, producing several sprained ankles, one broken leg and two bullet-riddled twelve-foot pythons. In other spots the troopers shinnied down sixty-foot aluminum ladders swaying from Chinook copters overhead, one special Reconnaissance Team slid down a rope in seven seconds from a copter hovering a full hundred and fifty feet above the jungle carpet.

The 1st Air Cav's mission was to determine if the Communists were indeed using Cambodia as both funnel and sanctuary for troops infiltrating from the north. If so, the First Team hoped to provoke an attack, giving the US a chance to act on last month's warning that pursuit across the Cambodian border would henceforth follow a continuing attack from the other side.

Doubt about the enemy's use of Cambodia was quickly dispelled. Beside one clearly defined crossing point on the river bank stood a camp with 400 lean-to structures, 200 foxholes and a small hospital— fit for a regiment and freshly evacuated. Gathered on the opposite Cambodian bank of the shallow river, only fifty feet wide at that point, were ill-concealed sampans loaded with ammunition boxes. At one point a GI patrol even caught sight of 12 uniformed North Vietnamese soldiers hastily paddling across the river into Cambodia. 1st Air Cav Lieutenant Colonel Kenneth Mertel took his helicopter down the middle of the narrow stream, hoping to draw fire, which presumably would have justified a US response. None came. But now that the US had penetrated right to the threshold of what had long been the enemy's privileged domain, chances were it would come soon enough.

The operation also received a quote from the Associated Press, published in the *Stars and Stripes* Wednesday, 12 January 1966. The item was headlined "Red in a Rush Neglects to Brush."

Along the Cambodian Frontier (AP). A Communist General was in such a rush to escape the Americans that he left his toothbrush behind.

Troopers of the US 1st Air Cavalry Division found the toothpaste and toothbrush in a blue and white checkered bag Saturday when they swooped down into a Communist hideout on the Republic of Vietnam border, less than 100 feet from the neighboring kingdom of Cambodia.

Pinned to the bag was a single silver star of a Brigadier General. It was retrieved when men of the "Jumping Mustangs" Battalion burned the camp big enough to house more than 1000 Communist soldiers.

It was the first time American fighting men in Vietnam had knowingly ventured up to the edge of Cambodia. Heretofore Americans had strict orders to stay at least three miles from the frontier to avoid charges of violating Cambodian sovereignty.

The Cavalrymen chose a spot where the frontier is well defined by the (Ton Le San) River about 40 miles west of Pleiku in South Vietnam Central Highlands and about 240 miles of Saigon.

A third quote from the Eugene *Register Guard*, Eugene, Oregon, 10 January 1966, headed "US Troops Strike Swiftly," by Eddy Adams of the Associated Press, included the following:

It was different than last time the Cavalry was in this general region. In November North Vietnamese regular soldiers slugged it out toe to toe in the Ia Drang Valley, southwest of Pleiku, close to Cambodia.

The Cavalrymen are not downhearted. Mertel noted wryly that 1965, the "Year of the Snake" in the Chinese calendar, is over, and added, "This is our year. It's the Year of the Horse."

Thus began the operation on the Cambodian border, providing the reason for the name of this book. The "Year of the Horse" came from the designation of the Chinese calendar for 1966 and also was given to honor the 1st Air Cavalry Division with its big yellow patch with the black horse's head.

The purpose of the operation was to determine whether there were any VC or NVA units in the area along the Cambodian border west of Pleiku. Intelligence reports indicated one main-force battalion of approximately 300 men. Additionally, there was one platoon operating in the area. The first landing zones selected would provide an opportunity to search out the general location of a reported Viet Cong way station and infiltration routes from north to south along the border. The mission of the battalion was to conduct an airmobile assault into its assigned sector and conduct a series of search-and-destroy operations.

It was anticipated that this operation would take two weeks, in which the Jumping Mustang Battalion, along with three other battalions of the 1st Airborne Brigade, would

search out an area forty miles in length along the Cambodian
border. In addition to the organic battalions of the Airborne
Brigade, one additional battalion from the 2nd Brigade was
under operational control for a portion of the operation.

The battalion moved by motor from the Lake Pleiku
area, having been relieved by the 2nd of the 5th, to an
assembly area in the vicinity of the Brigade Base near the
Stadium. The Stadium was the site of the old Brigade Command Post location during the Ia Drang Campaign. This area
would be used as a base on numerous future occasions. Many
will remember it as being near to a fine tea plantation, one of
the best in South Vietnam. The relief was completed and the
battalion closed in its new area by 1700 hours. Local security
was established. The battalion prepared to spend the night,
ready for the assault the following morning. Plans were
complete, orders were issued, and we were ready to go
again.

The first phase of the operation began at 0745 hours,
with a landing by A Company on a landing zone known as
"Bronco." This operation was intended to provide security for
the movement of B Battery, 2nd of the 19th Artillery to LZ
"Bronco" to provide support for the operation.

The assault on LZ "Bronco" was preceded by a thirty-
minute tactical air strike in which the Air Force's close
air-support fighters did an outstanding job in hitting likely
target areas in the vicinity of the landing zone. This was
followed by a two-minute preparation by the aerial artillery.
At the end of the artillery preparation, the flight of twenty-
four UH-1D helicopters from the 227th Assault Helicopter
Battalion landed on LZ "Bronco."

There was minimum enemy contact, with A Company
receiving only one casualty from a short burst of enemy
automatic weapon fire. The landing zone was secured by 0750
hours.

At this time B Battery, 2nd of the 19th Artillery, commenced landing by Chinook helicopter on LZ "Bronco." A
total of six guns were brought in. The battery was ready to
fire by 0850 hours in support of the operation.

Commencing at 0855 hours, B Company landed at LZ
"Stallion" and secured the landing zone. The assault was

preceded by an air strike from 0815 to 0835. This excellent strike was supported by tube artillery from LZ "Bronco" from 0835 to 0850. Upon lifting of the tubes, the ARA picked up the fire for the next three minutes, just prior to the landing of the twenty-four UH-1D helicopters on the landing zone. B Company landed without incident or enemy contact.

They were followed immediately by D Company from the Stadium to LZ "Stallion" and lastly by C Company, moving from Lake Pleiku area where they had remained for the night, not having been relieved of this mission until this date. With the closing of C Company at LZ "Stallion," the battalion completed its assault and occupied two landing zones along with a battery of artillery by 1040 hours. After landing, all units assumed defensive positions and made preparations for the second phase of the operation, the search-and-destroy mission within the area of the two landing zones.

A portion of A Company began a series of search-and-destroy missions around LZ "Bronco." At LZ "Stallion," the Reconnaissance Platoon moved out to the east, C Company to the north, and B Company to the west, forming a cloverleaf design around the LZ. Their purpose was to search out enemy personnel and equipment and, specifically, to look for evidence of the way station and the trails running through the area.

B Company discovered what appeared to be a way station at 1230 hours. An air strike was called, resulting in secondary explosions with a cloud of white smoke rising about 500 feet in the air. A Company spotted two Viet Cong suspects in green uniform and soft caps without weapons, but lost contact with them. A search by B Company of the way station could not determine the reason for the secondary explosion, but there was evidence that personnel had occupied this area a few hours before, and it definitely was a Viet Cong or NVA way station. There was also evidence of a trail system as had been reported through intelligence sources.

All units returned to their sectors prior to dark and set up defensive positions. An Active H and I program was conducted throughout the night by both artillery and mortars, and a series of patrols were sent out from each of the two landing zones.

A "Mad Minute" was fired during the evening hours

commencing at 1930 and again at 0600 in the morning—a one-minute firing of all weapons. There was no enemy contact during the night and the battalion spent a quiet night.

The Battalion Forward Command Post was on LZ "Stallion." The defensive fires were set up so that A Company could fire its mortars from LZ "Bronco" one mile away to LZ "Stallion." LZ "Stallion" reciprocated with mortars from D Company in support of A Company. During the adjustment of mortars late in the afternoon while I was sitting at the Command Post eating a C-ration, a round of high explosive suddenly burst in the middle of the landing zone 125 yards from the Command Post. My first reaction was enemy fire, but since there had been no evidence of enemy contact and I knew that A Company was registering its mortars, I was of the opinion that it was probably A Company's firing.

A radio call to Captain Danielsen verified that he was conducting registration. I relaxed and took another bite of C-ration, just as a second high-explosive round burst even closer, only seventy-five yards away. This was too much. I called Captain Danielsen and told him to cease firing; to find out what was wrong before he hit me; that I would not give him a third chance. Although he denied that it was A Company mortars, it was pretty obvious it was. It took many days and months for Captain Danielsen to live down this little episode of trying to knock out the Battalion Command Post.

We were fortunate in another episode concerning 81mm mortar ammunition. We had been getting some ammunition that was deteriorated and quite old, causing erratic or short rounds. D Company was adjusting mortars over C Company, which occupied the portion of the perimeter to the north. A short round from D Company landed right in the middle of C Company troops on the perimeter; however, it turned out to be a white phosphorus round, and owing to the softness of the ground when it hit, little damage or injury occurred to personnel or equipment. One man received a small piece of white phosphorus on his hand which burned considerably but did not cause his evacuation.

It was interesting to note that this short round could be heard by everybody within the perimeter, and it was obvious that it was going to go short. The cough of the mortar did not sound right.

Captain Tabb of D Company checked his mortars, found

no errors, and prepared to continue the registration. A second round was fired and fell in exactly the same place. This, too, was a white phosphorus. C Company, not quite sure what was going on with the mortars, had taken cover; therefore, no one was hurt this time. A quick order to Captain Tabb and a thorough check resulted in no more short rounds within the battalion sector. I was quite happy that these shorts had been white phosphorus and not high-explosive, or there might have been personnel wounded or even killed. Trouble with mortar ammunition continued to plague us for the future. C Company never quite forgave Captain Tabb for firing on them, and this caused some humor for a number of weeks.

It was interesting to note the names of the landing zones used by the Jumping Mustang Battalion. If a tendency toward the "horsey" set was noted, that was correct. Having the name "Jumping Mustang Battalion," we tried to select names for landing zones that had something to do with the animal itself. Our operations were labeled "Something Mustang." The designated names of operations by battalion ended within a few weeks, as higher headquarters began to designate each operation with the name of a President.

A recap of the day's activities that evening prior to going to bed indicated that the battalion had completed its planned air assault on schedule; the lift was performed exceptionally well; the fire support all came through as planned. We were disappointed in not finding more of the enemy, but there was sufficient evidence that he was in the area, or had been there. There were many trails that showed footprints and evidence of recent use. Food was located—in one case, fresh fruits and cooked vegetables, including rice, were found in the huts.

The battalion continued a series of search-and-destroy operations with searches in all directions around both LZ "Stallion" and LZ "Bronco." Negative enemy contact was made, but continuing evidence of the enemy was found. B Company found several hundred punji-sticks bundled, about three weeks old. The Recon Platoon found a series of eight to ten huts with sleeping capacity for eight to twenty men. These were destroyed. C Company found along the trails squad-size sleeping areas that appeared to be only three to five days old. In another case, B Company found twenty-three campfire sites. All units returned to the battalion area by dark and established defensive positions with "Mad Minutes" fired prior to dark. A good H and I program was planned to search out likely target areas found during the day and from continued air reconnaissance by myself and others.

During both the preceding day's operation and this date, I spent most of my time in the command helicopter in contact with the elements of the battalion as they searched the areas. Landing zones were readily available throughout the battalion zone; therefore, if a unit found something of interest, it was not difficult for me to land, move in, and join them. The usual Command and Control Team accompanied me during these flights.

In an operation of this sort, when it was mostly a search-and-destroy mission and there was little enemy contact, the battalion commander could spend four to five hours in the air in supervision of the operation.

My recons from the air provided the necessary information, along with the preplan for the mission, to determine exactly what we were going to do the following day. With the battalion assembled in the two landing zones, it was not difficult to make a quick flight to "Bronco" to see A Company to give Captain Danielsen instructions personally, or to visit the other company commanders at "Stallion" and lay out the next day's plan. I made it a point to go to the commanders rather than calling them to battalion, although occasionally this, too, occurred when we were in a close landing zone and it could be easily accomplished.

We had decided the day preceding that there was little point in searching further the area that we were in, since it was obvious that the enemy were no longer there. The next phase of the operation called for a battalion air assault from "Bronco" and "Stallion" to a new landing zone right on the Cambodian border, on the friendly side, to be designated LZ "Maverick."

The landing zone was named primarily because it looked as though it would be a difficult one. Major Floyd Worthland, A Company Commander of the 227th Assault Helicopter Battalion, and I had made a series of recons the day before to pick a landing zone that would put us in position near the

Cambodian border to search the high ground running along the river and to check the trails known to exist on the east bank. The landing zone selected from a study of the map and by our own reconnaissance appeared to be adequate. It was really the side of a hill—the lower or bottom portion. The LZ was covered with a heavy undergrowth which appeared from the air to be two or three feet high. We expected some difficulty in landing, but felt that in most cases the birds would be able to land for a short enough period for the troops to dismount. This proved to be incorrect; little did we know that LZ "Maverick" was appropriately named.

C Company had the mission of making this first air assault with twenty-four helicopters from A Company, of the 227th, into LZ "Maverick." The operation was preceded by a fifteen-minute close air support followed by twelve minutes of tube artillery from LZ "Bronco" and two minutes of aerial artillery. The tactical air strike was especially effective because the target was clearly defined, and once Captain Corey in the command helicopter arranged for the marking of the LZ, this time by a white-phosphorus round fired from the artillery into the landing zone, the Air Force fighter pilots went right to work. Napalm, bombs, and 20mm cannon, as well as machine guns, were used. We suspected that there might be enemy on the landing zone and did a thorough job of plastering the area, especially the high ground to the west that was really not part of the landing zone but dominated most of it.

C Company moved in and executed the lift successfully. The helicopters were unable to touch their skids to the ground, for when coming in it was found that the supposed three- to four-foot-high brush was actually twelve to fifteen feet in height. This necessitated the helicopters coming to a high hover, the troops actually bailing out, or jumping, from the skids of the helicopter to the ground. This was accomplished easily and C Company, with over 140 personnel, were on the ground in a matter of minutes with only one broken leg and two or three minor sprains, caused by the "parachute jump" from the UH-1D helicopters.

I was relieved to receive the call from Captain Smith that the company was on the ground; that although the landing zone was not quite what had been anticipated, they were able to carry out their mission of seizing the landing zone; that there was no enemy contact; and that personnel were proceeding immediately to improve the landing zone so that birds could touch down to let the troops off.

I decided to go on the ground and join C Company immediately. I, too, got credit for that first "parachute jump," as Major Propes, Captain Wolfsenholme, my radio operators, and I jumped from the skids of the hovering command helicopter into the brush. Most interesting was the "bail out" of my two radio operators. I jumped out and from the ground watched the other members of the control team dismount.

One radio operator, Corporal Jordan, jumped down with Corporal Hill ready to go. I thought Hill had cleared the helicopter when I gave a signal to the pilot to pull out. Hill was not completely ready to jump; therefore he more or less fell from the helicopter, landing on top of Captain Wolfsenholme, the Artillery Officer. This caused much confusion and amusement later, as the two of them were thrashing around in the brush.

Corporal Jordan lost his radio momentarily, dropping it to the ground first, himself following. He actually was standing on it and we were unable to locate it until minutes later. Within five minutes the command group was reorganized with all equipment assembled.

Then began the difficult job of hacking a way through the heavy underbrush to the top of the hill overlooking the landing zone, which was to be the Battalion CP. Lieutenant John B. Cater, one of the Assistant S-3's, had gone in with C Company to move to that location and initially set up the Battalion Command Post. I knew its location and started the command group forward, hacking our way through the brush with the machetes. It took us twenty minutes to reach that area, and it was necessary to follow a compass heading, or we would never have reached there. I personally learned the importance of a sharp machete, for the ones that my radio operators carried were not sharp. This was the last time they ever went on an operation with a dull tool.

The landing continued, with D Company executing its landing on "Maverick," followed by A Company from landing zone "Bronco," necessitating a shuffle between A and B Companies. A Company had been engaged in static operations on LZ "Bronco." The tube artillery remained in "Bronco" until sufficient area was cut away in "Maverick" to bring the battery in. I decided to make a switch with B Company moving by helicopter to "Bronco" to relieve A Company, A Company being the last unit to move in to "Maverick." This left the battalion disposed with B Company at "Bronco" along with B Battery, 2nd of the 19th Artillery, and the battalion minus on "Maverick."

The battalion initiated a series of search-and-destroy missions that afternoon with A Company operating to the east, the Recon Platoon operating along the river to the south, and C Company along the river to the north to search out the trails and see what was in the area. There was negative enemy contact throughout the afternoon; by 1800 hours all units had reassembled back at LZ "Maverick" to establish a perimeter defense for the night.

In reviewing the final reports of the day's operation, in spite of the roughness of LZ "Maverick," only three troopers were evacuated because of sprained ankles and one for a broken leg.

The primary mission of the Engineer Platoon working with the battalion and D Company minus the Recon Platoon was to improve the LZ to accept the maximum number of birds and to receive an artillery battery in the next day or so.

We were somewhat disappointed that we found no enemy, because we had surely expected them. On the initial landing on "Maverick" earlier in the morning, across the river we spied twelve Viet Cong with weapons moving rapidly from a small village deeper into Cambodia. We could not fire on them, since they were on the Cambodian side of the river.

This close to the Cambodian border, and knowing that there were enemy across the river, we expected incoming artillery and mortar fire during the night. This did not take place.

I was proud of the manner in which the battalion had performed during this operation. Air assaults were becoming commonplace, employing both the UH-1D helicopters and the Chinook.

Defensive concentrations were fired in and an active H and I program was conducted. A "Mad Minute" was fired at

2000 hours and again at 0600 the following morning. There was negative enemy contact throughout the night.

The following day a series of search-and-destroy operations were conducted along the east side of the river, including overland movement both by foot and by Chinook helicopter to an appropriate landing zone. A Company air-assaulted into a two-bird LZ designated LZ "Lancer"; it conducted a search-and-destroy operation within that area and eventually returned by "Maverick."

D Company continued an overland mission to LZ "Cheyenne," south fifteen hundred meters along the river. C Company continued a series of operations to the north, finally joined up at LZ "Lancer" with A Company, and returned by Chinook helicopter along with A Company. Negative enemy contact was made, but D Company did discover a large cache of rice along a well-worn trail leading south.

During all of these operations we employed tactical air power and artillery extensively. Any movement into a landing zone was made under the cover of tube artillery, ARA, and tactical air strike, if possible. The weather was ideal during the entire period, both for airmobile operations and for the Air Force close air-support operations. During the operation we concentrated on the employment of fire power to smooth techniques, and improved our control procedures for the future.

The battalion returned to LZ "Maverick" for the night. Under the cover of darkness the Recon Platoon moved to an ambush site south along the river astride the main trail in the vicinity of the previously located regimental bivouac. This bivouac was capable of taking a whole series of troops. It was a most interesting installation, located astride both sides of the trail that ran along the east side of the river. It was well hidden in the trees and could not be seen from the air. The camp itself consisted of a series of one-man frame shelters from which a poncho could be stretched easily to make a small hut.

Many earth stoves designed for cooking so that smoke would be dissipated and heat could not be detected by infrared devices in the air were located throughout the area. There was evidence of chickens having been cooked recently, with feathers scattered throughout the area. In addition, the unit barbers had been at work, for in several locations human hair could be found lying around the stump or rock where the barbers had been plying their trade.

After landing in the regimental bivouac area during the day, I walked back up the trail that passed through LZ "Maverick" and had a branch running between the LZ and the river. This trail itself was wide in many places, wide enough for two men to walk abreast. There were bicycle tracks throughout, some of them with large, balloon-type wheels two inches in width. In many places on the trail, a two-wheel cart had been moved along, carrying heavy equipment.

The trail followed the natural bends of the earth and the stream beds, remaining under the heavy vegetation where it went up a hill, always in the least suspectible area. Looking up through the jungle canopy, one could not see an aircraft except in rare cases. From the air it was almost impossible to see the trail. This was the type of trail that extended on the east side of the river, north fifteen kilometers and south for another ten or fifteen kilometers. It was well used and passed through a series of way stations that abounded throughout the area as in the regimental bivouac area we found. We found little foodstuffs in this area, but our sister battalion, the 2nd of the 8th, north of our area and along the same river, found tons of rice and large quantities of ammunition.

The Recon Platoon was in position by 2030 hours that night, ready with their ambush. I was somewhat anxious about this unit being off alone, although it was within supporting range of the weapons and troops on LZ "Maverick." I was always reluctant to place a small unit, such as a platoon, off by itself. This platoon was a fine platoon, however, and at this stage did not have a Platoon leader but was led by an outstanding noncommissioned officer, PSG Donald Johnson. All three squads were led by fine soldiers, and the Assistant Platoon Leader, PSG Robert Grimes, was an equally outstanding trooper. I had great confidence in this platoon and they were rapidly becoming the best within the battalion. They had tremendous pride and spirit and were especially proud because they had found the largest enemy target, the regimental bivouac, on this operation.

Another night of H and I and intensive patrolling was continued without enemy contact. It was unbelievable that the enemy did not hit us or fire mortars and artillery from across the border.

Communications had been excellent back to the Brigade Base at the Stadium. Although we were operating forty kilometers distance from the Stadium, we were able to contact the Battalion Rear by PRC-25 radio. In addition, the Brigade set up a Forward Command Post at Duc Co, which was a little closer, twenty kilometers distant. We were able to easily maintain communication with the brigade.

My time was spent primarily at the Command Post and in the air keeping track of the units, visiting them, and seeing how the operation was progressing. The troops were beginning to get a little tired now, because we had been doing nothing but walking and hiking around with little chance of finding the enemy.

A Company made a deep air assault south, four miles distance, to search the lower part of the trail complex. C Company was working to the northwest again. The landing zone was prepared sufficiently to take a battery of artillery. This meant that we could close out "Stallion" and move the artillery to "Maverick" to support further operations, not only of ourselves, but also of the 2nd of the 8th. The artillery was moved in successfully, followed by the movement of B Company into an objective area to the east where they conducted a series of search-and-destroy operations prior to moving back into LZ "Maverick" overland that night.

A Company had their big day: during their foot movement, they captured three NVA captives. These prisoners turned out to be from the 33rd Regiment, which had been involved in the Plei Mei/Pleiku action six weeks before. They provided valuable information for our intelligence personnel.

The search-and-destroy mission of the battalion continued throughout the day with a series of air assaults by UH-1D helicopters and Chinooks. These operations had provided a good workout during the past few days, for each company conducted a series of company- and platoon-size air assaults and was able to employ the ladder technique efficiently on several occasions. Two Chinooks accomplished a tremendous job in moving troops to relatively secured areas or from one landing zone that had been secured to another. One bird moved a platoon; therefore, four birds or four sorties were required for one complete rifle company.

Word had been received that the next day the battalion would be extracted and moved back to the Stadium to secure the Brigade Base and stand by as both brigade and division reserve. The additional battalion working with the Airborne Brigade would be pulled back to return to its parent unit for another mission in the Bong Son area, east along the China Sea coast. In addition, the 2nd Brigade would be working forty miles north of our present location, in an area where enemy activity was anticipated. Our battalion would have the job of reserve force for this brigade as well as for the Division.

The Recon Platoon spent another night at the regimental bivouac area along the river trails in ambush, hoping to catch more prisoners. Results were negative. Beginning at 1200 hours, the battalion commenced its move back to the Stadium and the Brigade Base. The move was conducted with six Chinook helicopters. The battalion minus B Company closed back at the Stadium by 1400 hours. B Company remained at "Maverick" until later on in the afternoon when the artillery had completed a displacement by Chinook to Landing Zone "Sioux." When this was completed, B Company moved to join the battalion, closing by 1824 hours.

In addition to securing the base, we had the job of providing security for the 227th and 228th Helicopter Battalions in the helicopter lagger area near II Corps Headquarters referred to as the "Turkey Farm." The "Turkey Farm" was a large, open area where helicopters remained at night and during inoperative periods; where maintenance could be performed under a little more administrative-type conditions; and where lights could be employed, permitting nighttime maintenance. It was not desirable to locate this type of activity in the immediate vicinity of the Brigade Base, especially if there were snipers around, and since lights would invite artillery and mortar fire. It was customary for one rifle company from the reserve battalion to secure the area. The company could be employed by the battalion if needed to carry out the reserve mission for either the 1st or the 2nd Brigade or the Division.

The battalion remained in this reserve location until 17 January, at which time we returned to An Khe by Caribou and on Highway 19 by motor.

This period of occupying the reserve location was a welcome relief. It gave the troops a chance to relax, get some good chow, and clean up a bit. It also provided time for the staff, the company commanders, and myself to continue reconnaissance in the area for future operations and also to make contact with the 2nd Brigade to the north, west of Kontum, to be ready to reinforce the 2nd Brigade if need be.

In addition there was word of a forthcoming operation, probably in the Bong Son area. We were to begin to look at the maps and terrain on the China Sea coast side.

The Stadium had been vastly improved since the last time we were up here, during the Plei Mei/Pleiku operation. At that time, as one would recall, the 3rd Brigade CP was shelled by mortar fire resulting in several casualties. This time the 1st Airborne Brigade decided to improve the positions so that the Command Post could more easily be defended. The perimeter was well dug in with a series of trenches and foxholes, the trenches having been dug in the soft red earth by a ditch-digger. This automatic foxhole digger was a fine piece of equipment and certainly saved a lot of time and effort. The system of trenches had been dug all the way around the Stadium or the base itself; in addition a fine barbwire entanglement was being constructed. Our efforts during the next two or three days included continuation of the barbwire barrier and further improvement of the excavations and positions.

We had been eating C-rations during this past operation; therefore A-rations had stacked up. We started receiving large quantities of fresh meat and fresh eggs as well as some vegetables. During the period in reserve, on the first and second days we had steak three times a day. We almost became sick of it, but between steak for dinner and supper and fresh eggs with all kinds of meat for breakfast, the troops had a chance to fatten up a bit. Some beer and soft drinks were available and were issued to the troops. There was also a good opportunity to check equipment, clean it up, replace what had been lost or damaged, and get ready to go again. We had learned that anytime we had a two- or three-day period in reserve with relative inactivity, it meant that something was going to be happening in the near future and we would be going again soon on a combat mission.

A B Company sergeant recalled the Cambodian border action, including this reserve period.

> We went up to the Ho Chi Minh Trail and Captain Martin shot a big 200 pound deer. We skinned it, cooked some of it and had fresh meat. Then we carried the rest back to the Stadium. It seemed like that was the only time over there when we ever were issued steak, breakfast, dinner and supper. Of course, we threw the deer meat away.
>
> I do remember the time we were searching the river bed and a sniper was firing a few rounds at our security on the right blank. The battalion commander was there and the word got out that we were going to be calling artillery in on the left flank. I had just finished taking a quick shave for the first time in four days and we were going to stop for chow. After eating a quick C-ration and hearing about the artillery request, I personally sized up the situation and decided that we were on low ground and if artillery came in on the ground to our left, there was a possibility of some of them falling around us. Realizing we had some misfortune with artillery two times before, I decided to dig in. I dug a foxhole, (the only one who dug) and was accused of having the fastest entrenching tool in the battalion after that. I guess I dug more holes than any private in Bravo Company but that is why I'm still around for two wars in twenty years.

A couple of days later we had a chance to go over the details of the recent operation and see what mistakes were made and what was done well. The search-and-destroy operations did reveal numerous well-used trails considered to be the infiltration route, with many squad- and regimental-sized bivouac areas along these trails. Large quantities of rice were found throughout.

Two notable findings were the regimental-size bivouac found by the Reconnaissance Platoon, consisting of 300 foxholes and 400 lean-to's, showing recent use. Found also were a hospital, by C Company, close to the border, along the river. This hospital was hidden deep in the trees and included several wards with beds, several storage huts, a kitchen, and numerous supplies.

The three NVA soldiers, captured by A Company on 9 January, provided the best intelligence of the operation. This was the basis for a massive B-52 strike in the Chu Pong area. I was in position to watch the strike. It was spectacular to behold. One could not see or hear the bombers, but one could see contrails high in the air after they passed. Suddenly the earth simply opened up in the target area as the hundreds of bombs of various sizes fell simultaneously in a wide destructive pattern.

Weather throughout the area of operation favored airmobile operations. The terrain in the area provided excellent cover and concealment to a ground force. Landing zones were few and difficult to find, and in all cases required much effort and time to improve. This did not really cause a serious handicap, but did require the use of ingenuity and perseverance. The Ton Le San River proved to be an obstacle to cross except by air or boat. This river was deep and wide in numerous places. It was difficult to use a rope to cross under these circumstances.

Throughout the operation it was evident that the inhabitants of the area, though few, and the VC and NVA forces previously located in the area were moving one to two days away from the United States forces. Indications were that the area had been completely evacuated prior to our arrival. It was obvious that the enemy had prior knowledge of the entire operation.

Fire power was employed in phenomenal quantities. For example, in the assault on LZ "Stallion" and "Bronco" on 5 January a total of twelve sorties for tactical air power were employed. This included two A1E's and four B-57's used in the LZ preparation and a total of four A1E's and two B-57's used for immediate strikes throughout the day. Artillery fired over 100 rounds on that initial operation itself, plus seventy-five H and I that night. The second day of the operation a total of six tactical air sorties were used 6 or 7 January, four on 8 January, four on 9 January, and four on the tenth.

Artillery continued to be used in large quantities. On 8

January a total of forty-six rounds were fired in an LZ preparation, sixty during the day, plus fifty-eight rounds on the H' and I program at night. Large quantities of mortar ammunition were also fired by the 81 mortars.

A recap of damage to the enemy included twenty-one tons of rice captured or destroyed, 169 enemy huts destroyed, thirteen boats or dugouts destroyed, and three NVA captured.

Of interest was the large number of photographers and newspapermen with the battalion. Since this was the first United States battalion on the Cambodian border by design, and was a preplanned operation, the press had been invited. Expecting some interesting stories, they responded well and a total of thirteen joined the battalion.

These were the fighter-type newspapermen—the ones who like to get down with the units. Three of them, including some Australians, joined each of the rifle companies; one was with the Recon Platoon most of the time, the others were with the battalion. All major networks were represented, including CBS, NBC, ABC, and Associated Press. Mr. John Flynn from NBC was interested in taking footage on the Cambodian border. I joined him and moved from the regimental bivouac area which the Recon Platoon located to the shore of the river, where he photographed the opposite side. I spit in the river, as did Mr. Flynn.

The battalion received excellent publicity as a result of this operation and of our treatment of the press. I found that the simplest method to handle the press was to use Sergeant Major Herbert P. McCullah to see that they were taken care of, were guided or escorted where they wanted to go, and were helped with transportation. An Infantry battalion has little transportation, but in this case most of these reporters wanted to be with the troops and see what could be learned. All they really wanted was a place to park their gear and a C-ration to eat. This we supplied. In return we received excellent publicity that appeared in all the networks throughout the United States. Since the operation had been named "Ripping Mustang," at least by our battalion, most of the newspapermen picked up this phrase and also picked up the name of the Jumping Mustang Battalion, which appeared in print many times.

The episode of the capture of the general's toothbrush and toothpaste caught the imagination of two or three of the newspapers and resulted in wide publicity. A photographer, name unknown, took a fine picture of the Jumping Mustang Staff and the Brigade Commander, Colonel Elvey Roberts, who was with us. The picture became the basis for the cover of *Fortune* magazine, May 1966 issue, which we were delighted to see, since we could all be easily identified in the picture. A good picture of Sergeant Major McCullah was taken in the hospital area which C Company captured as he washed his face in a trough, part of the running water system, the water pouring out of a bamboo tube from a central container. I was happy to see this publicity for the battalion because it gave recognition to the unit, something the troopers all richly deserved.

The Division received tremendous publicity as a result of the Plei Mei/Pleiku campaign, and some units had their share. However, in most cases the publicity for the Division simply referred to a battalion, or a company, without designating the unit. The troops were always happy, of course, to see the 1st Air Cavalry mentioned. They knew what unit was involved, but they were personally more pleased if their own battalion or their own company designation appeared in print, especially for the personal consumption of their families and friends back in the United States.

*   *   *

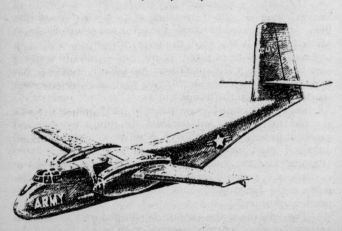

Caribou

We moved by convoy and Caribou back to An Khe. The movement took place with the troops moving by Caribou, with vehicles and equipment moving in a convoy about midday. The battalion closed in at An Khe by 1700 hours.

The movement over Highway 19 was without difficulty or incident. I flew back in the command helicopter after overseeing the movement of the convoy and the departure of the majority of the troops from the area. Major Herman, the New Executive Officer, remained at the Stadium until the last elements of the battalion had closed out.

There had been a change in the battalion organization. Major Eberhardt was promoted to Lieutenant Colonel during the latter part of December and moved to Division to assume a job on the staff. Major Herman moved up to be the Executive Officer and Captain Norm Propes became the S-3. Both Major Herman and Captain Propes performed well in their new capacities.

A recap of our accomplishments throughout this important operation gave me great confidence in the battalion. We were exceptionally proficient at this stage of air assault and in small-unit tactics. I was pleased with the success in the use of the trooper ladder—its use in getting in and out of the many inaccessible landing zones that we had to operate in. In addition, the companies were operating both at company and platoon level in a fine professional fashion.

The OH-13 scout helicopters from the 1st of the 9th were effective in screening flanks and the rear on a continuing basis and provided a great deal of intelligence through spot reports. The teamwork of the OH-13 Scouts working with a rifle company proved to be an outstanding success, not only in guiding the unit, but also in finding suspicious areas that the rifle unit could search out.

Artillery support was outstanding and continued to typify the excellent relationship set up between the Infantry and our own artillerymen in the 2nd of the 19th. ARA performed well as it had been customarily doing.

The engineer support was outstanding in this operation, with the engineers busy cutting out landing zones every time a move was conducted.

I was most pleased with the forty-eight tactical air sorties flown and the tremendous job that Captain Charles Corey performed as the Air Force Liaison Officer.

We used many LZ's of all shapes and sizes. The pathfinder operations performed by the team that worked with the battalion from the 11th Aviation Group did an outstanding job. Their performance helped materially in guiding aircraft into the new LZ's during an assault and was outstanding in assisting the smooth flow of the aircraft, including the movement of the artillery and logistics aircraft as well as night medical evacuation.

I was pleased with the operation of the skeleton Command Post, consisting of the Hex tent and the small battalion aide station. This proved to be satisfactory. Communications was excellent, using the PRC-25 radio, although I was criticized somewhat for not bringing the vehicles in with some of the heavier radio equipment. I considered this unnecessary as long as my Communication Sergeant could provide communications from battalion to the companies and I was able to maintain communications with the brigade. This caused the brigade to perform a little harder in some of their communications efforts, but it simplified the mobility of our unit.

After arrival at An Khe on the seventeenth, we remained in reserve for four days prior to assuming our first mission on the "Green Trace" as of the twenty-first. This was an excellent opportunity to check equipment, get cleaned up, and rest a little bit.

On the twenty-first we assumed responsibility for two-thirds of the Division area of the "Green Trace," including that formerly occupied by the 2nd and 3rd Brigades. The most interesting aspect of this operation was the offensive action by one company north of the Barrier where the 2nd Brigade had been engaging without success a squad to a platoon for some time. We would only be there a few days, for the Division was now engaged in a major operation in the Bong Son area. The 2nd and 3rd Brigades were there now. We were scheduled to move the latter part of the month and were already making plans and continuing the recons in that area. Our next battle would be on the China Sea coast.

13

CHINA SEA COAST—BONG SON

The battalion mission was operation of the Barrier with two companies, with one rifle company on the Picket Line. The mission at the Barrier became more a burden for one unit, as the number of units employed on the Barrier was reduced. It had now reached the stage where one Infantry battalion occupied most of the Barrier and was responsible for patrolling for a distance of five kilometers. Companies were rotated every two or three days in order to provide a change of pace and to keep fresh companies engaged in the platoon- and company-size combat operations.

D Company attached the Anti-tank Platoon to one of the rifle companies to assist on the Barrier. In addition, the Recon Platoon operated independently under battalion missions, on patrols beyond the Barrier itself. The Mortar Platoon was in position in a central location within the An Khe Base where it could provide mortar fire to the critical areas to the north and northwest.

In the area formerly occupied by the 2nd Brigade there had been frequent enemy contact almost every night, with snipers and squad- and platoon-size attacks. The 2nd Brigade was never able to locate and destroy those small elements, which were believed to be a local force reconnaissance company. We expected trouble from that unit.

Duty on the Barrier itself was pretty monotonous. The troops spent their time during the day improving positions, stringing barbwire, or providing labor details to the engineers who were supervising the construction of the Barrier itself. A certain amount of progress had to be made each day. The

Division finally came up with a master plan for construction of the Barrier under the direction of the Division Engineer. Qualified engineer NCO's supervised each phase to include bunker building, construction of the wire barrier, and installation of mines at such time as they would be installed. A master plan was completed, and it looked as if we would probably make progress on the Barrier. Heretofore every time a battalion, and especially a brigade, assumed responsibility on the Barrier, there was a change in concepts and a change in plans. Much work that one unit completed was not satisfactory for the new unit. The master plan would help eliminate wasted effort.

At night, a 50 percent alert was required. That meant that 50 percent of the troops would be awake and in their holes. At night the troops' positions throughout the Barrier were supplemented by what were called "tenant units." The combat-support and service-support elements occupying the An Khe Base provided a specified number of trained riflemen who were in the daytime cooks, clerks, bakers, medics, and mechanics. These men reinforced a rifle company and provided a greater strength to protect the Barrier than could one battalion alone. In addition, certain of those elements were available as reinforcements and a reserve force in the event that the Barrier was hit and reinforcements were required. The defense of the Barrier came under the respective Brigade Commander whose brigade was in the An Khe Base. He was responsible for the Barrier, the Picket Line, and the An Khe area generally, including reinforcement of Special Forces camps within the immediate vicinity.

The battalion's sector or portion of the Barrier was commanded from the battalion operations at the Base. My daily tasks included a detailed inspection of all portions of the Barrier to check progress and to see if the troops were maintaining equipment as well as their own personal appearance and that weapons were in operating condition.

I was most interested in the patrolling conducted outside the Barrier because it was my belief that through an aggressive patrol system, both on foot and by use of the OH-13 scouts from the Air Cavalry Squadron, we would be able to detect the enemy trying to penetrate our positions and to destroy them before they could create any damage.

Duty on the Barrier provided a little free time for the

troops and also provided some effort to be expended in improving the Base Camp. The improvements in the Base Camp were progressing well. Captain Russell Ramsey supervised construction of the headquarters area and soon would have prefab tin-roof huts available for all of the troops within the Headquarters Company. Similar projects were carried on by the rifle companies; however, the rifle companies were not as interested in maximum amounts of prefab huts as in messes, supply rooms, and two or three buildings or frame tents to be used for the few troops that remain back habitually at the base.

Sergeant Major McCullah had completed the construction of a new NCO-EM Club, of which I was most proud. It was his job to monitor the club and, with the aid of the committee of NCO's and the Club NCO, to operate it. It was important that the club provide the best of services, including all the cold beer and soft drinks that we could obtain when we returned. Word was that we would soon be on the list for a new battalion-type mess hall that would be constructed by the engineers. One or two of these buildings were slowly springing up throughout the area; however, it appeared that it would be quite some time before we received one.

The progress of the Chapel during periods when we were on the Barrier moved forward rapidly. The Chapel initially progressed somewhat slowly because it was difficult to obtain the necessary timber and cement. The cement floor was finished by that time and the A frame was beginning to go up. The front and rear ends of the Chapel were made by a unique method. They were constructed of cement squares, each square having a hole in it. These holes were made with No. 10 cans. In effect, you had a large cement brick about eighteen inches long by twelve inches high with two holes in the center the same size as the No. 10 can. This provided an interesting appearance, very striking and one that would be unique with the Jumping Mustang Battalion.

Captain Ramsey was successful in obtaining scarce road graders and bulldozers to work on the road system within the battalion area. We had a U or circle that passed through the area, which was extremely muddy during a rain. We dumped I don't know how many truckloads of gravel and sand in it, but the road still continued to sink out of sight. Captain Ramsey and Sergeant Major McCullah were finally instrumental in securing transportation and gravel and completed the project.

The battalion area itself was beginning to look nice. I tried to improve the area to the maximum so that when the troops came back for the relatively short periods of rest, they would have an area in which to relax and the finest creature comforts that we could provide.

B Company conducted aggressive patrols, from platoon-size up to company-size, in the area to the northwest where the 2nd Brigade had encountered trouble. A platoon was out on ambush. They set up security and stopped for chow. As the "point" watched, down the trail came three Viet Cong walking casually along, the lead one with a rifle hung over his shoulder.

The alert "point" man shot all three of them, at which time the platoon was alerted and set out in hot pursuit of the remainder of the Viet Cong patrol. They pursued them over an open area for five hundred meters and there engaged them once more, accounting for at least three additional snipers in the trees. Additional bodies were seen being dragged off. At this time the remainder of B Company was committed by helicopter assault.

When in a status such as the battalion was in now, four to six UH-1D helicopters were maintained on an alert status within the helicopter battalion area. These were made available as required on short notice. The rest of B Company moved in and spent the remainder of the day searching the area. Aggressive patrols were conducted with a stay-behind patrol remaining out that night.

Activities were routine on the Barrier as the battalion continued its mission.

Last night A Company had a night ambush patrol out. At 2030 hours the Claymores were set off prematurely, when the patrol thought a number of VC had walked into the ambush. We had high hopes of having killed several, but the report turned out to be a false alarm.

The battalion was now responsible for the An Khe Airfield and the An Khe Pass area. We were relieved of the Barrier and that particular mission. One company was deployed at the An Khe Airfield to secure it. A company secured Highway 19 south to the An Khe Pass. A third company maintained the highway open toward Pleiku, about half the distance to the Mang Yang Pass. During this period on the An Khe Pass, there took place a bitter and unfortunate experience for the battalion. A C-123 on takeoff from the An Khe Airfield flew south with troops from the 2nd of the 7th en route to Bong Son, where the new China Sea coast campaign had opened, and crashed shortly after takeoff, plowing into the mountains of the An Khe Pass.

I was driving toward the An Khe Pass, to the west a mile away, when I heard the noise of a low-flying aircraft as it passed overhead. A few minutes later I heard the tremendous crash and explosion as the aircraft augered into the side of the mountain. The bird had apparently flown across the mountaintop and in the bad weather conditions, in which fog and haze shrouded part of the peaks, for some reason turned a forty-five-degree angle to the right, lost altitude, and plowed into the forward slope or eastern side of the mountain.

Our battalion was responsible for the security; therefore we had the job of providing immediate assistance to the crash scene, since we were the closest troops; to rescue any troops aboard still alive; and to evacuate the casualties. Within a few minutes, men from the battalion were on the scene, but the intense flames and the exploding ammunition prevented us from getting too near for a few minutes. It was obvious from the condition of the airplane, the explosions, and the fire that there probably were few if any troopers left alive in the aircraft.

I reached the scene fifteen minutes after the crash. It was a grim and discouraging sight. By that time the ammunition stopped popping sufficiently so that troops could get in, extinguish the fire, and make an assessment of what was going on. The first report, since it was difficult to find any bodies, indicated that the only ones aboard were the crew, and we hoped that we had only a minimum of casualties. However, it turned out that the aircraft was fully loaded with a mortar platoon from A Company, 2nd of the 7th.

The battalion spent the rest of that afternoon evacuating the bodies from the wreckage. It was not as bad to get killed on the battlefield, if one had to, and to see the wounded and the dead under those circumstances; but it was always grim to see fellow soldiers in circumstances such as this aircraft accident. The bodies were badly torn; they had to be placed in rubber bags and carried by the troopers several hundred meters to a spot where they could be evacuated by helicopter.

The battalion established security over the entire mountain pass area. The engineers assisted in cutting an LZ and cutting up the aircraft. We finally located all bodies and evacuated them back to the Division Base for proper care.

This was not the last crash on this mountain during our tenure at the An Khe Pass, for two days later a UH-1D helicopter crashed under similar circumstances, resulting in our again locating the wreckage, which was hard to do this time, and taking care of the evacuation of the bodies. Fortunately, one trooper was still alive, a young soldier flying as supply man on the helicopter, which was engaged in a resupply mission. Just before the aircraft crashed, he decided to jump, and he survived with minor broken limbs.

In the meantime the Battle of the Bong Son campaign was progressing. This forty-one-day campaign on the China Sea coast was an operation similar to that conducted in the Plei Mei/Pleiku area a few weeks previous. In this operation the 1st Air Cavalry Division engaged the Gold Star Division, a North Vietnamese division consisting of two NVA regiments and one Viet Cong regiment.

The operation, which was called by the Division the "Bong Son Campaign," was also known as "Operation Masher/White Wing." To begin with, the operation started on 25 January south of Bong Son to increase the security of Route 1, a north-south highway paralleling the China Sea coast. On 28 January, D-Day, the Division joined in an air assault and overland attack north of Bong Son. The campaign included the area east along the coast and west of Route 1 and taking in the high ground between the coastal plain and the An Lao Valley.

In the attack the Division was successful, in spite of bad weather, in finding and fixing and destroying enemy units as large as battalions who were defending strongly fortified positions. One notable example of coordination between the ARVN and the 1st Cavalry Division was when the ARVN provided armored personnel carriers in conjunction with an attack by the 2nd of the 12th. The Division Engineers also had the opportunity to build a fine air strip at a position known as "Dog."

The plan provided for securing the initial lowland valley along Highway 1, after which the Division focused attention on the high ground lying between the coastal plain and the An Lao Valley. This operation was conducted in conjunction with the Marine forces to the north, to make certain that the enemy escape routes out of the valley to the north were cut off. In addition, the 22nd ARVN Division blockaded routes to the south.

The Division attacked the An Lao area on 4 February with five Infantry battalions under the 2nd and 3rd Brigade. Bad weather caused a delay until 6 February, at which time the Marines landed a battalion by helicopter in the northern end of the An Lao Valley and the 1st Air Cavalry landed three battalions by air assault on the high ground west of the valley and attacked across country into the An Lao Valley from the high ground east of the valley with two other battalions. Division artillery was positioned in the high ground to the east as well as in positions on the coastal plain.

The attack on the An Lao Valley met only light resistance as the Division drove out the enemy that was present in the first few days. An intense psychological warfare program was conducted to offer to the people a chance to leave the valley if they chose to do so.

Approximately 4,500 out of the total population of about 8,000 inhabitants elected to leave their homes in the valley and move to an area under government control. 1st Air Cavalry helicopters flew more than 3,300 of these people to freedom. The 2nd Brigade had the mission of protecting this exodus while continuing to clear the enemy from the valley and the high ground to the east. In the process of killing and capturing a large number of the enemy, a sizable supply of 105mm artillery, ammunition, rice, and a large stock of salt was found in hidden VC caches.

The 3rd Brigade in the meantime began an assault into the enemy base itself. This area was dubbed the "Eagle's Claw" or "Crow's Foot." It was a series of valleys southwest of Bong Son that branch out from the Son Long River Valley much like the toes on the foot of a crow. The resemblance of this area to a crow's or eagle's foot was noticeable from the air.

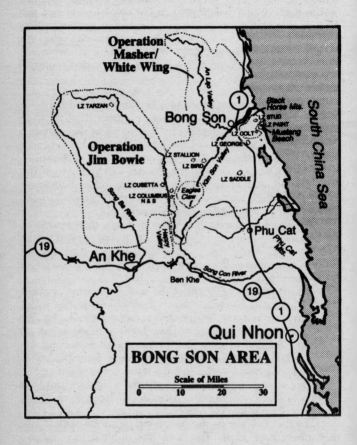

Operation
Masher/
White Wing

An Lao Valley

Route 1

Bong Son

LZ TARZAN

Operation
Jim Bowie

Song Be River

LZ CUSETTA
LZ COLUMBUS
N & S

LZ STALLION

LZ BIRD

Eagles
Claw

Happy
Valley

South China Sea

Black
Horse Mtn.
STUD
LZ PAINT
Mustang
Beach

LZ COLT
LZ GEORGE

LZ SADDLE

Kim Son Valley

Phu Cat

Phu Cat
Pass

An Khe

Ben Khe

Song Con River

19

19

1

Qui Nhon

BONG SON AREA

Scale of Miles

0   10   20   30

Into this enemy stronghold the 3rd Brigade air-assaulted and seized the foot of the crow, called "Position Bird," while simultaneously landing blocking forces in the toes to prevent enemy escape from the valleys. With this strategy, the brigade was successful in killing and capturing many enemy and taking over much equipment, including communications gear. They also succeeded in keeping the enemy bottled up in the overall area of the crow's foot.

The 2nd Brigade landed in the ridges in the high ground southeast of the crow's foot, when intelligence indicated that the enemy was hiding in strength and possibly had a major headquarters. The 2nd Brigade found the hidden enemy in an area known as the "Iron Triangle" and gave him a sound beating. In this fight the 2nd Brigade employed all their organic weapons plus much supporting artillery, tactical air, tear gas, and a B-52 strike. The actions of the 2nd Brigade accounted for many enemy killed or wounded and captured plus many large weapons captured or destroyed. In addition, there was extensive evidence that the enemy installation did include a Viet Cong regimental headquarters.

The 1st Brigade relieved the 3rd Brigade on 18 February and began a series of assaults and sweeps through the high ground around the "Crow's Foot" and then moved into the high ground along the east and southeastern sides of the Bong Son Valley. Here the brigade encountered elements of the 18th NVA Regiment, including a regimental headquarters and a heavy-weapons company. The Airborne Brigade took a heavy toll of these units and captured many crew-served weapons plus communications equipment and a hospital and medical supplies.

The 1st Brigade was joined by the 2nd Brigade in executing a series of air assaults and sweeps out from its positions in the eastern end of the Son Long Valley during which it destroyed enemy in small-unit engagements. Throughout the action of the 1st and 2nd Brigades, the eyes and ears of the Division, the 1st of the 9th Cavalry ranged along the perimeter of the coastal area, killing or capturing enemy who tried to leave the killing zone established in the crow's foot.

The end of February, the 1st Airborne Brigade returned to An Khe, leaving the 1st and 2nd of the 8th with the 2nd Brigade to continue operations on the Black Horse Mountains, known as they Cay Giep Mountains, south of Bong Son between the ocean and Highway 1.

The final phase of the operation, called Operation "Black Horse," was aimed at destroying whatever hostile forces were in the forest-covered mountain stronghold. The assault was made by bombing holes in the heavy jungle canopy that covered most of the mountain, and then by helicopter rappel and use of Chinook ladders assaulting into the dominant high ground to sweep down the hills. This was accomplished in conjunction with simultaneous sweeps and blocks by the 22nd ARVN Division and by two battalions of the 2nd Brigade in the low ground south of the mountains. No large numbers of Viet Cong were killed, but many were captured and the myth of this being a strong enemy base was exploded. In this operation, as throughout the forty-one days, the three helicopter battalions of the Division performed magnificently.

The Bong Son operation ended on 6 March after a total of forty-one days in continuous combat. The division had made a 360-degree traverse around Bong Son in which for the forty-one consecutive days we had been in contact with the enemy. In these forty-one days, 140,000 Vietnamese were returned to government control. The inhabitants of the An Lao and Son Long valleys were given a chance to be free of the VC domination by moving to areas under government surveillance. Over half of these people did leave their homes and moved to the area controlled by the government.

A hard blow was struck at enemy units which had long threatened the Bong Son area and Route 1 from Quin Nhon to Bong Son. The Division fought all three regiments of the enemy Sao Vang Division, also known as the Gold Star Division. In this fighting there was conclusive evidence that five of the nine Infantry battalions of the three regiments were rendered ineffective, and additionally, the mortar company and the recoilless rifle company of the 2nd Viet Cong Regiment were put out of operation. The anti-aircraft company and the signal company of the division were also rendered inoperative. Three field hospitals were captured.

In this campaign a total of 1,342 enemy were killed by body count, with an additional 1,746 estimated killed; over 3,000 were estimated wounded; and 593 were captured. The

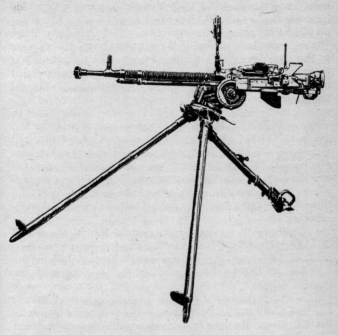

12.7mm Anti-Aircraft MG

captured included a battalion commander, a mortar company commander, and an executive officer of a regimental headquarters company.

A total of 1,060 enemy suspects were detained and 483 VC cadremen surrendered under the Chieu Hoi Program. As for weapons, a total of 203 individual weapons were captured, plus 52 crew-served, including one 105mm howitzer, ten 12.7mm anti-aircraft machine guns, and three 50-caliber anti-aircraft machine guns. Large quantities of ammunition, including 126 rounds of 105 howitzer ammunition, were captured.

A total of over 1,250 pounds of enemy documents were captured, of which 150 pounds proved most useful to intelligence. Large quantities of communication equipment, including Chicom AM/FM receivers, our own PRC-10 radios, Angry 9's, field telephones, wire, radio parts, and PA systems, were taken over. A total of ninety-one tons of rice and, most important, over fourteen tons of salt was captured and evacuated for refugees.

As a result of the Bong Son campaign, the Sao Vang or Gold Star Division was rendered ineffective for a period of several months. Our Commanding General, General Harry W. O. Kinnard, summed up the accomplishments of the Division.

> We obtained much tactical intelligence useful to ourselves and provided the basis for higher headquarters to glean much technical and strategic intelligence. The tactical intelligence we obtained enabled us to locate the enemy and to maintain contact every day for forty-one consecutive days.

> We again demonstrated an ability to air assault into even the most difficult of terrain. Using this capability, we surprised the enemy by landing above and behind his hillside defenses and surprised him also by entering the areas where he felt himself protected by his fortification and the ruggedness of the terrain.

> We again emplaced our artillery, and the 155 mm howitzers for the first time (these by the Flying Crane), on the hilltops and other unlikely spots and made tube artillery support constantly available to our Infantry and cavalry units.

> Our engineers built two fine airfields, one north of Bong Son, one west of Ho Cam.

> We continued continuous psychological operations which produced prisoners and Chew Hoi, and also kept the inhabitants of the area informed as to what was happening, and what they should do to avoid harm, to return to the government control.

> We fought in a densely populated area, strongly defended by the Viet Cong, and yet did remarkable little damage to the friendly or potentially friendly inhabitants of the area. This was a great tribute to the careful way in which the Commanders at all levels explained and enforced the rules of engagement, and a tribute to the individual trooper in carrying out those difficult instructions.

We cooperated and coordinated with the ROCKS, ARVN, US Navy, US Marines, and US Air Force, in prolonged and complex operations. This enhanced the confidence and mutual respect of each of these forces for the other.

We kept at least four of our Infantry battalions and six for the majority of the period, in sustained operations for forty-one days at an average distance from our Base at An Khe of approximately sixty-five kilometers. We laid to rest any residual doubt about our ability to conduct sustained combat operations.

We transferred battalions and switched brigades with far less loss of momentum than heretofore and were thus able to keep constant pressure on the enemy.

As individuals and as units, you performed like true professionals. Your teamwork within and between units was topnotch. The newly arrived members of the division acquitted themselves very well. Our old-timers were superb. I rated the division's overall performance as being at least 50 percent better than in our other long campaign in Pleiku, and we emerged from these forty-one days of sustained combat in far better shape than we ended our thirty-five days combat in Pleiku. In short, sky troopers of the 1st Air Cav, you have placed the name and the fighting reputation of the first team at the very top of the roll of Army divisions. You have again given the Army and our country cause to be proud of you. Well done. I salute you.

The Bong Son operation was most important. This is the reason I have taken time to detail a little bit more of the concept of the entire operation. Within the past six months, the 1st Air Cavalry Division had engaged in a major campaign along the Cambodian border in the Pleiku area and put out of action one North Vietnamese division of at least three regiments. A few weeks later another major operation in the China Sea coast—the Bong Son operation—had put on the ineffective list the second division within II Corps. The method of operating in the future was to consist of air assaults and movement back and forth throughout II Corps. Any time the enemy were discovered, a full force could quickly move in and locate and destroy them.

The outstanding mobility of the Air Cavalry Division enabled it to move anywhere in the entire II Corps Tactical Zone, extending 100 miles north of An Khe and 100 miles south, and from the China Sea coast to the Cambodian border, at will and on short notice. It became customary for a battalion when back in the An Khe Base as a matter of course to be prepared to move a company within minutes and a battalion minus within two hours. On many occasions, battalions moved out when word was received that the enemy had been located, conducted an operation, killed or destroyed large numbers, and returned to the An Khe Base, all within twenty-four hours.

The II Corps Tactical Zone became known jokingly amongst many in Vietnam as the "Pasture of the First Horse," and within the coming months the "First Horse," or the 1st Air Cavalry, learned to know that pasture as any horse does his own local pasture. The Viet Cong and the NVA would also come to know this "First Horse" well.

On 18 February the battalion moved as part of the 1st Brigade to the Bong Son area to relieve the 3rd Brigade, specifically the 1st of the 7th. We flew by Chinook and Caribou and eventually landed at a landing zone called "Bird" which would be the Brigade Base. The mission was to secure the Brigade Base, the Brigade Command Post, and the Artillery.

Prior to the initiation of this move, during the last few days on the Barrier and on the An Khe Pass, a series of recons had been made by the staff and myself, and also the company commanders. The terrain on the China Sea coast side was different from that to the west around Pleiku. First of all, the ocean was beautiful, with great sandy white beaches. There were three large mountain areas that extended from the town of Quin Nhon north toward Bong Son.

The first mountains, which lay just a few miles north of Quin Nhon up the China Sea coast between Highway 1 and the China Sea coast, were referred to as the Phu Cat Mountains. These were near a small Special Forces Camp where the Division constructed an airfield. This area also was the scene of the first action that C Company had with Task Force Amos back in October.

Next there was another series of mountains fifteen kilometers north, followed by the third one another fifteen kilometers further north called the Black Horse Mountains. This latter range was the area where the battalion fought in the final stages of the Bong Son operation. Midway between the southernmost and the northernmost mountains described and to the west of Highway 1 lay the "Crow's Foot." The initial operation for the battalion and the location of "Bird" was in the "Crow's Foot" area.

The terrain along Highway 1 was relatively open with many rice paddies. On both sides of the highway the mountains sprang up. The mountains were characterized by what I called "bald-headed mountains." These were steep-sloped mountains in most cases, completely bare of trees and smooth on top. There were exceptions. The Black Horse Mountains were heavily forested with jungle growth consisting of trees 100 and 150 feet high. This was the area where our method of entry into combat would be by blowing the tops off the mountains and rappeling troops in from the UH-1D helicopter followed by Chinook ladders.

There did not seem to be a rhyme or reason why certain mountains were bare and others were covered with heavy vegetation. About three-quarters of the mountains were bare. The bald-headed mountains provided landing spots almost at will for using the technique earlier employed by landing troops by helicopter on top of the mountains and working down. This technique, along with blocking forces which were positioned at the bottoms of the valleys, were most useful in destroying the enemy as they tried to escape from the attacking forces moving purposefully down the hills.

Position "Bird" was formed by a loop in the river—a complete U shape—in which two-thirds of the battalion area or perimeter was formed by the river bank. The top part of the U, to the north, included a small rise in elevation. "Bird" had been seized by air assault by the 3rd Brigade when they moved in initially, and the enemy village in that area had been pretty well destroyed. There were dead cattle and pigs lying around throughout the area, causing considerable smell and desolation.

Upon moving into Position "Bird" that afternoon, a rapid reconnaissance was made of the next area three miles to the north at the upper end of a valley that the Jumping Mustangs were scheduled to air-assault into the following morning. This area, designated LZ "Stallion," included an assault by the battalion minus C Company, who assaulted into another LZ, designated "Renegade," across the valley. The order was firmed up rapidly. As the planning was completed, I took the company commanders on a recon in the command helicopter to show them the objectives and the landing zone. Reconnaissance had already been completed with the assault helicopter unit commander.

LZ "Stallion" was a large hill mass covered with heavy vegetation. In the center or top of the hill mass was a low depression extending two or three hundred meters from the crest, forming a bowl. In the center of this bowl was a large, open rice-paddy area with two low hills in the middle. The bowl appeared to provide the only LZ in the hill mass. Since enemy intelligence indicated that probably there was an enemy company or elements of a battalion there, landing on top of the mountain seemed the most likely way to go it, instead of fighting up the hills from the valley floor.

Across the valley to the east and following the river were a series of trails which appeared to be an excellent avenue of approach for escaping NVA or Viet Cong. This was the reason for the selection of "Renegade," where C Company would land and conduct a series of search-and-destroy missions in an area reported to have at least one platoon of Viet Cong and possibly a hospital.

The battalion spent the evening in preparation for the forthcoming battle.

The first part of the next day's assault was the landing of C Company on LZ "Renegade." The operation commenced at 0900 hours as H hour. It was preceded by a thirteen-minute artillery preparation with tube artillery followed by two minutes of aerial rockets. C Company's mission was to establish a blocking position astride the valley, secure the landing zone, and conduct a local sweep operation of the valley. There was negative enemy contact, and within a short period of time the assault landing was completed, a total of twenty-four UH-1D helicopters being employed.

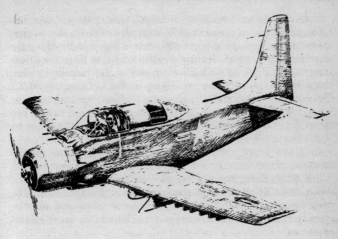

A1E "Spad"

The second phase of the operation began at 1005 with B Company air-assaulting into LZ "Stallion." Owing to the anticipated enemy in the area, this assault was preceded by a thirty-minute tactical air strike. During the strike, six A1E and F-100 fighters displayed an outstanding demonstration of how to conduct effective close air support. The edges of the bowl surrounding the LZ were covered with bombs, napalm, machine guns, and rockets, as were the two little hills in the center of the landing zone. Evidence of the bombing precision would be seen later on arrival in one particular area where a 750-pound bomb had blown a hole thirty feet across by twenty feet deep.

The tactical air strike was followed by a thirteen-minute artillery preparation employing over 150 rounds, followed by two minutes of aerial-rocket artillery prior to the landing of twenty-four UH-1D helicopters. The landing was without incident, there apparently being no Viet Cong or NVA in the immediate area. B Company secured the landing zone until the Forward Command Post and D Company closed in, landing by 1109 hours. At that time D Company assumed the mission of security while B Company initiated immediate search-and-destroy operations.

D Company was followed by A Company, and by 1230

hours the entire battalion, minus C Company still down in
the valley, was in position. A Company was given the mission
of securing the high ground 400 meters north overlooking the
landing zone and of clearing a two-bird LZ to facilitate future
operation. Prior to dark all elements of the battalion closed
back in on the perimeter defense, as did C Company at LZ
"Renegade," established defenses, and set up ambushes in
the area. Concentrations were registered and an active H and
I program was prepared and conducted during the night by
both the artillery and the mortars.

I was happy with the conduct of the operation, for the
pattern of air assaults which we had repeated many times
during this Bong Son Campaign were executed smoothly and
with little effort by the companies and by the staff. The
coordination with the assault helicopter units and all elements of the battalion team was performed in an excellent
manner.

In the first hours of the following day at 0115, an
estimated VC squad with automatic weapons and grenades
probed a portion of the perimeter in B Company sector.
Appropriate elements returned fire and the VC withdrew to
the north. Mortar and artillery fire was directed along the
route of withdrawal with unknown results. At first light the
area was searched for VC bodies and equipment, but with
negative results. Unfortunately, two of B Company's troopers
were seriously wounded and had to be evacuated to assure
their survival.

The medical evacuation was accomplished by lift helicopters from A Company, 227th Assault Helicopter Battalion,
under adverse weather conditions. It was difficult to get
regular medical evacuation helicopters into the area because
the pilots were not familiar with the new landing zone and
the weather was bad back at the base where the medical
aircraft were located.

I called Major Herman at our base at Phu Cat and told
him we must have medical evacuation up to pick up these
two young soldiers during the night, and to get hold of Major
Worthland and see what could be done. Major Floyd Worthland,
Company Commander of A Company, was an outstanding
aviator and soldier. He performed in the manner I expected
and under tremendous difficulties caused by deteriorating

weather flew to the vicinity of LZ "Stallion." There the haze
was such that it was almost impossible to see our small
landing zone on the top of the mountain. By talking with
Major Worthland, we worked out a system in which the 81
mortars fired illuminated shells straight up. The illuminant
marked the location of the landing zone and provided light in
the haze that permitted Major Worthland to slide down
through a narrow slot in the clouds to make the pickup.

The first try did not work well because the light reflecting
against the haze blinded Major Worthland. However, on the
second try he was successful in making the pickup, retrieved
the two wounded men, and flew back to the Battalion Base,
where expert medics were available.

This was a vivid example of the cooperation customary
between the Jumping Mustang Battalion and the 227th Assault Helicopter Battalion, especially A Company, who habitually
worked with us.

Captain Martin, B Company, was upset over the attack of
the VC against his positions. It appeared in later reconstructing
the attack that the VC squad had not known that the United
States forces were in that area. The VC moved down the trail
and encountered our lead elements on the perimeter. The
Fire Team Leader saw the Viet Cong and for some unknown
reason did not shoot, but stood up to call to them, apparently
thinking they were friendly. When he stood up, he was fired
upon and immediately shot down by the Viet Cong, causing
the first casualty. This gave warning to the remainder of the
VC squad, and before the remaining men in the fire team and
squad could shoot, the VC melted away. This little incident
led to tightening some of our procedures to assure that in the
future when an enemy approached our position, we stayed
put, let them get close, and then blasted them.

The rest of the day was spent in a series of search-and-
destroy operations by A and B Companies throughout the
mountain of which LZ "Stallion" was part. C Company down
in the valley conducted a series of search-and-destroy operations and captured one VC who gave a report of three
machine gun positions in the area. These enemy positions
were located further up the valley in the direction in which
we planned to move C Company.

A small, bald-headed mountain in the vicinity provided
an excellent place to emplace the mortar platoons. C Compa-

ny mortars were picked up by helicopter and emplaced on top of this hill, where they could provide excellent fire support for all of C Company operation, as well as provide complete visual observation of the entire area.

A tactical air strike was conducted at 0955 hours and again at 1027 hours on the suspected VC platoon. At 1335 hours C Company made contact with an estimated squad in the vicinity and took them under fire as the VC began to withdraw. Additional tactical air was called in on the fleeing Viet Cong. Some sniper fire was received as C Company made contact with an estimated platoon as they proceeded further up the valley. By 1700 hours C Company had cleaned up the situation, at least for the evening.

Results of the action were heartening, with only one friendly minor WIA. At least six Viet Cong were killed by body count, one was wounded, and an estimated eight were killed and an estimated twelve wounded. One rifle was captured. C Company reorganized and established its defenses for the night, including a series of ambushes in the event that the VC should attempt to come back and pick up or retrieve bodies and weapons.

Captain Mozey recently assumed command of C Company and was running this operation. This had been his first combat. I was pleased that it had been successful. In combat, everyone looks at and watches the new commander, wondering what kind of leader he will be and whether he is going to be a lucky leader or an unlucky leader. Captain Mozey proved that C Company was a fine company and that he could contribute to its further effectiveness.

I was concerned as dark began to approach and C Company was still cleaning up the tactical situation. However, resupply was in on time, and one casualty evacuated, and C Company was finally set for the night. During this battle we were uncertain what size enemy forces we were dealing with, and I was concerned because C Company was off some three kilometers from the battalion. Although we could provide fire support, it would have taken some time to reinforce by helicopter in the event they bit into something a little too large.

There was negative contact throughout the night, both with C Company at LZ "Renegade" and with the battalion minus on LZ "Stallion."

*   *   *

During the next two days the battalion continued a series of search-and-destroy missions within the area. Mortars from both D Company and two rifle companies were positioned on the single bald-headed mountain that C Company originally landed on. These mortars provided tremendous fire power.

B and C Companies continued an assault, with C Company working on up the valley to the northeast; B Company conducted an air assault into a landing zone called LZ "Stud" beginning at 0800. B Company established a blocking position and served as the anvil as C Company, acting as the hammer, moved down through the valley with the expectation of trapping a number of Viet Cong between the two.

During this battle, one of the best uses of fire power I had ever witnessed occurred. C Company, on the left portion of the zone to the west, employed tactical air power, conducting air strikes close in to their positions as the company moved forward. In addition, C Company mortars from the hill, a fine observation post for the entire action, were firing to the right side of their sector. In the B Company area, still in the battalion sector further to the east, tube artillery was falling. In between the B Company and the artillery and mortar targets of C Company, gunships from the 227th Assault Helicopter Battalion provided fire power for a patrol working in that area. Thus within the same battalion zone, in an area 2000 meters wide, simultaneously there was an air strike in progress, mortar firing, tube artillery fire falling, and gunships in operation. All of this was accomplished safely and under the control of the respective units.

I could not help but contrast this with some of the earlier reports of units in Vietnam where at any time when artillery was falling nothing else could operate in the area; and where, if there was an air strike in the vicinity, no other indirect fire weapons could be employed. I was always annoyed to see tactics of this sort, because it was wrong to curtail the fires of one or two groups of weapons simply to employ the other. The objective should be to employ all means of fire power on the appropriate targets simultaneously if that was the requirement. It could be done as was demonstrated here today, and quite simply. It required that fire-control personnel be on the ball, know their target areas, and have good communications.

C Company found a cave, and it was searched. It had evidently been occupied by a number of VC, but the cave had a rear exit and they had escaped. One rifle and a large quantity of documents were found. C Company continued to work in the general area and found various individual items of combat equipment, medical supplies, and an estimated company command post, as well as a battalion-size hospital area.

A Company continued assaults on their portion of the zone in a search-and-destroy operation, with negative results. They landed three miles deep to the northwest, in a steep valley, to serve as a hammer and to move down against B Company which was in the stopper of the cork, so to speak. In effect, B Company was a stopper for a two-opening bottle, with C Company at the base of one and A Company at the base of the other. A Company's landing had been on top of the bald-headed hills overlooking the river. They moved down the steep banks to the river valley and moved toward B Company.

I hoped that A Company would be able to move rapidly, but the going was extremely rough. The valley was a narrow defile which precluded fast movement. It appeared that the Viet Cong had not gone out through this area where we hoped to trap a number of them. A Company was not able to reach by dark the objective where B Company, the stopper, was emplaced. At that point I had intended to retrieve or extract A Company by helicopter. This was not now possible, for LZ's were not available. Supplies had to be lifted in by helicopter, using a slingload in the HU-1D. By this method we were able to resupply the company with the essentials for that night.

The battalion ended up that night split into three separate company perimeters—A Company to the north, B Company to the west, and C Company to the east. The Battalion Command Post was on the hill with the mortars, now known as Mortar Hill, overlooking and within the area of operation. At the same time, the Battalion Forward Base was retained back at LZ "Stallion" with elements of D Company acting as security. There was minimum enemy contact throughout the night with an active H and I program conducted by all three companies, especially their mortars.

All three rifle units continued their previous missions

from the day before. C Company found various items, such as rice, money, and clothing, during their sweep to join up with B Company. There were negative results from both A and B Companies. All units closed on the stopper where B Company was located by 1340 hours and were air-lifted back to LZ "Stallion," where the last elements of the battalion closed at 1600 hours. A perimeter was reestablished for the night with negative enemy contact.

The following day B Company air-assaulted into an LZ to the east of objective "Stallion" to conduct search-and-destroy operations, with negative contact. They were extracted at 1600 hours and returned to "Stallion." B Company continued the defense of the landing zone with a series of short search-and-destroy operations. A Company conducted an assault down into the south valley and by 0940 hours found five huts and bunkers which were destroyed. At 1135 hours they encountered two Viet Cong with weapons and pursued them, but the VC escaped into the jungles. At 1628, a total of five Viet Cong suspects were captured and evacuated back to brigade. The company had negative contact for the remainder of the day and was extracted back to LZ "Stallion" by nightfall. C Company remained at LZ "Stallion" in battalion reserve and assisted in the security of "Stallion" for that day.

At 1745 we received a brigade warning order to move one company immediately back to the Brigade Base as security position for "Bird," attached to and under the operational control of the 2nd of the 8th. At 1750 C Company began the airlift back to "Bird." Weather conditions were bad and the Brigade Commander felt that he might end up with the 1st of the 8th in static positions without being able to employ us for the forthcoming operation.

This feeling continued to persist, and at 1755 hours the Brigade Commander alerted the entire battalion for a move to "Bird." A continual helicopter shuttle was executed to close the battalion into "Bird," several kilometers away, prior to darkness. At the termination of the shuttle, A and C Companies were with the Forward Command Post, located at Position "Bird," under the operational control of 2nd of the 8th, who assumed security for the northern perimeter. The battalion minus, with B Company, remained at LZ "Stallion" for the night. There had been insufficient time prior to darkness, with bad weather closing in, to extract the entire battalion.

I was concerned with the fact that the VC, if there were any in that area, might have noticed that we had a majority of the troops out of the area and might try to conduct an attack on the battalion positions which represented only one-half of the battalion. An active H and I program was conducted during the night with negative contact, except for five VC who were spotted at 1840 hours, prior to dark. They apparently were a patrol and were taken under fire. A search was conducted, but we could not capture them. The result of our fire was unknown.

The battalion continued its extraction from LZ "Stallion" in the morning hours and closed in on "Bird" by 1000 hours. This reformed the entire battalion in Position "Bird" in reserve, prepared for missions the following day. The day was spent in reconnaissance, making the necessary plans, and issuing the orders for the forthcoming day's actions. The 1st of the 8th also assumed responsibility for the security of Position "Bird," and the 2nd of the 8th moved out on the beginning of this new phase of the battalion operation.

As you will recall, over one-half of Position "Bird's" perimeter was formed by a medium-size river. During the afternoon I walked the perimeter where the troops were continuing preparations for the night, cleaning themselves and their weapons and equipment. It was a pleasure to be near the water, and a great many of the troops were involved in baths, shaving, and relaxing. Halfway around the perimeter, the water looked so refreshing we all had a swim. One of the radio operators took a turn as guard while the rest of us stripped to dive in. Two or three hundred yards further around the perimeter during this time a sniper shot one of the bathers, wounding him slightly and causing us to be more alert as we swam in the inviting stream.

The forthcoming phase of the operation would prove to be a challenge. We would again make landings on the steep, bald-headed mountains which surrounded a picturesque valley with a small village, in which we had reports of at least a Viet Cong company and perhaps some kind of headquarters. Our mission was to go into the valley, search it out, seize any documents, and try to capture as many Viet Cong as possible.

The operation was to consist of three individual air assaults from the north, east, and west as we landed on the bald-headed mountains to work our way down the fingers to the valley itself. This was one of the first operations where a battalion commander could sit on top of a hill overlooking the valley and observe each one of the units as they moved down the fingers, seeing all activity within the valley.

Mortars were emplaced on two of the hills overlooking the objective area so that all of the battalion's mortars could be massed within the target area if need be. This included the D Company mortars. The observation post I selected and spent quite a bit of time on the next day proved to be popular with the Brigade Commander and the Division Commander, who dropped in on several occasions to observe the action. This observation post was much in the tradition of previous operations in Korea and in World War II where a battalion commander's best method of control was to find an observation post where he could see what was going on and command his operation from that point. This technique was rare in Vietnam, although we had exercised the same method to a certain degree in the last operation a few days previous. Each one of the hilltops had room for one or two helicopters to land, but this did require careful air traffic control to clear one bird off in order to make way for the other. We had one area down the slope a little further where several birds, including the command helicopter, could land while awaiting use.

The operation was initiated by the Reconnaissance Platoon, who conducted a small air assault to a position called "Mac," with a mission of providing security for A Battery, 2nd of the 19th Artillery. The landing went off without a hitch. It was not anticipated that there would be any trouble there, since it was a relatively open area. The platoon secured the landing zone and was followed by Chinooks bringing in the artillery within a short period of time. A Battery provided artillery support for this operation.

Commencing at 0900 hours, B Company assaulted into a landing zone called "Bronc." They were preceded by a thirteen-minute tactical air strike, followed by aerial artillery. After securing the landing zone, B Company conducted a search-

and-destroy operation in the sector. Next A Company conducted an air assault employing similar techniques into a landing zone called "Lancer," with the mission of conducting search-and-destroy operations within the sector. At 1010 hours, a tactical air strike was conducted, followed by D Company air-assaulting into LZ "Saddle," which was secured by 1035 hours as the landing zone for the Battalion Command Post. At 1116 hours C Company conducted an air assault into LZ "Stirrup" to continue a search-and-destroy operation in the sector.

The air assault of the battalion placed A Company down in the valley, with B Company moving down the ridge to conduct a search of the village. C Company moved along the ridge to the south and ultimately down the ridge to form a blocking position at the mouth of the valley to keep the Viet Cong from escaping. B Company was doing the same thing to the north, but their movement down the ridge and in the vicinity of the objective, or LZ "Saddle," was primarily to secure that landing zone for a Battalion CP.

A Company reported numerous foxholes and fortified areas. By 1410 hours C Company had captured three Viet Cong in a cave and discovered six huts with a United States Army mortar aiming stake in it. By 1610, A Company had captured another Viet Cong in green fatigue pants and also had reported numerous caves in the area. By 1800 hours, A and B Companies reached the village in the valley, secured it, found no enemy but evidence of their having been there, and established a company perimeter for the night. C Company reached the blocking position and apprehended two Buddhist priests; after interrogation verified their identity, these were released.

The battalion was thus disposed by dark with A and B Companies in position in a perimeter, C Company in a separate perimeter, and D Company securing the Battalion Command Post. Some sniper fire was received during the usual air resupply missions at 1800. Mortars and small-arms fire on the enemy positions stopped any further snipers for the night.

I spent the night on the side of the hill at the Battalion Command Post, a steep hill where one had a tremendous view of the area and where it was difficult to find a flat space to place an air mattress to sleep. The mattress had to be dug into the side of the hill on a stairstep as one would terrace a hill for farming.

A and B Companies continued their search-and-destroy operations, with C Company conducting a search of the draws to the northeast and south of their blocking position. A new phase of the operation commenced in the afternoon of the 26th, beginning with the airlift of A Company to Landing Zone "Thunder" followed by B Company at 1640 hours to Landing Zone "Champ." Both companies secured these landing zones on top of the high mountain peaks that were east of our last landing area.

There were again bald-headed mountains where it was easy to land with relative security. The two companies occupied adjacent peaks, with a saddle in between, in preparation for a movement to sweep down the valley to search out an area where it was believed that Viet Cong might be escaping from an action that the 2nd of the 8th had initiated to the north of the Jumping Mustang positions. C Company and the Battalion CP remained in their original positions. An active H and I program was conducted during the night within both areas. This left the battalion split, disposed on both sides of the large valley.

At 1022 hours one scout ship from the Air Cavalry Squadron was hit by small-arms fire. The scouts returned fire and the Forward Observer from C Company in an OH-13 adjusted mortar fire on the Viet Cong snipers, resulting in two VC KIA's. There was no other enemy contact that day or for the remainder of the night.

A and B Companies continued their search-and-destroy operation, moving down the valley. C Company was in position to serve as a block for this new action. Actually, C Company had had to move their position only a little, serving as a block or stopper for the original action of A and B Companies from the south yesterday and now a similar action from the north.

A tactical air strike was conducted at 0835 and 0900, in advance of both A and B Companies as they moved down the hill. In the movement, B Company's mortar platoon encountered three VC with weapons who tried a small assault on the mortar position. B Company took the VC under fire and estimated they wounded two, but they did capture one rifle and one pack.

By 1515 hours the battalion initiated its movement from present locations to a new objective area three miles to the northeast, called position "George." The entire battalion was to assemble prior to dark on position "George," with the initial mission of securing two artillery batteries and preparing for an attack to the east along the China Sea coast the following day. This was the last phase of the operation with the 2nd Brigade.

The 1st Brigade was concluding its operation and preparing to return to An Khe. The 1st and 2nd of the 8th were placed under operational control of the 2nd Brigade. This movement was to position us for the final phase on Black Horse Mountain. The battalion closed in on position "George" by 1814 hours and established a perimeter. An excellent H and I program was planned, and we were ready for the night should there be any enemy.

Position "George" was a mile from the base of the huge mass that makes up the Black Horse Mountains. It was a rather pleasant area. Sandy soil made digging easy, and there were dozens of palm trees around which provided shade to the troops within the perimeter. Position "George" had been occupied for several days without any attacks on the area. We spent a quiet night with little enemy activity.

It was planned the next day that the battalion would make an overland movement from position "George" to seize objective areas in the vicinity of the China Sea coast. This was an operation in which four battalions would move into positions to begin their assaults on the mass of the mountain itself. In connection with the movement to position "George," a quick reconnaissance had been conducted, the plan developed, and orders issued. A reconnaissance was conducted by each of the company commanders. The battalion remained in position "George" for one additional day, the eighth. This gave us a chance to clean up both personnel and equipment and to verify our plans for the forthcoming operation.

This new operation, known as Operation "Pistol," had four subtitles: Pistol-South, Pistol-North, Pistol-East, and Pistol-West. The battalion participated in three phases and was the last battalion out of the Bong Son Campaign. It was becoming traditional within the 1st Air Cavalry that the 1st of

the 8th was always the last battalion out of any major operation.
This had been established in the Plei Mei/Pleiku operation and now would happen again in the Bong Son operation.

March 1st, commencing at 0800 hours, the Anti-tank Platoon moved on foot to an LZ one mile away to secure a position for the movement of B Company mortars by air assault to support the remainder of the operation. At 0900 hours, B Company moved overland to secure a new objective, Objective "100." The Recon Platoon conducted an air assault on top of the high ridge of Pistol-South into a small landing zone known as LZ "Ken" at 1201 hours to improve the landing zone, to be followed by A Company, who had the mission of searching out the high ridge and coming down from the northwest to join on Objective 100. The assault was preceded by a twelve-minute artillery preparation on LZ "Ken." The landings of both the Recon Platoon and the A Company were made without difficulty. C Company remained in reserve at Position "George."

On this operation a new technique was employed which had been developed in the past; however, it was really emphasized here. In a heavily forested area where there were no landing zones, precision bombing was initiated with 100- and 500-pound bombs to blow trees down and blow the limbs off to permit a small hole in which UH-1D helicopters could bring in troops to rappel down and secure the area, to be followed by Chinook helicopters with the trooper ladder. The rappel and ladder technique had been used effectively by the 1st Air Cavalry on numerous occasions. It was further employed on this operation with great success by other units of the Division as well as our own battalion.

I had a chance to make recons on the twenty-seventh and twenty-eighth of February, having been told to be prepared to go into Pistol-East, West, and North. The first flight over the heavily forested area resulted in little enemy information and knowledge of the terrain. In the first pass, it seemed almost impossible that landing zones could be obtained and a likely area found for the precision bombing technique to be employed. However, within a short period of time the plan began to develop. Colonel Lynch, the 2nd Brigade Commander, in furtherance of the Brigade plan, selected two of the highest peaks of the Black Horse Mountain and landed air cavalry elements from the Air Cavalry Squadron with engineers to begin the improvement of landing zones on the two peaks. These LZ's were to help further operations of the battalion and the brigade in the near future.

Commencing at 1400 hours C Company began its ground movement in the same direction as B Company on a parallel path to the south, to seize a blocking position on the high ground overlooking or about midway between position "George" and objective "100," to be prepared for a further pickup and continuance in a new mission that afternoon in conjunction with Pistol-East. Owing to the rough terrain, A Company up on the high ridge was unable to reach its objective, and by 1703 hours it was obvious that they would not be able to move on down to objective "100." They were directed to establish a landing zone to receive resupply and to prepare positions for the night. With the help of the small engineer detachment present a one-bird landing zone was constructed on the knife-edge ridge that permitted one bird at a time to make an approach, bring in supplies, and pick up casualties.

During B Company's movement through the area toward the objective "100," several booby traps were encountered. These apparently were our own hand grenades which had been rigged as booby traps by ARVN forces in the area some time previously. They proved to be quite a problem, as there were many mines and booby traps established and little if any information was available as to whose they were or where they were located.

At 1705, helicopters picked C Company up from their forward position and moved them to a new landing zone designated "Colt," one of the previously prepared LZ's on top of the highest mountain overlooking the objective area for Pistol-East. This was done to position them for the forthcoming operation the next day, in which they would make an assault as part of Pistol-East. B Company closed in and assembled on the objective area; the Battalion Forward CP began to close in; the last portion arrived at 1930 hours, immediately prior to dark.

At 1822 hours, B Company in the north sector of the objective, as well as the new battalion perimeter, received automatic-weapons fire. The fire fight continued for approximately twenty-three minutes and was silenced by Infantry mortar and artillery as well as ARA fire. The enemy encountered were estimated at platoon size, approximately thirty to forty men. We continued to receive sniper fire during the rest of the evening, and at 2130 hours resupply aircraft were fired upon by enemy automatic weapons. The enemy were taken under fire with machine guns and mortars which silenced the firing.

The battalion spent a somewhat restless night. We knew there were VC in the area, yet we could not get our hands on them. At 0005 hours, a blocking position which had been established by B Company was probed by Viet Cong. The platoon returned fire and killed one VC. Again at 0331 sporadic sniper fire from an estimated VC platoon was received on the battalion perimeter. This was silenced by controlled machine-gun, mortar, and artillery fire. It appeared that the VC in small numbers were trying to feel out the battalion and locate our weapons. As a result of this action, total VC body count was six KIA's, with an estimated five more killed and ten wounded.

Again the battalion was split, A Company on the high ground to the northwest, C Company to the north in the Pistol-East area, and the battalion minus at objective "100" ready for the forthcoming operation.

An interesting fact was vividly demonstrated during this evening's operation. I always liked to have the units in position and secured for the night prior to dark. This included resupply and evacuation of casualties. If one did not do this, snipers—and there were always two or three in the area—as soon as darkness fell began to harass and cause trouble. Conditions were always worsened by darkness, and one or two snipers shooting at the resupply helicopters or at the medical evacuation birds could complicate matters considerably, resulting in a tremendous amount of effort expended to find a simple solution. This was vividly brought home this night because it took until 2000 hours to finally get the battalion settled down, resupply ammunition and food, and evacuate the one or two casualties. A Company spent a quiet night up on the ridge, and the battalion continued its plans and thoughts for the forthcoming operation on the morrow. Enemy contact through the remainder of the night was negative.

A Company continued search-and-destroy operations,

moving down the ridge to join up with the battalion at objective "100." B Company continued security of the objective area or landing zone and conducted a search-and-destroy mission. By 1025 hours they had captured three Viet Cong suspects and a small amount of expended small-arms ammunition. A Company encountered several Viet Cong with carbines at 1310 hours and returned their fire, with unknown results; however, one rifle was captured, along with a few grenades and packs. A Company was on a trail 200 to 300 meters above the flat valley floor that moved toward the China Sea coast side to the east and into the area of Pistol-East.

At 1400 hours, B Company executed a search-and-clear operation in a village along the shallow lake adjacent to the battalion landing zone. This was a fine village search operation conducted in conjunction with the Psychological Operations personnel and the Vietnamese Civilian Police. The village was surrounded by the company to cut off escape. Then personnel moved through the village and searched out every hut and checked every person, the Civilian Police checking for identity and documents and B Company personnel providing the security and helping in the search of the huts themselves. We believed this village to be dominated by the Viet Cong, but it appeared not to be true, for the actual results of the search were negative, except for two Viet Cong suspects that were captured trying to flee the area.

I observed the operation from the command helicopter and was impressed by the way Captain Martin commanded and controlled his organization during this critical search. If men were trigger-happy when entering a village of this sort, a large number of civilians could easily be killed. This would be unfortunate not only for the civilians killed, but because of undue criticism of the unit and the Army.

Commencing at 1640 hours, A Company was picked up at a landing zone they had selected, having moved down off the ridge. They were moved to Landing Zone "Stud," which was the second peak I have earlier described that the Brigade Commander had under preparation. The two peaks, "Colt" and "Stud," which A and C Companies had occupied, overlooked the Pistol-East valley that we would start down into the following morning. The rest of the battalion closed back in on the battalion landing zone and spent a quiet night preparing for the next day's operation.

During the day, the recons were completed, the plans made, and the orders issued for the Pistol-East phase. The plan included the movement of B Company to Position "Stud," now occupied by A Company, down the ridge to the north, closing in on the central objective within the Pistol-East area, a big valley with a small village and intelligence of one platoon and rumors of probably a battalion. A Company was to move down the immediate ridge directly toward the objective, designated Landing Zone "Paint." C Company to the south would perform in a similar manner. The mortars for C Company were to be left on "Colt"; A Company and B Company's mortars, at "Stud." The D Company mortars remained on position "Colt," with all mortars of the battalion in position to support the operation.

D Company, reinforced with one platoon of B Company, would make their first air assault on the objective area at the village in the center of the valley. Thus the plan included a coordinated attack involving the overland movement of three rifle companies down the ridges, and the air assault by a fourth company, D Company, on the objective itself. It was hoped that the assault would start Viet Cong moving away from the objective area and they would be policed up by the converging rifle companies. This proved to be classic operation.

The operation itself was observed easily from both LZ "Stud" and LZ "Colt." Again this LZ served as the focal point for the Brigade Commander and the Division Commander, General Kinnard, to observe the operation.

The next morning commencing at 0700 hours, A Company and C Company started down off the mountain ridges toward the objective "Paint" in the valley below. B Company executed their airlift commencing at 0915 hours and started their foot movement down the ridge to the north. The advance Command Post was airlifted to LZ "Colt," commencing at 0915 hours.

A tactical air strike was initiated on LZ "Paint," the objective, at 0815 and 0840 hours. A series of air strikes were conducted during the morning, a fine display of tactical air. The Brigade Commander positioned artillery all around the Black Horse Mountains so that tubes could fire from any direction except the China Sea coast side.

At 1250 hours, C Company in its movement encountered

three Viet Cong trying to escape toward the mountains. They killed one VC and captured two carbines. At 1259 D Company, reinforced by one platoon from B Company, conducted the air assault into "Paint." In addition to the air strikes conducted intermittently throughout the morning, the air assault itself was preceded by a fifteen-minute artillery preparation followed by two minutes of aerial rockets.

The landing itself was conducted in classic manner and was one of the better assaults by the battalion, even though it was the first one conducted by D Company under Captain Tabb. About thirty minutes later I moved my Command Post from the high ground at "Stud" to LZ "Paint," the center of the battalion perimeter.

The rest of the operation proceeded according to plan, with three rifle companies converging on the objective secured by D Company. A series of small patrols were conducted by D Company to assure our security. The entire battalion closed into LZ "Paint"; the new battalion perimeter was established by about 1730 hours; resupply was then executed and the battalion prepared for another night's activity. Aggressive patrolling was conducted throughout the night with negative Viet Cong contact.

A highlight, after the battalion had been secured and all preparations completed, was the opportunity for an hour and a half or so on the beach to swim and clean up. This was one of the most beautiful beaches I have seen in Vietnam. The hills formed a U shape, closing right up to the water on the China Sea coast in which this little village and landing zone "Paint" were the focal point. The wide beach was composed of soft white sand. The water was extremely pretty, cool, and invigorating. Establishing security at both ends of the beach and with scouts overhead from the Air Cavalry Squadron to assure that we were not surprised, I gave permission for the entire battalion, less those on guard to go in the water.

Mustang Beach, as we designated this beach, became the Mustang Nudist Colony, as all of the troops stripped and had a glorious time in the sunshine and the clear salt water. My command group and I spent a few minutes in a similar occupation.

Plans were completed for the following day's operation, called Pistol-West. This was to be similar to today's operation; however, the bombing techniques would be employed by preparing two landing zones, one called LZ "Bit," into which A and B Companies would conduct an air assault; the second one, LZ "Stirrup," in which C Company would land. The companies would then move down the long fingers to the valley floor to search out that part of the Black Horse Mountains, looking for Viet Cong.

Toward noon on the following day, one platoon of A Company rappelled into LZ "Bit" with negative enemy contact. The operation was preceded by a tactical air strike using precision bombing methods, primarily 100 bombs, that blasted the jungle cover from the top of the hill. An artillery preparation preceded the initial movement of the platoon by A Company rappelling in, followed by the remainder of A Company, using CH-47's with the trooper ladders. The company closed by 1220 hours.

Almost simultaneously but following one phase later at 1145, one platoon of C Company rappelled into LZ "Stirrup." Similar techniques were employed. There was negative enemy contact. The air strike was conducted simultaneously in both LZ "Stirrup" and LZ "Bit," as had the artillery preparation. A longer artillery preparation was continued on LZ "Stirrup," because there had to be a slight shuffle in the use of the aircraft to land first A Company and then C Company. B Company followed A Company into Landing Zone "Bit" with the CH-47's closing back by 1400 hours. All three companies then conducted search-and-clear operations toward the valley to the west with negative enemy contact. D Company remained on LZ "Paint," securing the Forward Base, since we were scheduled, barring unforeseen circumstances, to return to "Paint" that night.

I controlled Pistol-West platoon from my command helicopter, working in close conjunction with Colonel Jack Cranford, the commander of the 227th Assault Helicopter Battalion. At one critical phase during the operation my command helicopter was almost out of fuel, which meant that I had to go on the ground someplace where I could control the operation. Colonel Cranford overheard my conversation on the radio, called me, and said he could pick me up. I dropped down on one of the positions overlooking the Pistol-East and West area, where we left the mortars in position to provide fire support. Colonel Cranford came in and picked me up and we flew together, as pilot and copilot, to control the crucial completion of the tactical air, the artillery, and the rappelling by helicopter and the Chinook ladder.

This was one of the best examples of close coordination between the aviation commander and the Infantry commander that occurred throughout my entire tour in Vietnam. Colonel Cranford was a fine soldier to work with and very cooperative. Between the two of us we were easily able to solve all of our problems. I controlled through my Command Post the fire power, that is, the artillery, tactical air, and mortars, and he controlled the UH-1's and the Chinooks.

During our conduct of this phase of the operation, we had a real scare as word was received from my Artillery Officer that the preparation on LZ "Bit" had been lifted so that Colonel Cranford and I could make a short run into LZ "Bit" to make sure the area was satisfactory for the UH-1D's to initiate their rappel mission. We started in toward LZ "Bit" when a hurried call over the radio informed me that one battery had a single round left in each of four tubes and had just fired. I did not know which one of the two LZ's it was going into, but we were right in the middle of LZ "Bit." We counted the time of flight seconds until the rounds hit. I think all of us offered a silent prayer as we observed over to the right the rounds landing in the adjacent landing zone, LZ "Stirrup." This again documented the case, "if you are going to go, you're going to go," because here we were in one of two landing zones when just by chance the artillery fired. It could only hit one. We were in the correct one in this case and avoided the barrage. Had the rounds fallen on LZ "Bit," we would have surely been destroyed.

The rest of the operation continued without enemy contact, with the companies finally moving to their respective landing zones, prepared for pickup. Darkness approached, and again the battalion was in the difficult position of possibly not being able to complete the extraction. I faced the decision of whether to stop the extraction and keep the troops in their position, or try to proceed with it and get everybody assembled back at LZ "Paint." There were few enemy in the area, but I did not like the idea of one platoon or perhaps a company remaining by itself. I preferred to have the battalion in one or two positions at most. I decided to go ahead with the lift, and with some help from Division in obtaining additional Chinook helicopters, we were able to extract all three companies and return them to LZ "Paint" prior to dark. Resupply was completed and a quiet night was spent on LZ "Paint."

The Brigade Commander informed me that the operation was about to draw to a close, and that beginning the next day the battalion would be airlifted back to LZ "Two Bits," which was the 2nd Brigade Base. We would secure the base for one or two days, oversee the security of the evacuation of the brigade elements, including the logistical portions, and then return to An Khe. He did inform me that we would move out of our present position at LZ "Paint" at 1100 in the morning. This provided a wonderful opportunity for two or three hours on the beach.

Plans were completed for our move to LZ "Two Bits," commencing at 1100 hours. We cleaned up equipment and especially men. I gave maximum numbers of troops time off to go on the beach and relax. My radio operators and I stripped and spent about two and one-half hours with the Command Post on the beach, alternating in the clear blue water and in the brilliant sunshine. This was probably a funny sight to many—a battalion of nude soldiers roaming around on the beach. My radio operators were horrified when we got word that the Brigade Commander was flying in to join us. I put on my shorts; they were concerned that I was not in full uniform to report to the Brigade Commander. Colonel Lynch was a fine soldier and excellent to work for. He knew the value to the battalion of these few hours on the beach; therefore he had left us there for that purpose. As I talked to him, he expressed the regret that he could not join us for a few hours, relaxation himself.

We continued relaxing in the sun. I can't think of anything that was more glorious and more pleasant after days and days of sweaty and dirty clothes than the opportunity to wash and clean up, to be able to relax in the water, and to have the wonderful sunshine on your body. It was glorious.

At 1100 hours, the battalion began its airlift back to LZ "Two Bits" to secure that area and the Bong Son airstrip. The battalion closed on "Two Bits" at 1245 hours. I made the customary pass in my command helicopter over LZ "Paint" to assure that no one was left behind as we departed this pleasant area. We would all have fond memories of this operation, and especially of Mustang Beach, which became a highlight of the Jumping Mustang history.

A quick check of the "Two Bits" area, and security was established. The battalion continued its preparation for the final move back to An Khe. An active H and I program was conducted during the night in the event that the Viet Cong or NVA might attempt to catch us short as the division executed a withdrawal. This situation was not as critical as it had been in the Plei Mei/Pleiku area, because Bong Son had a number of Vietnamese troops in the area and quite a bit of artillery. We were supplementing them.

Commencing at 0800 hours, the battalion initiated its airlift back to An Khe, using Caribous. A three-hour delay was caused by receipt of an additional mission to hold security at LZ "Two Bits" while other elements of the 2nd Brigade Forward Support Element cleared. By 1735 hours the battalion was released and the last element returned to An Khe. Thus the Bong Son operation closed with an efficient campaign.

Results of this more favorable action for the battalion were a total of 25 enemy killed by body count, an estimated 23 killed, 41 estimated wounded, 6 Viet Cong captured, 40 Viet Cong suspects captured, and 7 weapons captured. Most important in this fifteen-day operation, the battalion lost only one man killed with 12 wounded. We lost no equipment. We captured 35 packs belonging to the Viet Cong—approximately 600 pounds of medical supplies—and captured over 15 tons of rice.

The operation was a success both in destroying the Viet Cong and in furthering the training of troops in air-assault techniques. Employing airmobile assaults into landing zones, the battalion again utilized the rappel and troop ladder techniques to get into difficult landing zones, and the troop ladder for extraction from small pickup zones. The experience gained by these techniques continued to enhance our over-all capability.

Intensive tactical air support was employed, using over forty-three sorties throughout the operation with outstanding results. The availability of tactical air afforded the Infantry the extra support required to exploit operational areas and combine arms effort. During this operation all Infantry companies experienced the effect of close air support through our directing strikes within 100 meters of their positions. This greatly enhanced the confidence of the troops as to the capability of obtaining close effective tactical air support. Tactical air was also efficiently employed in clearing dense jungle areas to provide a small landing zone in order to rappel troops into the operational area.

Air Cavalry was effective in screening flanks, rear, and landing zones on a continuing basis and provided a great deal of intelligence through spot reports and gave assistance to ground units in searching the area.

Artillery support was outstanding throughout the entire operation, including the use of ARA's to provide overhead cover while landing or extracting troops, and providing fire on Viet Cong closely engaged with friendly troops.

The engineer support was outstanding. Support ranged from improving a landing zone to completely clearing one. Their organization ranged from separate teams attached to rifle companies, to the composite team used in one major effort in combination with D Company. Pathfinders performed their usual outstanding work.

In some instances, the quick response of Medivac remained a problem; however, a new technique was developed, that of using the CH-47 winch and basket, employed for the first time with outstanding success. The CH-47 has a fine winch plus a wraparound basket developed for lowering through the trees on the winch cable. The wounded soldier was placed in the basket, securely lashed, and then hoisted up through the jungle cover into the Chinook. C Company employed this method on "Pistol-East" operation when halfway down the hill one young trooper fell and broke a leg. It would have been extremely difficult to carry the wounded soldier the remaining distance by hand. In addition, his condition required medical attention as soon as possible. A Chinook hovered against a deep draw, in close to the trees on the side of the steep slope down which C Company was moving. The winch was lowered and, after two or three tries, the trooper was successfully evacuated.

I was pleased with the operation and with the battalion. All commanders, all leaders, had performed in an exceptional manner. The Jumping Mustangs were probably at their peak at this time and ready to take on any number of enemy and to accomplish any objective with outstanding results.

We would remain at An Khe for a day or so and then continue on a new mission called Operation "Tarzan," which would take us to the area deep beyond Bong Son to the west.

A disturbing incident within the brigade had occurred during the past few days. Lieutenant Colonel Harlow Clark, the Deputy Brigade Commander, was flying the new Brigade Commander, Colonel John J. Hennessey, on a reconnaissance of the area. Colonel Elvey Roberts had moved to Saigon, where he had joined General Westmoreland as the Chairman of the Joint Chiefs of Staff.

The OH-13 landed and Colonel Hennessey made quick recon and got back into the bird. As Colonel Clark picked up the aircraft, apparently something caused the aircraft to tilt over on its right side, the side in which Colonel Hennessey was riding. The rotor mast of the helicopter bent, and the rotor blade came around, striking Colonel Clark on the head, killing him almost instantly.

This was unfortunate because Colonel Clark was a tremendous soldier and his loss was widely felt within the brigade.

Personally affecting me was a rumor now that, since Colonel Clark had been killed and a new Deputy Brigade Commander would be required, I probably would be moving up to brigade. It was quite an honor to be considered for such a job; however, I did not wish to leave the Jumping Mustangs at this stage, since I felt that we were reaching our peak effectiveness and I wanted to see through our continuing operations.

On to "Tarzan."

14

TARZAN—JIM BOWIE

On March 10th our new operation would be back in the Bong Son area, a few miles west of the previous operational area. Intelligence sources revealed that the Sao Vang Division (Gold Star Division), including unidentified transportation, quartermaster, ammunition, medical, and tactical forces up to regimental size, as well as an unidentified anti-aircraft battalion, were believed to be in the new area of operation. This area was probably the base for the combat units that we had engaged during the Bong Son operation. The Viet Cong and NVA thought we had terminated our campaign. They were in the process of recovering, taking care of their wounded, rearming and re-equipping. A brigade going back into the area, especially the supply and maintenance area, could cause considerable damage and further defeat the remaining elements of the Gold Star Division.

The 1st Airborne Brigade was given the mission. Since there were no friendly elements remaining in the Bong Son area, the initial landings, to be made by the 1st of the 8th, followed by the 2nd of the 8th, would be accomplished without supporting tube artillery. The concept was for the 1st of the 8th to move in by air assault, seize an area, establish and secure an artillery base, and continue search-and-destroy missions within the two- or three-mile radius of this base.

Weather conditions delayed the operation for three days, because of lack of tube artillery and the complete dependence on tactical air and the aerial rockets for fire support. The operation could have been conducted any day using the aerial rockets as the only fire support, since the weather did not preclude the flight of the helicopters, either the armed or the assault transports. The Commanding General felt it important that the operation not be conducted until tactical air support could be employed because the enemy situation was somewhat unknown. Since we were not really on any important timetable, we could well afford to wait two or three days.

Reconnaissance of the area was controlled by the Division Commander with limited flights by elements of my battalion, the brigade, and the supporting forces of the division. The assault would be made by both the 1st and 3rd Brigades. The 2nd Brigade was in charge of the Barrier and the An Khe area. The landings would be simultaneous, the 1st Brigade on the mountain ridges between the Bong Son area of operation and the deep ravine made by the Vin Thanh River, and the 3rd Brigade occupying the Vin Thanh River Valley, including the high terrain to the west. The reconnaissance was made, using a new technique for the first time, by key commanders and staff in a Caribou and flying over the area much as if one were on a transport flight. The Caribou flew over and about thirty minutes later returned to provide a limited view to the commanders and staff of the area of operations. This method of conducting a reconnaissance did not prove successful. The aircraft was too high and it was difficult to see out of the small plexiglass windows in the Caribou. This bird was never designed as a reconnaissance aircraft, and even though this method might be desirable as a deception measure, it did not accomplish the primary purpose.

Additional limited reconnaissance was authorized, using a flight of two UH-1D helicopters: a combined flight by key commanders, staff, and supporting commanders within the 1st Airborne Brigade. The flight of two UH-1D's passed over the area of platoons to pinpoint objectives and, most important, the landing zones. A flight back a few minutes later at low level close to the ground for a distance of ten or fifteen miles gave a detailed view of the terrain without divulging the reconnaissance plan.

I believe this method did not arouse enemy interest as to what our intentions might be within the area. There had been so much traffic in the Bong Son area, and since this area of operation was between Bong Son and An Khe, it was easy to make the recon. Prior to the Bong Son operation, with two or three days in the An Khe area, I and my key staff had made

several other recons of this area. Therefore, we were ahead of
the game considerably and had already spotted landing zones.
Originally the recon had been for the Vinh Thanh Valley, the
3rd Brigade sector, so we were now completely familiar with
both brigade sectors.

The terrain that the 1st of the 8th was to make the initial
assault into was characterized by bald-headed mountains, the
tops completely bare except for the high grass; deep, wooded
jungle ravines; and many little valleys and numerous folds in
the terrain. Landing zones were not a problem because the technique to be employed would be to land on top of the bald-
headed mountains, establish a base, and search out the
valleys and the rest of the peaks. The valleys themselves, two
or three cross compartments running from the "Eagle's Claw"
back into the Vinh Thanh River Valley, were the areas we were
most interested in.

The initial landing zone selected, designated LZ "Columbus," was large enough to make a landing with the entire
battalion and establish two artillery batteries on the tops of
the hills. This LZ was bowl-shaped with a ridge running
almost all the way around the bowl. The northern portion was
large enough to establish the two artillery batteries, with the
rim of the bowl providing the perimeter.

The original plan called for the landing of A and D
Companies on "Columbus-South" with B on "Columbus-
North." The distance between the two, the southern and the
northern portions of the bowl, was 1000 meters. This caused
a large perimeter, but owing to the height of the terrain and
the relative freedom from vegetation, it would be easy to
defend. C Company was to conduct a landing on an LZ called
"Cusetta" 1500 meters further northwest down in the valley.

Final preparations were completed. We were ready.
Chaplain Spear led us in a battalion prayer, offered in thanksgiving for having successfully guided us in the months before.

Chaplain Spear

> Our Heavenly "Commander-in-Chief," we would
> give thanks to Thee, not as our forefathers who
> weathered the stormy seas of the Atlantic, the treach-
> erous first winters in the colonies, and the Indian
> raids and final friendships, but we give thanks that
> we have weathered combat with a minimum of

casualties. We give thanks for Thy Presence in the foxholes, Thy nearness in the mountain's sweep, in the muddy assault of the rice paddies, and Thy Presence wherever we are and whenever we permit Thy Presence.

As the artillery has arched its way overhead, we have been reminded of the first arch of promise, the rainbow. Our "artillery rainbow" reminds us of the uncertainty of life, the suddenness of destruction, and the eternal quality of Thy promise. As the rainbow reminds of Thy promise and faithfulness, may the whistling artillery remind us that the rainbow of promise continues over the battlefield. That You are present.

Life to us is dear. Flak jacket security is comforting. The shelter of the bunker is our hope. Our training and weapons are a help, and yet life is not so dear that we would preserve it at the cost of dictatorship, enslavement, or at the sacrifice of our loved ones on the altar of the enemy. Our "Purple Heart Valour" demonstrates this faith. Life is not so dear that we would sacrifice our faith and freedom to worship at the hands of a God-less philosophy.

We "Mustangs" will keep marching, seeking Thy presence, thanking Thee for the past, and depending on Thee for the present and future, so help us God. Amen.

The operation began with the assault at 1000 hours by B Company on LZ "Columbus-North." The landing was preceded by a tactical air strike and the usual ARA preparation. There was no enemy contact and B Company made it landing, using twenty-four UH-1D helicopters, without incident. A Company was next into "Columbus-South," followed by D Company. The battalion command group was located on a piece of high ground in the vicinity of "Columbus-North." The initial landing in "Columbus-North" was immediately followed by the Chinooks with 105 tube artillery to provide support for the landing of C Company a few minutes later and to support the landing of the 2nd of the 8th and the 1st of the 12th adjacent to the Jumping Mustangs.

"Columbus-North" and "South" were secured by 1250

hours. C Company completed its assault into LZ "Cusetta" without major enemy opposition, although there was some sniper fire from the ground at the helicopters as they made their landing at the LZ. LZ "Cusetta" could take only four birds at a time; therefore, the flights were in echelons, one minute between flights, so that the four birds could touch down, troops could unload, the helicopters could clear the small LZ, and the next wave of four could come in.

By 1325 hours, both landing zones, "Columbus-North" and "South" and "Cusetta," were secure and the search-and-destroy operations began. The first phase was the immediate search of the "Columbus-North" area by B Company and of the "Columbus-South" LZ by A and D. C Company conducted similar search-and-destroy operations and established ambushes in the vicinity of "Cusetta." Negative enemy contact was made during the day, and all units returned to their respective landing zones prior to dark. An active H and I program was conducted during the hours of darkness, with both mortars and artillery.

By this time the sight of cannons sitting on top of bald-headed mountains was a common one for the 1st Air Cavalry. This was not the technique taught at the Artillery

F-100

School at Fort Sill, Oklahoma, for generally artillery was seldom in a position where the target area could be seen, but was usually emplaced on the reverse slopes of hills to provide protection from incoming rounds, counter-mortar, and counter-artillery, and also to provide protection from enemy air. In this case there was no artillery, little enemy mortar, and no enemy air bothering these batteries. Therefore, cannon emplaced on top of the hills provided the most effective fire, were easily resupplied by Chinook helicopter, and could easily be extracted.

The first look at a bare hill with six cannons sitting there was quite a shock. This method was a most effective technique within the 1st Air Cavalry Division. In addition to the 105-tube artillery positioned within the 1st of the 8th area, a battery was similarly employed within the other battalions of the brigade. A 155-howitzer battery of four tubes had been brought in by the Flying Crane and was within the area of the 2nd of the 8th to provide support for the entire Airborne Brigade.

The landings had not been without casualties. Although there was no enemy contact, a number of men were wounded by punji-sticks, which were liberally emplaced all throughout "Columbus-North" and "South," though not so many in the "Cusetta" area. They were placed on top of the bald-headed mountains by the thousands. The initial casualties came on the first assault landing as men jumped from the hovering helicopters, moving quickly to seize the area. Fortunately, not many of the punji-sticks wounds were serious. In one case, a young soldier impaled himself in the fleshy part of his lower leg, fell, and pierced an arm with another. It was not uncommon to have two or three punji-stick wounds, especially if a man should fall. By this time the medical personnel had learned how to care for punji wounds, so that after care in the local division hospital for seven to ten days the wounded soldier returned to his unit at the An Khe Base for light duty; within a few days he was ready to go back into combat with his unit.

The Battalion CP was located on a beautiful little bare hill on which we had been able to carve out two landing spots for the command helicopter and the OH-13s working with the battalion. These two landing zones were cut on the pinnacle of the hill. The Battalion CP was deep within a clump of heavy trees and brush, which made it easy to defend and yet concealed it from the observation of the enemy.

These two landing zones were constructed by use of the baby bulldozer brought in by a Sky Crane at 1600 hours in the afternoon. Within thirty minutes, the two landing zones had been so flattened that the helicopter could rest its skids easily on the pinnacle and were big enough to facilitate loading and unloading of supplies and personnel. This technique was used throughout the bald-headed mountain area; the crane bringing in the baby bulldozer which then carved out a landing zone.

A series of four stairstep landing zones were cut on "Columbus-North" with similar LZ's on "Columbus-South." This permitted a platoon of four birds at a time to land, pick up troops, and unload supplies.

Since we were using the hilltops as a base to reduce the number of troops required for defense, the technique for the next few days would be to pick up units and move them out to appropriate landing zones where they could search out the suspected target area, be retrieved prior to dark, and be brought back to their base. Additionally, if an area that a unit was in showed little evidence of the enemy, the search could be called off. A landing zone could be quickly selected and necessary brush cut with machetes; birds came in, picked up the troops, and took them to the next landing zone in the plan to continue the search. In this manner little effort was wasted on a dry hole.

B Company on "Columbus-North" and A Company on "Columbus-South" launched a search-and-destroy mission to the west through a series of valleys that we expected, and intelligence indicated, to contain enemy base locations. C Company continued search-and-destroy missions within their area of operation. Tactical air strikes were conducted in conjunction with the movement of A and B Companies, using F-100's and B-57's. From my helicopter and from vantage points on the battalion observation post at the CP where one could see the entire area of operation, a good view of the tactical air operation was also revealed. The B-57's put on a tremendous display of close air support, using bombs, napalm, 50-calibers, and rockets. The noise of the bombardment echoed and reechoed through the narrow valleys and vibrated repeatedly around our hilltop position.

Various campsites were discovered by companies of the battalion, ranging from platoon to company in size, with several small rice caches being found and destroyed. Only two sightings of the enemy were made during the day and mortar and artillery were called in on these distant targets which were out of range of small arms. The companies set up blocking and ambush positions for the night with an active H and I program planned.

C Company conducted a series of platoon-size ambushes to 1500 meters around position "Cusetta." There were indications of numerous NVA or Viet Cong in the area, but other than some sniping, there were few results up to this time.

B Company located for the evening in a fine area, having progressed 2000 meters during the day. They were easily resupplied and secured for the night.

A Company was another question. Their routing had taken them down a deep ravine, so steep and narrow that it was impossible to bring in UH-1D helicopters for resupply and, most important, to retrieve casualties. A Company kept moving right up to dark in order to try to reach a valley where they would be able to receive supplies and arrange for the evacuation of casualties. It was obvious that this would not take place.

A Chinook helicopter was obtained and, using the winch and the wraparound basket, after a number of tries they were able to hoist the few casualties up to the helicopter and evacuate them. At the same time, C-rations were lowered down through the heavy jungle canopy right up to dark, meeting with little success owing to the time and effort involved and the small amount of C-ration cases that could be suspended by the cable. Finally, with darkness almost upon them, the crew elected on my order to simply toss the remaining C-ration cases from the helicopter. These rained down through the 150-foot trees, with a majority of them landing intact and in serviceable condition.

I was concerned with this resupply effort, for the battalion had a reputation of never failing to resupply its units, regardless of the conditions, either day or night. It looked at this time, because of the approaching darkness and with it the low ceiling, that we would have our first failure. I was pleased when we were able to accomplish this mission.

The battalion was somewhat scattered that night, with C Company still at LZ "Cusetta," B Company in its new area of operations, A Company in the ravine I described, and D Company securing the base, "Columbus-North" and "South," reinforced by the Reconnaissance Platoon from the 1st Airborne Brigade. The Brigade CP was located at "Columbus-South"; therefore there were a number of troops in that area who could be employed in the event of an attack at night. The 1st of the 8th was in charge of the security of the Brigade CP as well as the artillery and the battalion installations.

B Company and A Company continued their operation to search out the remaining portions of the valley. A Company moved 1500 meters to a landing zone on top of a bare hill, from which by the end of the day they were extracted and moved to a new landing zone called "Trigger," which would be the base the following day for a series of search-and-destroy operations to the north to join up with C Company. B Company continued its search, reaching by late afternoon a small one-bird LZ from which it was extracted to assemble on LZ "Trigger." The battalion was finally deployed with A and ·B Companies on LZ "Trigger," D Company back at "Columbus-North and South," and C Company at "Cusetta."

To assist in securing LZ "Rope" for A Company, the Anti-tank Platoon—that versatile rifle platoon—was used in a small air assault to seize LZ "Rope" until A Company arrived, at which time the platoon was recovered and moved back to "Columbus-South." They were used later on in the day to secure LZ "Trigger" prior to the arrival of A and B Companies.

LZ "Trigger" was deeply imbedded with hundreds of punjis, and several men were wounded. The entire operation would see fifty-eight men wounded by punji-sticks. This gives an idea of the number that were in the area and how difficult, despite our precautions, it was to keep from stepping on one.

At 1100 hours my command helicopter dropped me in the small landing zone selected by B Company where, with Jordan and Hill, I joined B Company for the rest of their movement overland during the day. This was an interesting trip through the valley. We found a number of huts and little villages that had been occupied by the NVA. There was evidence of rice and recent fires, only a few hours old, indicating that the enemy had been in this area and were rapidly moving out.

We received an excellent idea of the denseness of the jungle and terrain as we cut our way through the deep brush and the jungle trees, which by this time were thinned out somewhat, appearing to be mostly seventy and eighty feet in height. You could clearly see the double canopy, common in this area: the first made by small trees, twenty to thirty feet tall, the remainder, or second canopy, by the taller trees. In many areas, especially the new landing zone called "Tarzan" thirty kilometers to the north to which we would soon be moving on a continuance of this operation, we would see triple-canopy jungle, with the highest canopy averaging 150 feet in height.

The extraction of B Company that afternoon was not easy. It was difficult to find a landing zone; thus the side of a small hilltop had to be improvised, with much cutting by machetes to clear a path for one or two birds. The temperature was over 100 degrees. The fact that this landing zone was deep in a ravine made it difficult for the helicopters to pick up a normal load. On the extraction, three and four troops were the limit for the pickup. Coordination was effected quickly as the pilots came in and made their landing; the troops were positioned ready to dash to either side of the two birds. The crew chief or gunner in each door indicated the number of personnel, one or two, that he could take on his side. If the signal on the right side was two, then two troops dashed quickly to mount, so that the bird could move rapidly out of the way. Within thirty minutes, a total of eight UH-1D helicopters made the short shuttle of three kilometers and extracted B Company. I remained with the company commander and departed with the next-to-last platoon.

A short visit was made to LZ "Trigger," where A and B Companies were assembled, to go over our plans for the following day, to see how the troops were doing, and to chat informally with a number of them. A few minutes later my command helicopter arrived at my call to pick me up and take me back to the Battalion Command Post.

During our initial landing at "Columbus-South" a UH-1D helicopter came in to land atop the pinnacle or ridge that

was our LZ. There as it touched down the helicopter lost
power and flopped over on its back. Unfortunately, several
men were nearby, having dismounted from another helicopter. One young soldier was in the way of the flailing rotor
blade, which cut both of his legs off midway between the
knees and hips. One of the company aide men in A Company
was on his feet and with quick thinking put tourniquets on
both stubs and stopped the bleeding. The medical evacuation
helicopter came in, picked up the young soldier, and evacuated him direct to the Medical Evacuation Hospital at Quin
Nhon, where he was cared for and lived.

Several other men were seriously injured inside the
helicopter, but none were killed. I later visited at the hospital
the young soldier who lost his legs and was impressed with
his positive attitude, for he knew he would not be able to
walk again on his own legs, but could on artificial legs. He
was already making his plans for the future. It was inspiring
to see a man who had lost so much, who had given so much
for his country, and yet was not down and out, was not
discouraged, and was ready to drive on and adapt to his new
way of life in the future.

The night passed, with an intensive H and I program
throughout the night and without enemy contact.

The following day C Company continued a series of
search-and-destroy operations combined with platoon air as-
saults to converge with A and B Companies moving down off
LZ "Trigger." A and B Companies moved out down the long
fingers to the valley floor. By the end of the day they were
both extracted and returned to their respective positions in
"Columbus-North" and "South." At the end of the day C
Company was retrieved for movement back to "Columbus-
South." Thus the battalion reassembled with D Company on
"Columbus-North," and B and C Companies at "Columbus-
South," and A Company back at "Trigger," which was within
supporting distance of "Columbus-North." The purpose was
to prepare for the forthcoming operation.

Effective tactical air strikes were conducted on suspected
targets throughout the sector of all companies. Negative
enemy contact was made during the operation. All elements
closed back by 1750 hours and the battalion was established
in a perimeter defense on LZs "Trigger" and "Columbus." An

intensive H and I program was conducted during the night with no enemy contact.

In the meantime, plans were prepared for the assault on 17 March to a new landing zone thirty kilometers to the northeast, beyond the 3rd Brigade area of operations. This landing zone was designated "Tarzan." LZ "Tarzan" was selected as the center of an area of operations for the 1st Airborne Brigade deep within enemy territory near the I Corps Tactical Zone boundary, along a route on which it was believed NVA had been moving from the Bong Son area back into the Laos area. "Tarzan" received its name from the recons and the map study, which revealed extremely heavy jungle with trees extending 150 feet into the air. "Tarzan" itself was a large, bare mountaintop, almost a meadow—an island surrounded by rain forest. It was large enough to land thirty-six UH-1D helicopters simultaneously, although we would not initially use that many.

The operation was to be conducted out of the range of tube artillery; therefore tactical air would be most important, as would the ARA.

The assault began at 1300 hours, with C Company leading the way from "Columbus-South" for the initial landing.

A tactical air preparation of eight fighter-bombers was planned; however, it was not accomplished owing to difficulty in the fighters' locating LZ "Tarzan" and failure of communications between the Forward Airborne Controller and the fighters. A total of two birds did show up and executed a limited attack on LZ "Tarzan." The high ground to the north, which dominated the upper slope that made up LZ "Tarzan," was hit effectively with bombs, napalm, and rockets.

The air attack was followed by aerial rockets, preceding the landing of twenty-four UH-1D's. C Company was on the ground with little difficulty and no enemy contact. Owing to the distance involved and the delays in the tactical air support, the fuel in my command helicopter had reached a dangerous level; therefore, I landed with the command party to join C Company immediately after they landed and seized the LZ.

The assault helicopter lift proceeded back to pick up the remainder of the battalion, which would come in to consolidate the security of LZ "Tarzan." My command helicopter returned to "Columbus-South" for fuel and came back to join me within a short period of time.

Aerial-rocket artillery remained in the air to cover the last of the landings, as did an Air Cap which had arrived to replace the two fighters that had conducted the initial preparation. The entire battalion was assembled on "Tarzan" by 1650 hours.

Immediately after my landing, I received a call from General Kinnard, saying that he was coming in if the area was secure. The area was secure, since there had been no enemy contact whatsoever and, interesting enough, there had not even been a punji-stick. I believe the Viet Cong and NVA thought that this area in their own territory was relatively free from enemy attack and had not anticipated United States actions.

General Kinnard dropped down, with members of the Division staff, to join me for a few minutes. We discussed future plans and I briefed him on the present battalion situation.

Fires on the ground had been started from shooting aerial rockets into the dry grass that made up a major portion of the landing zone. A Chinook helicopter coming in a few minutes later made an approach directly over the burning fire to land sling-loaded tube artillery. The rotor wash, tremendous winds up to eighty or ninety knots from the rotor blades of the helicopter, fanned the fire, causing it to race rapidly across a major portion of the LZ, burning off most of the grass.

The fire quickly swept through the Mortar Platoon of C Company before the ammunition could be evacuated. We had to abandon some of the ammunition until the fire burned itself out, in the process of which three 81mm high-explosive mortar rounds exploded. The exploding shells created some degree of interest and activity in the landing zone, as personnel nearby had to take cover until the grass fire died down. The mortar-platoon leader and company commander did not live down this little episode for some time to come, although it was not entirely their fault. The first was almost out when the Chinook made an approach over the remaining embers, fanning it into brilliance. I was most happy that General

Kinnard had departed a few minutes prior to this little incident. That was the major activity for the day on LZ "Tarzan."

A perimeter was established for the night with the usual H and I program and an extensive series of patrols.

Plans for the following day were a series of search-and-destroy missions out 1500 meters to thoroughly search out one suspicious location, believed to hold at least a platoon of NVA.

Prior to leaving "Columbus-South" and the Brigade Command Post, Colonel Hennessey, the new Brigade Commander, called me in and stated that he had decided to move me up to brigade to become the Deputy, replacing Colonel Harlow Clark, recently killed. I was to be prepared on 20 March to turn over my battalion to the new commander, Lieutenant Colonel Barney Broughton, after things had calmed down on LZ "Tarzan."

I did not react too enthusiastically to the proposed change in assignment, although moving up to Deputy Commander was an honor and would be a most interesting job. I did hate to lose the battalion.

Search-and-destroy missions continued without enemy contact, resulting in a lot of exercise for all companies as they fanned out to search the area. Over to the west the 2nd of the 8th initiated a landing, as had the 1st of the 12th to the south. The 1st Airborne Brigade would spend two or three days in the area to see what could be found. The operation was to be concluded about 21 or 22 March.

I described earlier the tremendous jungle trees, towering 150 feet in height. Generally where there was heavy vegetation of this sort, the underbrush was almost nonexistent. Therefore, in this entire area foot movement was relatively free.

One of the hazards of the jungle area was the mountain leech. The leech was a small, inch-long, worm-like creature with a mouth seemingly on either end with which it could inch its way along, looking for blood. The only readily available product in the area was the troops of the Jumping Mustangs, and our major battle was conducted with these leeches.

The battalion CP was located on the uphill portion of the

landing zone in a heavily jungled area. We had a nice bivouac
with the usual stripped-down Command Post and the Hex
tent, and we were trying for the first time a handful of the
jungle hammocks. These were a lightweight hammock made
of silk and reinforced with a built-in mosquito net. Suspended
between two trees, they were handy for getting troops off the
ground, especially during wet weather. In this area, because
of the many readily available trees, the hammocks worked
satisfactorily. I tried one for the two or three nights and it
worked out well, primarily in its ability to keep the leeches
away.

The first night I spent sleeping on my air mattress with a
poncho pitched overhead. I was amazed how leeches dropped
down on the poncho and crawled up the inside; then when
they were over the exposed portion of your body, face, or
hands, they dropped down, latched onto you, and sank their
teeth in.

PFC Jordan was horrified the next morning when we got
up; stripped to check for leeches, he found two huge ones
embedded in his back near his waist belt. They had swollen
up to almost three or four times their regular size from the
blood they had absorbed during the night. I found one under
my wristwatch and another on the back of my neck. They
were more horrifying than actually dangerous and would
immediately let loose the flesh with the touch of a cigarette
or, better yet, the excellent insect repellent that we all carried. A squirt of insect repellent and a flick of the finger, and
they would quickly back out and were gone.

The area into which B Company made their search-and-
destroy operation was most heavily infested with leeches;
every man was covered with them by the time he got back.
We tried a number of things, such as spraying boot tops with
insect repellent. This helped somewhat, but the leeches still
found you. The only solution was, when one returned, to
strip one's clothes off and help each other remove any and all
leeches. As for medical or physical dangers, Dr. Odom said
there were none.

We fired another "Mad Minute" this night, customary
morning and evening, but by this time the Brigade Command Post had moved in from "Columbus-South" to join us
here on "Tarzan." There was one group of young soldiers, an
MP Squad, that apparently had not been with the Jumping

Mustangs before nor received word of the "Mad Minute." Just prior to dark the "Mad Minute" was executed. These young soldiers were in the process of eating C-rations and making leech searches, some of them having most of their clothes off. When the firing broke out, there was a mad scramble of confused soldiers for rifles, certain that the enemy were coming in on them and that all was lost. In the future we were careful to make sure that all of our newly attached or supporting elements were notified of "Mad Minutes."

LZ "Tarzan" was pretty well occupied now, although it was a large landing zone, 1500 feet in length and 800 feet in diameter. It included two artillery batteries, the Brigade Command Post, a portion of the Forward Support Command, and a fueling and landing point for the assault helicopters. The primary base of supply was still An Khe sixty miles away, from where resupply came by Huey helicopter late each afternoon.

During that time of the year, in the late afternoon the weather could get pretty severe and there was a continual shower every afternoon. We were wet daily, and it seemed as though rain always fell the last thing in the day, conflicting with the arriving resupply aircraft, which thus far had managed to get in even though the weather had been bad, slipping in between clouds and the jungle-covered terrain. Worst yet, one got wet prior to trying to attempt a few hours' sleep. Although the weather was not cold, when you were wet any slight decrease in temperature, especially in the mountains, was strikingly noticeable at night.

With the evening chow came a cold beer, which seemed to me the most wonderful thing I had all day—in fact, for the last several days. There was nothing like the uplift that one received from good hot chow and perhaps a cold beer after a long hot day when you were about to settle in for the night and relax a little bit from a rigorous day.

The night passed on with no enemy contact and considerable noise from our H and I program.

Another day of search-and-destroy missions, C Company with a deep search to the north, D Company's two-platoon search to the west, A Company with a deep search to the south to a landing zone and later extraction back to "Tarzan," and B Company with a series of platoon searches to the east. The battalion closed back in "Tarzan" by nightfall, with its primary mission still the security of the Brigade Command Post and the artillery.

Another quiet night except for the leeches, rain, and outgoing artillery and mortars.

March 20th was my last day in command of the "Jumping Mustangs." The battalion conducted limited patrolling action and concentrated on its perimeter-security mission. The change-of-command ceremony was scheduled for 1100 hours.

LTC Barney Broughton had been with me the last couple of days to look over the battalion and be briefed by the staff, as well as to receive my own personal briefing. He had previously visited the battalion rear at An Khe to get up to date on those facets of the battalion. Major Herman, the Executive Officer back at the base, came up to the LZ "Tarzan" and remained with LTC Broughton for the next few days to assist him in assuming command.

With my radio operators, Jordan and Hill, I made a quick final tour of the battalion area to say goodbye and take one last look at my command. It was good to see the Corporal, now Sergeant Ballew, who approximately one month previous transferred to C Company, where he was again a Fire Team Leader in the 1st Platoon of C Company.

Sergeant Ballew had accomplished a tremendous job as my radio operator. I had promised him that before I departed he would be sent to a rifle company where he would have an opportunity to demonstrate his abilities as a Fire Team Leader, and if he could do the job, he would be promoted to sergeant. The highest grade he could achieve as my radio operator was corporal. He performed a fine job for Captain Mozey, the company commander, and was later promoted. It was good to see him and note the progress that young soldier had made in the past few months. He would be getting out of the Army when his tour was up. He would be a loss to the Army and I would have liked to see him remain, but I had not been successful in my recruiting efforts.

The radio operators that remained with me were SP 4 Jordan, who had been with me since a change from PFC

Desner two or three months ago; and my second operator, a new one, Corporal Hill.

General Kinnard was to be present for the ceremony. We had a reduced-size ceremony on a broad portion of the landing zone. One platoon from each company was present, forming a somewhat dispersed square. Company commanders were present. Since there had been little activity and no danger of incoming mortar fire, I felt safe in having this small formation on the landing zone itself.

General Kinnard arrived. Present also were the Brigade Commander, Colonel John Hennessey, General Richard T. Knowles, and General Jack Wright. I was most pleased to see all of these senior officers of the Division come to witness my change-of-command ceremony.

A few minutes prior to the changeover, I took over the battalion formation for the last time and made a short speech to the men and officers of the battalion and visited each one of the company formations to shake hands with the company commander and the 1st Sergeant.

At 1100 hours General Kinnard arrived at the formation site, having been up on the hill at the Brigade CP with the Brigade Commander and the other dignitaries. LTC Barney Broughton was present. The General removed the Jumping Mustang Crest and the green tabs of command from my shoulder and pinned them on LTC Broughton. General Kinnard then made a fine speech to the battalion, praising the Jumping Mustangs for the tremendous job they had accomplished since their activation on 1 July 1965. This speech in itself was a climax to the battalion's operation and actually the last phase of this book. The reassuring comments as General Kinnard recited some of the recent history of the battalion and its accomplishments made me feel good indeed that the battalion had performed such an outstanding job. I was most proud. The ceremony was over.

LTC Broughton assumed command and made a short speech to the battalion. I joined the Generals and Colonel Hennessey at the Brigade CP for coffee and cake and the presentation of two or three awards from company commanders of the battalion. C Company presented me a fine Chinese rifle, a copy of the Russian SKS, with a plaque indicating that it came from C Company. In addition, a plaque was received from the officers of the battalion which I highly treasure. It

had the name of every officer in the battalion and the crest of the Jumping Mustangs. A similar award was received a few days later from the noncommissioned officers of the battalion, an award of which I was even more proud. B Company presented a crossbow captured on a recent operation, which hangs in a treasured spot in my home.

Colonel Joe Bush, commander of the 2nd of the 19th Artillery, gave me an eleven-gun salute during the ceremony. This was the first gun salute that I ever received; I was most proud of the feelings this salute represented between the fine artillerymen of the 2nd of the 19th and the Jumping Mustang Battalion.

At 1200 hours I jumped into the command helicopter for the last time and flew back to An Khe to spend a couple of days at the battalion base prior to assuming my new duties as the Deputy Brigade Commander of the 1st Airborne Brigade. Arriving back at the base, I spent a quiet afternoon cleaning up, collecting my thoughts, and getting my gear organized to move to the Brigade Command Post.

In looking over the operation, I could not help but think how successful it had been, even though there had been little enemy contact. Much was gained from the training it afforded the newly arrived personnel, getting them better oriented in their assault operations.

Tactical air was used extensively throughout the entire operation, with thirty-three sorties expended during the period. Air cavalry was used effectively to screen the front and flanks and rear elements and afforded a much better chance of locating targets that might otherwise have been bypassed.

Artillery was used extensively through the operation, and especially the ARA's, where tube artillery was not in supporting distance of our battalion.

I was especially pleased with our engineer support this time. Owing to the nature

SKS Rifle

of the terrain, the carving of hilltop landing zones or improvement of them was a major accomplishment of the engineers. The baby bulldozer brought in by the Flying Crane assisted greatly in leveling off the helipads on tops of the ridges.

Pathfinders were most effective in the control of the air traffic in conjunction with the use of supporting artillery within the area. Medical evacuation was the best yet, using the conventional UH-1D medical evacuation ships and especially the CH-47 with the wraparound basket on the end of the winch.

The photo coverage on this operation had been outstanding. An excellent photo was taken by the Mohawks prior to the operation which detailed and outlined the entire LZ and minimized the necessity for actual recon and possible revelation of the operation to the enemy.

Our actual enemy accomplishments were not so great. We only killed one VC by body count. By this time we had stopped estimating wounded because this was a rather artificial figure that one could not be certain of. We had not captured any VC or weapons. We had suffered a total of 85 casualties on this operation, 58 of them from punji-stick wounds and the remaining 27 from other types, including the UH-1D that rolled off the side of the mountain. We destroyed more than 55 huts and structures which were definitely used by the NVA and Viet Cong.

The use of the CH-47 to resupply a rifle company and the techniques involved, using the winch for the lowering of supplies, were a major accomplishment. We did find that there had to be improvements in the sling and an increase of the weight limitations of the winch. In spite of these problems, this method was most effective when no LZ's were available and the height of the jungle canopy precluded dropping supplies from a helicopter.

I had a quiet drive down to Quin Nhon to the Medivac Hospital to see the wounded Jumping Mustangs and say goodbye to all of them. It was always an inspiration, when one visited the hospital, to see how the men reacted, how well they had recovered, and to see the eagerness which so many demonstrated to return to their units and, strange as it seems, to combat.

I saw the young soldier whose legs had been cut off a few days before. His progress and attitude were remarkable.

I also saw many of the longer-term casualties who had been more seriously wounded and were awaiting improved medical condition prior to evacuation back to the states or to other hospitals within the Pacific area.

It was pleasant making the drive down to and from Quin Nhon, one that I had made several times. I had my regular jeep with SP 4 Jordan driving, since he had come back with me from "Tarzan," as he was to be discharged in the near future and would soon be rotating back to the United States.

I made a visit to the 2nd Mobile Army Surgical Hospital in the An Khe Base to say goodbye to the young soldiers there from the Jumping Mustangs. Here were the great majority of the punji-stick wounds that had been received during the recent operation. It was good to see these men and to chat with them prior to my departure.

A final tour around the battalion area and a last look at my old battalion as the battalion commander, then a jump into the jeep and a drive up to brigade and to assume my new duties as Deputy Brigade Commander.

The activities of the brigade from this point on, as far as I am concerned, merit a book in themselves. I could not do justice to what had been accomplished by the brigade and its units in the short space remaining in this book.

During the next chapter I will try to highlight a few of the activities of the brigade—mostly of the Jumping Mustangs as they carry on in several splendid operations, particularly one in the famous battle, Crazy Horse, which came in May and June. The battalion continued to drive on in the tremendous manner in which I knew it would, making me extremely proud as it continued to cover itself with glory, especially in Crazy Horse and in operations further south between Quin Nhon and Tuy Hoa in July.

I could have no greater tribute than to know that this battalion, which I had nurtured from activation in the United States to Vietnam and had fought with during the past six months, would carry on in the splendid manner that it had already done. I was proud of every officer, NCO, and trooper.

15

DRIVE ON—ALL THE WAY

The Jumping Mustangs Battalion "drives on" under its new commander, Lieutenant Colonel Barney B. Broughton. From my vantage point at the 1st Airborne Brigade Headquarters and my new job as Deputy Brigade Commander, I watched the Jumping Mustangs embark on the next operation, designated "Lincoln." This was to be a reconnaissance in force back to the area of the Plei Mei battle against the North Vietnamese in October-November of last year.

The purpose of the operation was to interdict the Viet Cong and North Vietnamese Army logistical points, infiltration routes, and units operating along the Cambodia-Vietnam border in Pleiku and Dalat Provinces. Intelligence reports indicated movements of the 32nd and 66th Regiments from their base area near the Chu Pong Mountains, south and into our area of operation, where they had been operating for at least a month. The 33rd Regiment was reported in the vicinity also. These were the three regiments that made up the NVA division which the 1st Air Cavalry Division decisively defeated in October-November.

The brigade operation began with the air assault led by the Jumping Mustangs into the area jut west of Plei Mei. The initial assault was by B and C Companies, by UH-1D helicopter. The remainder of the battalion and an artillery battery moved by Chinook helicopter. This operation began at 1200 hours; the battalion closed by 1300 hours. The assault was preceded by the usual tactical air strikes, artillery, and aerial artillery preparations. Negative enemy contact.

The remainder of the brigade headquarters and the 2nd

of the 8th battalion combat team moved by convoy on Highway 19 from An Khe to the base established near the Stadium, site of former Brigade CP of the Plei Mei campaign, now designated "Oasis." The Task Force included an artillery battery and the Brigade Forward CP.

The 1st of the 12th battalion combat team arrived by C-130 aircraft, landed, and was immediately deployed by UH-1D assault helicopters, plus some CH-47's, from Duc Co to a new area of operations west along Highway 19 in the vicinity of the Cambodian border.

They had flown initially from the An Khe airfield to the Duc Co airfield in the Duc Co Special Forces Camp. In addition, the 2nd of the 19th Artillery Battalion minus was included.

The operation was an airmobile move of 100 nautical miles in which one battalion moved by assault helicopter, a second battalion by C-130, and a third battalion by road and which took less than six hours to complete. This was probably the fastest move made by an entire brigade of 3500 men yet witnessed within the 1st Air Cavalry Division.

The brigade continued its reconnaissance-in-force operations to search out enemy within the area. Two attachments joined in this operation, a tank company from the 25th Division Tank Battalion and an armored reconnaissance company from the same division. They were attached to the Airborne Brigade and performed in an excellent manner.

The brigade operation was characterized by little enemy contact during the first portion. The 1st of the 12th contacted a few Viet Cong, captured five or six, and killed two or three more. During this phase we did identify five different regiments from the North Vietnamese Army, which indicated that the North Vietnamese were continuing to feed units and replacements for existing regiments down through Cambodia across the river.

The second phase of the operation was to move into the Chu Pong beginning 1 April. The Chu Pong was the huge mountain mass of the Plei Mei operation on the slopes of which the 1st of the 5th had been mauled in November. This action was a combined operation of three brigades: our own, the Airborne Brigade; the 3rd Brigade; and the 3rd Brigade of the 25th Division.

The 3rd Brigade of the 25th operated to the north of the

Chu Pong, our own 3rd Brigade on the east of the Chu Pong mass, and the 1st Airborne Brigade in the south. We moved in and encircled the mountain for the assault of the massif itself. By the use of airmobile techniques, troops were landed on all the high peaks of the massif with the usual technique of working down the slopes, scouting for the Viet Cong.

On the afternoon of 30 March, the 1st of the 12th attempted to rescue a rifle platoon of the 1st of the 9th Cavalry that had landed just south of Chu Pong to capture three Viet Cong. The three Viet Cong were located first by the OH-13 Scout Team, the White 'leam. These called for reinforcements, and the Blue Team, a rifle platoon, moved in to try to capture the Viet Cong. The platoon ran into at least an enemy platoon or company and were heavily engaged.

A Company, 1st of the 12th, was committed to secure the elements of the cavalry troop, extract them, and continue the mission to develop the situation and destroy the enemy in that area. The rifle platoon of the cavalry troop was extracted, but A Company was heavily engaged and suffered a number of casualties. The situation prevented extraction prior to dark had the Brigade Commander desired to do so.

In the meantime, four UH-1D's from the Cavalry Squadron were shot down, three of them total losses. An effort was made to extract the rifle company, but one CH-47 trying to make a landing in the only available small landing zone was seriously damaged by fire. It managed to land safely but could not be flown out again.

The Brigade Commander made the decision to leave the company there. A sporadic fire fight continued throughout the early hours of the evening. Ammunition resupply was dropped in by low lex from two Caribous that made low passes over the landing zone just prior to dark. Low lex was a method of loading cargo into a Caribou with a small parachute attached that was used to extract the cargo from the rear of the bird with just enough buoyancy to ease the cargo to the ground.

During the early part of the evening, it was obvious that there was more enemy in the area than first anticipated. It was possible that A Company, 1st of the 12th, would run into trouble during the night as the Viet Cong reinforced their present positions. The company was out of range of tube artillery and was depending entirely on aerial rockets and tactical air support. Although this fire was being directed effectively as required, it was still desirable to have tube artillery if possible.

Colonel Jack Hennessey, the Brigade Commander, along with the commanders of the 227th Assault Helicopter Battalion, LTC Jack Cranford; the 1st of the 8th, LTC Barney Broughton; and the 2nd of the 19th Artillery, LTC Joe Bush, made plans to execute a night air assault of one rifle company from the 1st of the 8th and secure an LZ close enough to the present area of operations in order to move an artillery battery in by Chinook to provide artillery support for A Company, 1st of the 12th.

By chance, A Company, 1st of the 8th, was in reserve. They were picked by LTC Broughton to make the second night air assault in the history of the 1st Air Cavalry Division, the Jumping Mustang Battalion, and this one company.

The 1st of the 8th assaulted into the area without any prior recon, either by the company commander or the battalion commander and, most important, without any prior recon by the aviators of the 227th Assault Helicopter Battalion. Colonel Jack Cranford led the flight of helicopters and personally landed his bird to drop off two Pathfinders in the landing zone to set up instruments to guide the rest of the flight in.

The landing was attempted initially with the use of flares dropped from a CH-47. However, timing was unsatisfactory and finally efforts were made to drop flares from UH-1D helicopters. These were successful and provided sufficient light for Colonel Cranford to make his initial landing. He overshot the landing zone on the first pass and had to make a second entry. Fortunately the immediate area was occupied by few enemy and within an hour the landing zone was secured, the artillery battery moved in by Chinooks, and A Company, 1st of the 12th, was receiving artillery support.

Most interesting from the Mustang view was that A Company, 1st of the 8th, was the unit on this preplanned mission—this night air assault—the first actual planned night air assault in Vietnam by the 1st Air Cavalry Division and the second one executed by this company.

Operations continued in the Chu Pong area with the rest of the 1st of the 12th going in the following day to reinforce its actions and the remainder of the 1st of the 8th moving in also to expand the landing zone and conduct search-and-clear operations. This incident led to the operation to clean out the Chu Pong.

The entry into the Chu Pong and the thorough search were somewhat discouraging because we found few Viet Cong and little evidence of their presence. The Chu Pong was the bogeyman of the Plei Mei Campaign because it was believed that perhaps many of the Viet Cong had escaped into the mountains. This was probably not true. Although we did not thoroughly search the massif at that time, there was little evidence now of the Viet Cong having been deep in the Chu Pong.

Some of the old battlefields, especially "X-ray," still remained. Abandoned weapons and a few remaining skeletons from NVA bodies not recovered had not been touched. Had the Viet Cong or the NVA been in that area, they certainly would have secured the weapons and the ammunition left behind.

A combined operation of the three brigades did have the good effect of at least determining that there were no enemy in the Chu Pong. It did verify that they were across the border in Cambodia. A number of telephone wires were found running across the border itself, especially from the area where the 1st of the 12th had been engaged.

The operation terminated on 7 April, and with good results. The brigade killed over 350 Viet Cong by body count and estimated an additional 500 killed. In addition, a large amount of equipment had been captured.

Operation "Mosby I" began as an operation that took the brigade and the Jumping Mustangs back to the area they were operating in when the "Year of the Horse" began. The 1st and 2nd of the 8th were in assault with the 1st of the 12th in division reserve.

The 1st of the 8th made an assault landing again into LZ "Maverick" of fond memories. "Maverick" was heavily punjied and there was evidence of locals recently in the area. However, there was little enemy contact and no indication of major enemy units.

The 1st and 2nd of the 8th continued their operation and found few Viet Cong. The 2nd of the 8th found a large quantity of ammunition—approximately seven tons—probably

one of the largest caches found in the Vietnamese War by the
1st Air Cavalry Division. This ammunition was found by a
patrol moving along a trail near the Cambodian border.

A little side trail wandered off to the left of the main trail
for approximately 400 meters. The patrol followed this small
trail, which led to a Vietnamese hut. In the hut they found
4500 rounds of 50-caliber ammunition; 28 rounds of 120mm
mortar ammunition, complete with fuses, including a new-
type fuse; 40 rounds of 81mm mortar ammunition, both HE
light and HE heavy, plus some WP. There were 40 cases of
explosives and approximately 40 cases of hand grenades,
potato-masher type, with both long and short handle. There
were two brand-new AM radios and a series of 1 master and 4
slave switchboards, brand new, that had not been used and
were the type generally employed for a Division Command
Post. A quantity of other small-arms ammunition was also
found. Most significant were the communication equipment
and one item that all helicopter pilots were glad to see
captured, the cache of 50-caliber ammunition.

The rest of the operation continued to be a series of
search-and-destroy operations with no enemy contact. A few
days later, on 17 April, the brigade commenced its withdrawal from "Oasis" back to An Khe, moving by C-130 aircraft
everything but one rifle company, B Company, 1st of the 8th,
which remained at "Oasis" overnight as security for remaining
logistical elements.

I watched the entire operation from the Brigade Forward
Command Post and on the numerous visits to the Jumping
Mustang Battalion. I was happy to see the battalion carry on,
under its new battalion commander, without ever missing a
beat—if anything, improving its performance.

One highlight of Operation "Lincoln" on 25 March was
the establishment of a Caribou landing strip within four hours
at "Oasis," followed in three days by the construction of a
C-130 strip 4000 feet in length, covered with the new mem-
brane that provided an all-weather capability. This was the
first time this system was employed in the 1st Air Cavalry area,
although it had been quite common in air assaults in the Carolinas back in 1965. The strip received large numbers of C-130's
on 17 and 18 April without damage and with ease. C-130's
were able to take off and land on the field strip, moving
large loads of troops and equipment to An Khe. Again

the Caribous were handy in this operation and worked well with the C-130's to return the entire brigade.

Operations "Lincoln" and "Mosby I" were good operations. We killed a large number of Viet Cong in the first phases of the operation and showed again that there was not a Viet Cong or NVA behind every bush. We discovered new units. We found that the Viet Cong and the NVA continued to avoid making contact with the American forces. We were able to employ the tank company from the 69th Armor of the 25th Division to good advantage. This was the first time American armor had been used extensively in this area. The Cavalry Troops from the 25th Division, C Troop of the 3rd of the 4th, did a fine job opening roads and facilitating cross-country movement.

The division was the first to employ the use of 175mm guns and eight-inch howitzers, self-propelled, off roads down into and supporting the Chu Pong attack. Of most interest, we laid bare the falsity of the belief that there were two or three regiments in the Chu Pong. Maybe there had been at one time, but they had not been there for months. There was a shortage of water in the area at this time of the year. It was no place really for the Viet Cong or NVA to be. Obviously the VC were all across the Cambodian border, where they were safe in sanctuary, where they could come out and go ahead with their mission of attacking the Special Forces Camps at the time and place of their choosing.

We were prepared to return to Pleiku and this area, and maybe it would be a good idea if the VC did come out in the open and attack one of these camps, because if we could, with our rapid reaction, land troops and fire power between them and the border, we might be able to destroy many more.

This past operation was quite an experience for me. Instead of being an active battalion commander, I sat back a little bit more as the Deputy. My primary job was to coordinate the brigade staff, make sure that everything worked in the brigade, and be prepared to step forward when needed. Colonel John J. Hennessey, the Brigade Commander, was a tremendous soldier to work for. I enjoyed it immensely. If I could not be a battalion commander or the commander of the Jumping Mustangs, then I certainly had an outstanding job as the Deputy Brigade Commander.

We would probably be in the An Khe are for two or three weeks and then go into another combat operation. By the way, the brigade call signs still remained the same, and in my new job I was known as "Quarterback 5."

The brigade began a new operation designated "Crazy Horse." This was an operation only eighteen kilometers to the northeast of the An Khe Base in an area called "Happy Valley." This valley saw one of the first operations of the 1st Air Cavalry Division back in September-October of the past year by the 3rd Brigade. The valley was cleared in a search-and-clear operation and a Special Forces Camp was installed by the Vietnamese Army. This camp, at the foothills of some of the most rugged mountains in Vietnam, was watched over by the 1st Air Cavalry and was in range of some of our medium artillery. In addition, the division had plans to reinforce this camp at the first indication of enemy contact.

The Bong Son operation in February and March saw the defeat of an entire NVA Division force on the China Sea coast. There was little current indication of enemy activity anywhere in the area. This was not really the case, for evidence gathered during Operation Crazy Horse verified that the Viet Cong forces were about to launch a massive offensive into the Vinh Thanh Valley, another name for "Happy Valley," sometime during the latter part of May. Furthermore, it appeared that the Viet Cong planned a full-scale interdiction campaign against Highway 19 in the vicinity of the An Khe Pass and against the Happy Valley road. It was also probable that the Viet Cong planned harassing actions against Camp Radcliff, the name of our base at An Khe, in conjunction with the offensive. The Viet Cong objectives were to increase their prestige and morale by regaining control of "Happy Valley."

On 15 May a CIDG Patrol from the Special Forces Camp ambushed a Viet Cong force and captured documents which revealed Viet Cong plans to attack the Special Forces Camp with 120mm mortars. It was probable that this attack would be in support of an Infantry assault to be conducted by the 2nd Viet Cong Regiment. The Special Forces teams reported to Major General John Norton, the new Division Commander, at An Khe that a platoon-size force planned to attack "Happy Valley." This estimate was quickly raised to a battalion, then to two battalions, and finally to at least regimental strength.

On 16 May, B Company, 2nd of the 8th, moved into the mountains east of "Happy Valley" and landed on LZ "Herford," to intercept the one or two platoon-size Viet Cong forces initially reported to be preparing to attack the Happy Valley Special Forces Camp. The company was immediately engaged in a fierce fight. It soon became evident that this unit was fighting more than two platoons. It was surrounded by at least two battalions of Viet Cong and was in one of the most vicious battles since LZ "X-ray" in the Plei Mei Campaign.

A Company, 1st of the 12th, assaulted in to relieve the embattled American company in the late afternoon of 16 May and took more than four hours to fight its way uphill to the current location of B Company, 2nd of the 8th. Early the next morning the entire 1st of the 12th moved by air assault into the fight.

Fierce fighting continued for the next three days as the rest of the 1st Brigade was brought into action. The fighting continued in a series of short, fierce contacts until early June. 1st Brigade troops ambushed and harassed units of the 2nd Viet Cong Regiment every day. Tube artillery, aerial-rocket artillery, tactical air, and B-52 strikes fired into the area daily. Assessment of damage to the enemy was made difficult by the thick jungle, but each day's body count was twenty to fifty enemy dead. Friendly casualties were light.

The Jumping Mustang Battalion was committed on the

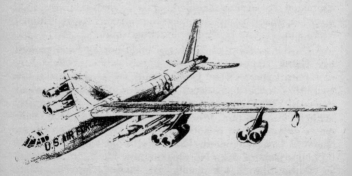

B-52

afternoon of 20 May to relieve the 2nd of the 12th at LZ "Horse," a landing zone deep in a steep valley, a route through which it was believed the enemy would try to escape.

On 21 May, A Company, remaining at the LZ as a security element, continued to receive sniper fire. In the meantime, B and C Companies moved toward the northeast on down the valley. At 0855, C Company killed one Viet Cong sniper. At 0940 B Company received heavy automatic-weapons fire from an area between them and C Company. Captain Mozey of C Company and Captain Martin of B Company maneuvered against the enemy, believed to be about squad-size. Artillery was called in, and the entire area was swept, with negative enemy contact. At 1510, A Company patrol engaged three Viet Cong wearing khaki rain jackets and black pajamas and armed with AK-47 assault rifles. One Viet Cong was killed, actual body count, and one wounded. At about the same time B Company engaged an estimated reinforced Viet Cong company with heavy weapons. Heavy fighting continued throughout the afternoon and night and lasted to about 0200 hours the next day.

Reports revealed that the Viet Cong were well dug in, were disciplined, and were using heavy automatic weapons and had excellent supplies and morale. Captured documents from the dead Viet Cong personnel identified the unit as the 8th Battalion of the 22nd NVA Regiment. Artillery was called in late on 21 May and during the morning hours of 22 May. B Company reported 30 Viet Cong killed by body count, an estimated 18 additional killed, and 19 wounded. By 1500 hours, a patrol by B Company encountered two additional Viet Cong digging along a well-defined trail.

On the morning of 22 May, a small enemy force probed LZ "Horse" from the southwest. This attack was repulsed by the security force. B and C Companies swept the area in the vicinity of their engagement and reported finding an additional 21 Viet Cong killed. At 1115 hours, C Company engaged an estimated squad and brought fire to bear, with results unknown. As of 1800 hours, a composite report from B and C Companies indicated a total of 60 Viet Cong killed by body count in the 21-22 May engagement. An estimated 20 additional were killed and 20 wounded. Two 30-caliber machine guns, two AK-47's, one M-1 carbine, one radio, and numerous quantities of ammunition and assorted uniforms were captured.

During this operation, Captain Roy Martin performed in such a heroic manner that on 12 September 1966 he was awarded the Distinguished Service Cross. The Citation reads as follows:

> For extraordinary heroism in connection with military operations against an armed hostile force in the Republic of Vietnam. Captain Martin was serving as Commanding Officer of Company B, 1st Battalion Airborne, 8th Cavalry, 1st Cavalry Division Airmobile. On 21 May 1966, his unit was assigned the task of routing an unknown Viet Cong force out of a nearby valley. While moving up, Captain Martin's unit came under intense automatic weapons and sniper fire from a well-dug in, reinforced Viet Cong battalion. As a counter-movement, the friendly defenders launched a frontal assault but were beaten back by the insurgents. Realizing the necessity of a break in contact with the hostile forces prior to darkness, Captain Martin withdrew his troops and called for aerial rocket artillery, mortar and artillery fire support. He then took his headquarters element and the 2nd Platoon and moved to within 30 meters of the Viet Cong's line of defense. A machine gun opened fire on the advancing platoon and Captain Martin, with complete disregard for his own personal safety, exposed himself to the intense fire, shot the gunner and threw a grenade into the emplacement, killing the three remaining Viet Cong. Continuing another 25 meters, Captain Martin eliminated two more bunkers which allowed his units to advance. Still moving up, he exposed himself three more times to kill snipers. Captain Martin's extraordinary heroism and gallantry in action are in keeping with the highest traditions of the United States Army and reflect great credit on himself and the military service.

The Distinguished Service Cross could not be awarded in Vietnam to Captain Martin, because a few days later, on this same operation, he was seriously wounded with a bullet in his hip, causing his evacuation back to the United States and to the Army Hospital at Fort Bragg, North Carolina. It would not be until November 1966 that Captain Martin actually received the award at Fort Bragg. I was privileged to be present and see him receive this well-deserved honor, along with four additional awards for his Vietnam service. The four included a Bronze Star for Valor, Air Medal, Commendation Medal, and Silver Star.

Sp4 David Dolby was the main hero of B Company action. A machine gunner in the 3rd Platoon, Sp4 Dolby took over command of his platoon when the platoon leader was killed and most of the noncoms killed or wounded. His citation for the Medal of Honor, awarded by the President at the White House on 28 September 1967, best describes both the action and Sergeant Dolby's bravery and heroism.

The Citation:

On 21 May 1966, Sergeant Dolby, then Specialist Four, was serving as a machine gunner of Company B, 1st Battalion (Airborne), 8th Cavalry in the Republic of Vietnam, when his platoon, while advancing tactically, suddenly came under intense fire from the enemy located on a ridge immediately to the front. Six members of the platoon were killed instantly and a number were wounded, including the platoon leader. Specialist Dolby's every move brought fire from the enemy. However, aware that the platoon leader was critically wounded, and that the platoon was in a precarious situation, Specialist Dolby moved the wounded men to safety and deployed the remainder of the platoon to engage the enemy. Subsequently, his dying platoon leader ordered Specialist Dolby to withdraw the forward elements to rejoin the platoon. Despite the continuous intense enemy fire and with utter disregard for his own safety, Specialist Dolby positioned ablebodied men to cover the withdrawal of the forward elements, assisted the wounded to the new position, and he, alone, attacked enemy position until his ammunition was expended. Replenishing his ammunition, he returned to the area of most intense action, single-handedly killed three enemy machine gunners and neutralized the enemy fire, thus enabling friendly elements on the flank to advance on the enemy redoubt. He defied the enemy fire to personally carry a seriously wounded soldier to safety, where he could be treated and, returning to the forward area, he crawled through withering fire to within fifty meters of the enemy bunkers and threw smoke grenades to mark them for air strikes. Although repeatedly under fire at close range from enemy snipers and automatic weapons, Specialist Dolby directed artillery fire on the enemy and succeeded in silencing several enemy weapons. He remained in his exposed location until his comrades had displaced to more secure positions. His actions of unsurpassed valor during four hours of intense combat were a source of inspiration to his entire company, contributed significantly to the success of the overall assault on the enemy position, and were directly responsible for saving the lives of a number of his fellow soldiers. Specialist Dolby's heroism was in the highest tradition of the United States Army.

I was privileged to be present along with several other Jumping Mustangs when the Medal of Honor was presented, the third won by the 1st Air Cavalry in Vietnam and the thirty-fourth in the history of B Company. I was most proud of Sergeant Dolby, B Company, and the Jumping Mustangs.

Captain Mozey, C Company, performed in a very outstanding manner during Operation "Crazy Horse" and received considerable credit for the fine job his company performed. A total of six Silver Stars were won by B Company for this action, and two Silver Stars by C Company. I know that Colonel Broughton was proud of the Jumping Mustangs, as I was in watching this operation from Brigade.

At the end of "Crazy Horse," which concluded 10 June 1966, more than 500 enemy were killed. Much ammunition was captured and destroyed. Several caches of hospital equipment, food, and salt were also liberated from the enemy. "Happy Valley" was believed to be the home station of the rear elements of the 2nd Viet Cong Regiment, and if so, this attack disrupted their logistical and communications base.

The attack also broke up an enemy attempt to overrun the Happy Valley Special Forces Camp and, from the size of the units involved, perhaps prevented an attack on the 1st Air Cavalry Base at An Khe.

The Brigade completed the twenty-one-day Operation "Crazy Horse" and returned to An Khe to continue defense of the base until the next operation, which began on 20 June as far as the Jumping Mustang Battalion was concerned and little bit later for the rest of the Airborne Brigade.

A recap of Operation "Crazy Horse" revealed some interesting facts. First, the operation was conducted in almost impossible terrain, with peaks running up as high as 3000 feet, steep, razor-back, and covered with heavy jungle vegetation. This operation required the utmost in ingenuity to perform the outstanding airmobile role conducted. Weather was extremely bad throughout the operation, curtailing tactical air support from time to time and interfering with the airmobile operations.

A summary of the fire power expended during the twenty-one days was phenomenal. A total of 260 tactical air sorties were flown. Of these 106 were immediate request and 154 were preplanned. Ordnance employed included general-purpose bombs, fragmentation bombs, CBU, and napalm. In all, the tactical Air Force dropped over 346,540 pounds of ordnance during the operation. In addition, there were a total of three B-52 strikes involving twenty-one B-52's.

Artillery fire during the operation was probably the largest in number fired by anyone since the division arrived in Vietnam. Approximately 80,000 rounds of tube artillery were fired, in addition to over 30,000 rounds of aerial rockets. Fires included 105 and 155mm howitzers, 175mm guns, and eight-inch howitzers. Over 55,000 rounds of 105mm artillery alone were fired, and almost 10,000 of the heavier-caliber 175 gun and eight-inch howitzer.

Another interesting part of this battle was the use of allied forces during the operation. These forces were composed of two Vietnamese Army scout companies, plus an armored Infantry company and an Airborne company. The 2nd Battalion, 1st Cavalry Regiment, Republic of Korea Capital Division, operated with the brigade, plus four CIDG companies for the Special Forces. In addition to these allied forces and the three battalions of the Airborne Brigade, a

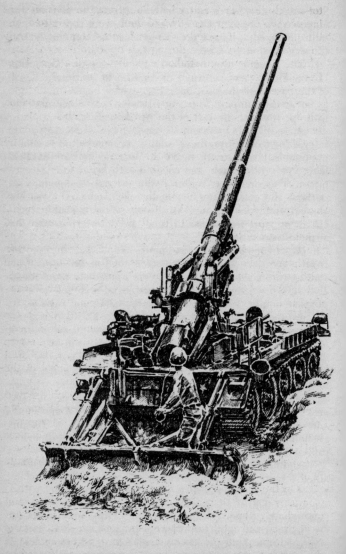

175mm. Self Propelled M-107

total of three other Infantry battalions from the division were involved in the operation. Two of them were committed, the third one kept in reserve. Colonel John Hennessey truly commanded a large force during this operation—six US battalions, a Vietnamese battalion equivalent, and a Rock Tiger Division battalion.

On the 20th of June the Jumping Mustang Battalion joined with the 3rd Brigade in Operation "Nathan Hale," a search-and-destroy mission in the Tuy Hoa area.

A North Vietnamese regiment infiltrated from the Cambodian border across South Vietnam in an attempt to interfere with the rice harvest in the Tuy Hoa area. The Tuy Hoa Valley, a beautiful area, well-watered, was one of the richest rice-producing areas in the Highlands. The rice had been under control of the Viet Cong for many years. During the past year, a brigade of the 101st Airborne Division had driven most of the Viet Cong and NVA from the valley. The movement of the enemy regiment was an attempt to regain for the Viet Cong the rich rice harvest. The operation began with an attack on the Special Forces Camp near Tuy Hoa and led to the employment of the 3rd Brigade, 1st Air Cavalry Division, later to be reinforced by the Jumping Mustangs.

The Jumping Mustangs moved by C-130 aircraft to the airfield at Tuy Hoa-South, closed by 1700 hours, and immediately moved into the operation. They worked in conjunction with C Company, 2nd Battalion, 327th Infantry of the 101st Division, which came under the operational control of the Jumping Mustangs.

At 1535 hours, B Company, 1st of the 8th, moved overland a short distance into an LZ designated "Eagle" to join forces with C Company, 2nd of the 327th. At approximately 2315 hours, B Company began receiving heavy mortar and recoilless-rifle fire which resulted in minor casualties. The night was quiet except for sniping and the usual friendly H and I fire.

On the morning of the 22nd, B Company, along with C Company, 2nd of the 327th, conducted a "Mad Minute" and immediately came under heavy ground attack from the northwest, west, and southwest by an estimated two companies of NVA. At one point the enemy assaulted to within six feet of the United States perimeter. Tear gas was frequently used by the United States elements. The two units were engaged with the enemy for approximately four hours. Aerial-rocket artillery and tactical air was called in and the enemy finally withdrew from the battle area. At no time was B Company perimeter penetrated.

Again at 0820 hours B Company became engaged with the enemy at close range and asked for commitment of the reserve company, A Company, 1st of the 8th. At 0917 hours, B Company reported holding but again receiving heavy 82mm and 60mm mortar fire. At 1030 hours, B Company, 1st of the 8th, and C Company of the 2nd of the 327th reported the situation well in hand, with a large Viet Cong body count in front of their positions. At approximately 1045 hours, a Viet Cong was captured and initial interrogation revealed that he was a lieutenant from the 1st Platoon, 3rd Company, 2nd Battalion, 66th Regiment. His platoon consisted of thirty personnel, armed with three sub-machine guns and twenty-seven other rifles.

A recap of this action indicated that one rifle company, reinforced, planned to attack the location of C Company, 2nd of the 327th, a small company, reduced in numbers by casualties and in poor condition to continue the fight. The NVA were not aware that B Company had moved in overland to reinforce the landing zone. The NVA made preparations and plans during the night, moved up to surround the position, ready to attack at first light. They were in the final process of initiating the attack when the "Mad Minute" was set off by B Company.

The "Mad Minute" caught the NVA in the open with our own troops standing to, all in position on their weapons and firing. This battle resulted in 127 Viet Cong killed by body count, with only seven wounded in B Company's action. In addition, large quantities of ammunition and weapons were captured. The NVA company commander was found at the conclusion of the battle sitting on a rock holding his head in his hands, repeating to himself in Vietnamese words to the effect that "All is lost, all is lost."

Captain Jerry Plummer recently had assumed command of B Company, having returned from Walter Reed and the United States a few days before. He arrived at brigade just prior to the wounding of Captain Martin and his subsequent evacuation. He took over the company and, as evidenced by this action, performed an outstanding job for which he was awarded the Silver Star a few weeks later.

B Company was fortunate to have had two such outstanding commanders: Captain Martin, who won the Distinguished Service Cross for heroic actions in "Crazy Horse," and now Captain Plummer with the Silver Star. This battle was a most successful battle with the highest kill rate ever attained by any unit in Vietnam, 127 to 0.

This action concluded the "drive on" of the Jumping Mustang Battalion, for a few days later I completed my service with the Airborne Brigade and moved to Headquarters of the 1st Air Cavalry Division to work for the Commanding General, General John Norton.

As I look back over that period, from 20 March when I left the battalion to my departure from the brigade, I could not help but leave glowing with pride in the Jumping Mustang Battalion for what they had accomplished for both LTC Broughton, their present commander, and me. We were both fortunate to command a battalion such as they. The battalion truly accomplished every mission in Vietnam that either LTC Broughton or I asked, with a dedicated "Drive on, all the way." It marked deep into the history of its own unit as well as contributed to the history of the 1st Air Cavalry Division. A job well done.

Proof of the tremendous success of the remarkable airmobile concept and the 1st Air Cavalry Division in Vietnam was evidenced by the Presidential Unit Citation for the Plei Mei action in 1965, awarded by the President at the White House on 15 September 1967, almost two years later:

TEXT OF CITATION

THE WHITE HOUSE
Washington, D. C.

By virtue of the authority vested in me as President of the United States and as Commander-in-Chief of the Armed Forces of the United States I have today awarded The Presidential Unit Citation (Army) for extraordinary heroism to the 1st Cavalry Division (Airmobile) and attached units.

The 1st Cavalry Division (Airmobile) and attached units distinguished themselves by outstanding performance of duty and extraordinary heroism in action against an armed enemy in the Republic of Vietnam during the period of 23 October 1965 to 26 November 1965. Following the attack on a Special Forces camp at Plei Mei, in Pleiku Province. on 19 October 1965 by regular units of the Army of North Vietnam, the 1st Cavalry Division (Airmobile) was committed to action.

The division was initially assigned the mission of protecting the key communications center of Pleiku, in addition to providing fire support both for an Army of the Republic of Vietnam (ARVN) armored column dispatched to the relief of the besieged camp, and for the camp itself. The 1st Cavalry Division (Airmobile), having recently been organized under a completely new concept in tactical mobility, and having arrived in the Republic of Vietnam only a month earlier, responded quickly with an infantry brigade and supporting forces.

Using air assault techniques, the division deployed artillery batteries into firing positions deep within enemy-held territory and provided the vital fire support needed by the ARVN forces to accomplish the relief of the Special Forces camp. By 27 October, the tactical and strategic impact of the presence of a North Vietnamese regular army division in Pleiku Province necessitated a change in missions for the 1st Cavalry Division. The division was given an unlimited offensive role to seek out and destroy the enemy force. With bold thrusts, elements of the division pursued the North Vietnamese regiments across the dense and trackless jungles of the west-central highlands, seeking the enemy out in his previously secure sanctuaries and giving him no quarter.

In unfavorable terrain and under logistical and tactical conditions that would have stopped a unit with less capability, motivation and esprit, the cavalrymen repeatedly and decisively defeated numerically superior enemy forces. The superb training, unflinching devotion to duty, and unsurpassed gallantry and intrepidity of the cavalrymen, individually and collectively, resulted in numerous victories and succeeded in driving the invading North Vietnamese division back from its positions at Plei Mei to the foot of the Chu Pong Massif. There, in the valley of the Ia Drang, the enemy was reinforced by a fresh regiment and undertook preparations for more incursions into Pleiku Province.

The 1st Cavalry Division deployed by air its men and weapons to launch an attack on this enemy staging area, which was 35 kilometers from the nearest road and 50 kilometers from the nearest logistical base. Fully utilizing air mobility in applying their combat power in a series of offensive blows, the men of the division completely defeated the numerically superior enemy. When the enemy finally withdrew his broken forces from the battlefield, the offensive capability of the North Vietnamese Army in the II Corps tactical zone had been blunted. The outstanding performance and extraordinary heroism of the members of the 1st Cavalry Division (Airmobile) and attached units, under the most hazardous and adverse conditions, reflect great credit upon themselves, the United States Army, and the Armed Forces of the United States.

> LYNDON B. JOHNSON,
> *President of the United States*

September 15, 1967

No finer tribute to a new concept, a division, and the Jumping Mustang Battalion could be asked for.

APPENDIX

JUMPING MUSTANG DECORATIONS

Medal of Honor
  Sgt David C. Dolby   B Company

Distinguished Service Cross
  Major Roy D. Martin   B Company
  Sp4 Raymond Ortiz   Hq Company
  *Sp4 Michael G. Vinassa   C Company

Silver Star
  Sp5 Arnold A. Arrellano   B Company
  *2Lt Robert H. Crum   B Company
  Capt Theodore S. Danielsen   A Company
  1Lt John B. Hanlon   A Company
  2Lt William D. Hughes   B Company
  *Sp4 David M. Jolley, Jr.   C Company
  Sp5 Nathaniel Lindsey, Jr.   Hq Company
  Major Roy D. Martin   B Company
  1Lt William L. McCarron   B Company
  Col Kenneth D. Mertel   Hq Company
  Sp4 Raymond Ortiz   Hq Company
  Maj Gerrell V. Plummer   B Company
  Pfc Gregory M. Ratliff   Hq Company
  *Pfc Allen J. Ritter   B Company
  Sfc Kenneth Riveer   A Company
  PSgt Mario Rodriguez   B Company

Awarded posthumously.

Sp4 Jimmie Sampson   C Company
*Pfc Nels W. Swanson   C Company
1Sgt Grady Trainor   C Company
2Lt Frank R. Vavrek   C Company
*Sp4 Michael G. Vinassa   C Company
Sgt David C. Dolby   B Company

Awarded posthumously.

GLOSSARY

A1E—World War II/Korea single-reciprocating-engine fighter
capable of carrying a large bomb load with long flight
endurance and slow speed, flown by Air Force, Navy,
and South Vietnamese. Ideal for close air support.

Air Cav—Air Cavalry; applied to the 1st Cavalry Division,
Airmobile.

ALO—Air Force Liaison Officer. An Air Force officer attached to an Infantry battalion or brigade to coordinate
close air-support fire power.

Arty LO—Artillery Liaison Officer. An Artillery officer attached to an Infantry brigade or battalion to coordinate
artillery fire power.

Barrier—Primary base defenses at the An Khe Base Camp.

Bird—An aircraft, specifically a helicopter.

Bubble (OH-13)—Small two-man observation helicopter
employed for scouting.

Cannons—Howitzers and guns of the artillery.

Chinook (CH-47)—Next to the largest helicopter in the Army
inventory, capable of carrying one rifle platoon internally
or 9500 pounds externally.

CIDG—Civilian Irregular Defense Groups. South Vietnamese
trained by U.S.-advised Vietnamese Special Forces.

Click—A kilometer.

Coiled—A unit prepared for movement into combat. Ready
to attack or strike, similar to a snake.

Cow fence—Applies to the Barrier—a five- to six-foot-high
barbed-wire fence.

Door gunner—A soldier in a UH-1D or CH-47 helicopter,

firing a machine gun or automatic rifle to protect the helicopter when near the ground.

Dry run—A field or planning exercise in which live weapons firing is not conducted.

FAC—Forward Air Controller. An Air Force pilot generally flying in another aircraft in communication with the fighters conducting a tactical air strike.

Flying Crane—Largest helicopter in the Army inventory, capable of carrying nine tons externally suspended from beneath the crane.

Green Trace—Another name for the Barrier.

Grunt—Infantryman; rifleman.

Hex tent—A small hexagon-shaped tent—small size holding five men, larger size holding ten.

HUEY (UH-1)—A UH-1 helicopter.

Jump pay—A hazardous-duty pay that paratroopers earn in performance of a specified number of parachute jumps.

Jumping Mustangs, *or* Mustangs—Nickname for the 1st Battalion, Airborne, 8th Cavalry.

KIA—Killed in action.

LAW—Light anti-tank weapon. A small tube-like weapon that fires a rocket against tanks or point targets. It replaces the bazooka.

Leg, *or* Straight Leg—A non-Airborne soldier.

LZ—Landing zone. A designated area into which paratroopers jump or helicopters land to dismount airmobile troops, generally in an assault.

Mechanical Mule—A small four-wheeled vehicle with a low silhouette, capable of carrying 1000 pounds of cargo.

NVA—North Vietnamese Army.

On final—A term applied to an aircraft as it makes its final approach or movement to the ground for landing.

Pathfinder—A group of men with electronic aids who accompany the lead helicopter or make the first parachute jump in order to set up aids to guide the remainder of the aircraft or jumpers to the LZ.

Picket Line—The outer perimeter, six to seven kilometers beyond the base camp. An outpost line.

Pre-strike—Attack by artillery or air against a target previously planned.

Punji-stick—A small sliver of bamboo, stuck into the ground at an angle along trails where troops are expected to walk, so that they may accidentally impale themselves.

Pup tent—A small two-man tent.

PZ—Pickup zone. A designated area for helicopters to land and pick up airmobile troops.

Recon—Reconnaissance.

Rocket artillery—Artillery fired from rocket tubes mounted on helicopters or airplanes.

Rolling-barrage—Term applied to artillery or mortar shells whose range continues to be increased in front of an advancing unit.

Six-Two-Six—Refers to commanders, one talking to another.

Sky Trooper—A soldier of the 1st Air Cavalry Division.

Thunderbolt mission—A reserve force, waiting alongside helicopters ready for immediate employment.

Tube artillery—Conventional artillery fire in contrast to rocket artillery, which is fired from tubes mounted on helicopters or airplanes.

Unload ordnance—On a fighter aircraft or a helicopter, to fire or release its ordnance.

VC—Viet Cong.

WIA—Wounded in action.

INDEX

Join the Allies on the Road to Victory
BANTAM WAR BOOKS